GeekChic

Geek Chic

By Neil Feineman

Concept
Neil Feineman & Femke Wolting
Producer
Bruno Felix
Managing Editor
Femke Dekker
Contributing Editors
Rob Davis, Chelsea Kalberloh,
Matt Sammons, Erwin van der Zande
Visual Research
Coup, Daphne Dijkerman,
Bibi Fadlalla, Raymond Go
Production
Yaniv Wolf
Design & Cover Illustration
Coup (Peter van den Hoogen,
Simone Koller, Erica Terpstra)

Produced by
Stichting Submarine Media
Rapenburgerstraat 109
1011 VL Amsterdam
The Netherlands
T +31 (0)20 330 1226
F +31 (0)20 330 1227
www.submarinechannel.com
info@submarine.nl

First published in the United Kingdom in 2005 by
Thames & Hudson Limited
181A High Holborn
London, WC1V 7QX
United Kingdom
T +44 (0)20 7845 5000
F +44 (0)20 7845 5050
www.thamesandhudson.com

British Library Cataloguing-in-Publication Data
A catalogue record for this book is available from the
British Library.

ISBN-13: 978-0-500-28561-9
ISBN-10: 0-500-28561-6

Printed in Singapore

By Neil Feineman

GeekChic

 Thames & Hudson

The Rise of Geek Chic

Twenty centuries, give or take a decade or two, is a long time. But, at least as far as geeks are concerned, good things really do come to those who wait. After years and years of persecution, ridicule and never, ever getting the girl (or guy), geeks are finally, irrefutably, certifiably chic. They appear on the covers of magazines, win Oscars and Grammys, eat at the best tables in the best restaurants, drive Ferraris and Lamborghinis and elevate the price of real estate in every important city in the world.

Evidence of the transformation of the geek into le chic is embarrassingly evident. While writing this introduction, I wanted to take two days off and not think about geeks, geek culture or this book. But the minute I hit the sidewalk, I stepped over some graffiti scrawled on the pavement saying "nerds unite". It got worse by the time I got to the newsstand. There, on the cover of *Newsweek* were the two billionaire twentysomethings who founded <u>Google</u>. And over on the indie rack, the entertaining, post feminist manifesto, *Bust* Magazine featured Tina Fey, with the coverline (and theme of the issue), "Geek Chic". Later, I started reading two books for recreation, S.J. Rozan's award winning mystery novel *Winter and Night* and Peter Biskind's well reviewed history of indie films in the 1990s, *Down and Dirty Pictures*. Unexpectedly both turned out to be about geeks (criminals and sleuths in Rozan's case and big time Hollywood directors in Biskind's).

The parade continued on television. First, a mindless reality show, *High School Reunion*, introduced a self-described geek who had come to his 10-year high school reunion to see if his Texas classmates were still capable of making his life a living hell. Then, in the trashy but phenomenally successful TV soap opera, *The O.C.*, bimbo guest superstar Paris Hilton hit on the male geek hero, who had somehow ended up at a strip bar in Los Angeles. Her pick-up line involved a reference to Thomas Pynchon's *Gravity's Rainbow* ("it's his masterpiece," she said knowingly) and a confession that she was a closet-geek.

Earlier in the day, on MTV, uber-Geek *American Idol* megastar Clay Aiken's nondescript ballad, 'Measure of a Man', had topped the hormonally active TRL video countdown; while *USA Today* singled out the 2004 version of *Dawn of the Dead*, whose zombies had just toppled Mel Gibson, Jesus and The Passion from box office domination, as a prime example of 'geek chic'.

"We used to shun them, mock them, give them wedgies and snicker when they played <u>Dungeons & Dragons</u>. Those loser days, however, are as over as *Dumb and Dumber* prequels. Knowledge is power and geek is chic," concluded *USA Today*'s Susan Wloszczyna and Ann Oldenburg.

This journey from loser to winner represents a cataclysmic shift in what society considers cool. Ninety years ago, the best *Webster*'s could say about a geek was

Google
> page 135

Dungeons
& Dragons
> page 78

that he (or she) was: "A person often of an intellectual bent who is disapproved of. 2. a carnival performer often billed as a wild man whose act usually includes biting the head off a live chicken or snake." In normal circumstances, given the choice between a carney and an egghead, you'd think the carney would win every time. Yet despite its use in Katherine Dunn's cult novel, *Geek Love*, and the efforts of Ozzy Osbourne, who did, after all, bite off the head of a pigeon, we've pretty much retired the head-biter in favor of the nerd. (Speaking of which, the word 'nerd', which tends to be used interchangeably with geek, has an even more distinguished entomological pedigree, since it sprung from the mind of <u>Dr. Seuss</u>, who coined the term in his 1950 opus, *If I Ran the Zoo*.

In that book, the zookeeper, ever in search of exotic animals, sails to Ka-Troo, where he bags an It-Kutch, a Preep, a Proo, a Nerkle, a Seersucker and a bitter, fowl looking fellow called a Nerd.)

Back in the 1960s and 1970s, when computers were the size of buildings and the seeds of modern geek culture were being sown, it didn't matter whether you called them geeks or nerds because unless you were one yourself, they were pretty much invisible. While everyone else was partying at the frat house or hanging around their off campus apartments getting stoned, protesting the cause of the month, those other kids – the ones who spent their high school time in the A–V department or science club – were in the science hall, punching out data cards. They were there all day and all night: a pale group of distracted, unstylish, unathletic, uninvolved wallflowers who taped their thick, horn-rimmed glasses with duct tape, wore pocket protectors filled with mechanical sported pencils and ball point pens in nondescript polyester shirts and, if you asked anyone, wasted the best party years of their lives.

At least that's what we thought. But by the early 1980s, as computers and technology started having a more demonstrable impact on our lives, we weren't so sure. Suddenly, the stuff that Alvin Toffler had talked about in *Future Shock* was starting to come true and nerds were starting to look pretty good. Without any seeming historical antecedent, bespectacled, whiny, nebbishy <u>Woody Allen</u> had become a sex symbol – with Diane Keaton and then Mia Farrow in tow. And he wasn't the only one; gross, grotesque Henry Kissinger, a man the counterculture had no love for, was going to A-list parties with bombshell Jill St. John on his arm. Movies like *Star Wars*, *Star Trek* and *Tron* were giving the future a new, technological look; William Gibson wrote a compelling, at times baffling book, *Neuromancer*, which introduced us to cyberpunk; and a new group of actors such as Matthew Broderick were using wit, finesse and vulnerability to outfox the football players and get the girl.

Far more important changes, however, were happening under our non-geek noses, amongst the hackers themselves. The mainstream would get glimpses of it in books like Steven Levy's <u>*Hackers: Heroes of the Computer Revolution*</u> (1984) and, later, Douglas Rushkoff's *Cyberia* (1994), or from speeches such as <u>Al Gore's</u> famous introduction of the term 'information superhighway' in the *Washington Post*:

> "Just as the Interstate highway system made sense for a post-war America with lots of automobiles clogging the crooked two-lane roads, a nationwide network of information superhighways now is needed to move the vast quantities of data that are creating a kind of information gridlock. If we had the information superhighway we need, a school child could plug into the Library of Congress every afternoon and explore a universe of knowledge, jumping from one subject to another, according to the curiosity of the moment. A doctor in Carthage, Tennessee, could consult with doctors at the Mayo Clinic in Minnesota on a patient's CAT scan in the middle of an emergency. Teams of scientists and engineers working on the same problem in different locations could work together in a 'co-laboratory' if their supercomputers were linked."

Since his verbal styling had about as much flair as his campaigning skills, most people didn't have a clue what Gore was talking about, what computers did or what kind of people would get so obsessed by them. But a growing number did, and for them, the computer was creating a sense of community around it, and starting to change the geek tag from an epithet to a badge of pride.

As *The New Hacker's Dictionary* described it, computer geeks were people who ate (computer) bugs for a living. A geek, the dictionary continued, is "One who fulfills all the dreariest negative stereotypes about hackers: an antisocial, malodorous, pasty faced monomaniac with all the personality of a cheese grater. Cannot be used by outsiders without implied insult to all hackers; compare black-on-black vs. white-on-black usage of 'nigger'." This emerging sense of pride and identification was directly proportional to the increasing influence of computers. Mike McConnell in *The High-Tech Dictionary*, for instance, admits that geek began – and persists – as a pejorative term implying the person had considerable computer skills but was a social disaster. But, he adds, "As computers become more important in the average person's life, this term becomes more often a compliment than an insult."

This increasing sense of importance was being articulated by numerous preachers, even if they were primarily preaching to the choir. Few of the evangelists were as erudite as <u>MIT</u> Media Lab founder Nicholas Negroponte, who in 1997's book, *Being Digital*, wrote, "Computing is not about computers anymore. It is about living. As we interconnect ourselves, many of the values of a nation state will give way to those of both larger and smaller electronic communities. We will socialize in digital neighborhoods in which physical space will be irrelevant and time will play a different role. Twenty-five years from now (2020) when you look out a window, what you see may be 5000 miles and six time zones away. When you watch an hour of television, it may have been delivered to your home in less than a second. Reading about Patagonia can include the sensory experience of going there. A book by William Buckley can be a conversation with him."

That same year, *Wired* Magazine's Louis Rossetto, another head cheerleader for the cause, wrote that the digital revolution is creating "social changes so profound that their only parallel is probably the discovery of fire. Within 20 years the world will be totally transformed. Everything we know will be different. Not just a change from LBJ to Nixon but whether there will be a President at all. I think Alvin Toffler's basically right: we're in a phase change of civilization."

Three years later, <u>Jon Katz</u>, a respected journalist from Chicago and member of the *Wired* crew, wrote perhaps the contemporary definition of the geek. On both the back cover and beginning of his book, *Geeks: How Two Lost Boys Rode the internet Out of Idaho* (Villard, 2000), he laid it out in plain, irrefutable English: "Geek: A member of the new cultural elite, a pop-culture-loving, techno-centered Community of Social Discontents. Most geeks rose above a suffocating unimaginative educational system, where they were surrounded by obnoxious social values and hostile peers to build the freest and most inventive culture on the planet: the internet and the <u>World Wide Web</u>. Now running the systems that run the world. Tendency towards braininess and individuality, traits that often trigger resentment, isolation or exclusion. Identifiable by a singular obsessiveness about the things they love, both work and play, and a well-honed sense of bitter, even savage outsider humor. Universally suspicious of authority. In this era, the Greek Ascension, a positive, even envied term. Definitions involving chicken heads no longer apply."

As he made it clear, geeks were the gatekeepers of the new global economy. As an e-mail from one of his fans said, "We run the systems that run the world. Until recently, most CEOs wouldn't have let us in the door. Now we sit next to the

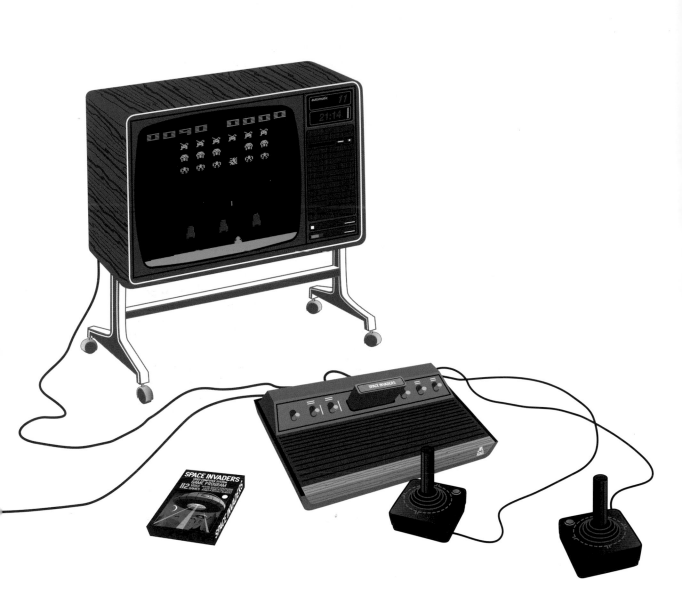

CEOs. We are the only people who know how the place operates, how to retrieve files, how to keep the neural systems running. We are the indispensables." Indispensability, of course, is not just about operating the system, but supplying it with content. As Katz breaks it down, the most narrow definition of a geek is the computer obsessed technician who "is building the infrastructure of the Net and its related programs and systems". The broader, more useful definition includes the brainy, single-minded outsiders drawn to a wide range of creative pursuits – from raves to Japanese animation – who live beyond the mainstream. These people are defiant of government, business or other institutions who want to shut down their freewheeling exchange of ideas, and represent a state of mind and a lifestyle that transcend traditional geography. For them, it is the Net that provides the boundaries to their lives.

As these brainy, creative outsiders began infiltrating the media, they started recasting the media portrayals in their own image. By the late 1990s, the movies, TV, publishing, videogames and even sports were getting hip to the message that geek was chic.

Pulp Fiction
> page 128

George Lucas
> page 92

While the major studios were turning out one bloated franchise action movie after another, for instance, the independent film movement, helmed by self-described geeks such as Kevin Smith, Wes Anderson, Todd Solondz, the Coen Brothers, and, most of all, Quentin Tarantino, whose film *Pulp Fiction* was the first independent film to gross $100 million, turned the film business upside down. Unlike their film school graduate predecessors – directors like George Lucas, Stephen Spielberg, Martin Scorsese, Francis Ford Coppola – these iconoclasts grew up with the VCR and cable television. This new breed didn't have to sit through boring lectures, film history and semesters of obscure foreign films. Instead, they got stoned, ordered pizza, rented handfuls of videos and got their own education. As Kevin Smith, whose early films were peppered with comic books, mallrats and video store clerks, tells Peter Biskind in his book, *Down and Dirty Pictures*, "I didn't grow up watching Eric Rohmer. I grew up watching John Landis. I don't think of myself as an artist at all, but I think I'm just kind of pigheaded enough to want to do stories my way, without any involvement, without any tips from somebody else." These self-educated, determined geeks threw their obsessions with science fiction, fantasy, comic books, cult horror, B movies and the French New Wave, into a blender and came out with movies like *The Matrix* and *The Blair Witch Project* that beat the major studios at their own game. "The new Hollywood directors are pop culture nerds who were virtually kids when they were touched by the wand of fortune and turned into frog princes of Beverly Hills," says Biskind.

The Matrix
> page 147

With geek auteurs behind the cameras, it was no wonder that the concept of the leading man was changing both in the movies and, even more obviously, on TV. Long a haven for guilty pleasures, television had been geek-friendly with shows like *Star Trek*, *Max Headroom*, *MacGuyver*, *Twin Peaks* and *Northern Exposure* for years. But by the mid-90s, the geek went mainstream. In *Beverly Hills 90210*, Brandon was the dreamy geek who worked at the soda shop in the afternoon, studied every night and earnestly tried to do the right thing. (He even went to a rave but, God help him, freaked out when his girlfriend gave him Ecstasy, which the show inexplicably renamed as Euphoria.) And the best of them all, *The X-Files* revolved around Uber-geeks Scully and Mulder's sexy war with the world.

Max Headroom
> page 107

The music business was undergoing less obvious but even more profound changes. While the major labels threw their money into recycled rock and roll acts, a generation of DJs and electronic dance artists with names like Fatboy Slim, the Aphex Twin, Moby, Sasha Coe, John Digweed and Paul Van Dyk had been making a fortune and creating a global fan base without any help from the major record labels, radio stations or MTV.

The X-Files
> page 127
Aphex Twin
> page 121
Moby
> page 122
John Digweed
> page 132

Underneath the mainstream's (and apparently customs officials all over the world) noses, the electronic music community flaunted drug laws, copyrights, radio formats and conventional ideas on what constituted a performance. The superstar DJs could make six figures a night and, using only underground channels of publicity, pull tens of thousands of club kids to out of the way, often makeshift venues. Like rap and rock before it, the dance community had its own subculture, including magazines such as *Urb*, *XLRSTR*, *BPM*, and *Ministry*, clothing lines like Fresh Jive, a new drug of choice (Ecstasy) its own record labels and its own distribution system (the Web). It even had its own spiritual identity (represented by the acronym PLUR, which stands for Peace, Love, Unity and Respect). Unlike rappers and rock stars, the DJ didn't sing or dance, but stood in a booth, often in darkness, for hours, manipulating records and sounds for hours on end. Despite their obvious charisma and wealth, the DJs remained remarkably accessible, mingling freely and often ending up on the dance floor, at an after-party and, later, at breakfast with their fans. It became almost a point of honor, especially since all the people in the club scene lived on the Web and wouldn't hesitate to blast anyone who forgot that the dance community, to quote Fatboy Slim, existed somewhere between the gutter and the stars.

A similar accountability was taking place in publishing. Early magazines such as *Mondo 2000* and *Wired* were soon joined by titles such as *Fast Company*, *Red Herring*, *The Industry Standard* and *Business 2.0*. As magazines have a habit of doing, each carved out its special niche and each pumped up the culture with a steady stream of soundbytes and updates. Book publishing was quick to jump on the demographic, with authors such as William Gibson, Douglas Rushkoff,

Douglas Coupland, Bruce Sterling, Neal Stephenson, Nicholas Negroponte, Po Bronson, Neil Gaiman, Frank Miller and Alan Moore churning out nonfiction,

fiction and graphic novels that resonated with the emerging geek culture. This was insignificant, however, when compared to the seismic shifts being created by the growth of the internet, its insatiable need for content and the number of people who began relying on the screen, rather than on the printed page.

Without going too McLuhan here, the medium is a huge part of the message. It is too soon to tell how this will all settle down. For now, it's enough to note that the internet has created a new way to read and to write and that the culture it is creating will no doubt be cast in its own image.

The growth of video game culture is equally astonishing. Although arcades, previously the lifeblood of the gaming industry, declined in recent years, games are more popular than ever, thanks to the explosion in home gaming consoles and computer games. According to *BPM* Magazine, in 1999, more households had a video game system than an internet connection; and Americans as a whole spent six times more money on game players and games than on American school library materials. It would be a mistake to dismiss games as just for kids, either, because increasingly graphic and violent games such as *Grand*

Theft Auto, *Postal* and *Gang Wars* are aimed at the aging gamer and sell out as fast as stores can stock them. Estimated total revenues for the videogame industry are difficult to come by, but $11 billion (US) is frequently bantered about. Regardless of the actual figure, the video game industry now outgrosses Hollywood. And that is only the beginning. With the growth of internet gaming and the increasing synergy between games and big film releases (many of which are inspired by video games), the game industry is certain to consolidate its position as a permanent player in the entertainment pantheon. Electronic Arts,

the biggest video game developer in history, made headlines in the spring of 2004 when they announced plans to hire 1000 people from the film industry to work at their new office in Los Angeles. And, never far behind, the University of Southern California, which has long been a leading film school, introduced a major in video game studies and found themselves with more applicants than they knew what to do with.

Even skateboarding, at one point perhaps the ultimate outsider activity, has been coopted by the geeks. The pioneer skaters of the 1970s were rebellious, drug taking outcasts, constantly running afoul of the law, the school system, their parents and their peers. Taking their cues from the surfers' "locals only" attitude, they developed a tight knit, closed hard-core industry and communication network, dedicated to keeping everyone they didn't like – which was everyone who didn't look or think like them – out. But the younger skateboarders, who came into their own in the 1990s like Tony Hawk and photographers like Spike Jonze, had no problem with broader ambition, investing their prize money in computer systems and DIY companies and willingly positioned skateboarding in a more mainstream, less threatening light. To see the difference, you need only compare today's hero, Tony Hawk, to Tony Alva, who was the face of skateboarding in the 1970s. Alva, who was the first pro rider to have a signature skateboard and start his own company. But like the punk rock stars he hung out with, Alva was fast living, intimidating, brash and unpredictable. Hawk, on the other hand, grew up with computers, championed a clean living suburban lifestyle and appeared – irony free – in a famous "Got Milk" campaign. While Alva shuddered at the idea of corporate sponsorship and spent his post-skate years in relative obscurity, Hawk got into bed with the *X-Games*, assembled a world-class team of Hollywood agents and managers, developed a multimillion dollar string of companies, including one of the best-selling and most influential video games, *Tony Hawk's Pro Skater* (a standard feature on the new Macs).

Some old-school purists bemoan this mainstream marketing as a loss of "soul" but others just chalk it up to the way things are today. Kurt Anderson, author of *Turn of the Century*, a novel chronicling the geek takeover of Manhattan and editor of *Spy* and *New York* magazines, found that out first hand when he helped start Inside.com, a website aimed at the digerati. The reaction among the press was quick: Anderson had abandoned his ethics and sold his soul for dot.com dollars. "No one feels guilty about being rich anymore and not caring about anything but money," he argued. "Unemployment is at a historic low. The kids come pre-sold out. A 21 year old today knows only the post-liberal Reagan philosophy, [and that] the free market won. They come into a landscape where their college friends make $5 million overnight. They see the rewards of capitalism directly – and they look good." These days, echoes Josh Schwartz, the creator of *The O.C.* and a self described geek, even if you are on the outside looking in, you do not grow up in today's world wanting less. Not being accepted, he continues, does not mean that you don't want what the others have. But it also means that you don't necessarily do what everyone wants just to be accepted. And, with role models as varied as Lisa Simpson, Clay Aiken, *The O.C.*'s Seth Cohen or Bill Gates, giving you encouragement, you might go about getting it in a different way.

And while high school is still a pretty rotten place where jocks, Abercrombies and power-mad adult authority figures call the shots and while feeling weird still sucks, for the first time in history, even if you're alone on yet another Saturday night, you can plug into the internet and talk about how much life sucks with people just like you, all over the world. While that could have become a scenario "misery loves company", the amount of information exchanged and web of relationships that develop accordingly has led to a virtual community that has dispensed with physical appearance, age, gender, race, location and, although probably to a lesser extent, class.

In the process, the internet has become as close to a meritocracy as we've seen. The deck is still stacked in favor of corporations with deep pockets, but those advantages can be circumvented by people with superior vision, skills and motivation. Say what you will, the internet is a community and, like any community, knows how to take care of its own.

Nowhere, one suspects, will this be seen sooner than in the increasing power of women in the geek world. The research for this book was, for the most part, an exercise in machismo, with white males from the Western world running the show. The women were hard to find; people of color, nonexistent.

But there are real reasons to think that it is changing and that women and minorities will soon be making their own indelible marks on geek culture. In Andrew Vachss's 1999 novel, *Choice of Evil*, the protagonist, Burke, is dependent upon the computer skills of one of his underworld connections. When Burke, Vachss's hero, asks her how she learned "all this stuff" she responds by saying:

> *"I had to pretty much teach myself. It's mostly men – boys, really – who understand it. And you can't get them to teach you much."*
>
> *"Why not?" I asked. "I don't mean to be offensive, but you're a pretty girl. I'd think those kids would be falling all over themselves to –"*
>
> *"The opposite." Xyla laughed. "Cyber-boys are always flexing their little muscles . . . Like, if I go to the beach . . . I walk by, guys show off . . . Well, it's he same thing in Cyberville. Only the muscles they have, they're not real. I mean, I can't bench-press four hundred pounds. But I can do anything on a computer they can do – it doesn't take strength, just knowledge. If they give me theirs, they can't . . . pose . . . As soon as I snapped to it, I realized I'd have to learn the cyber-stuff myself. So I did."*

That, in the end, is why the internet is a meritocracy, and why the future ultimately belongs to geeks. Simply put, it is one of the few arenas in modern life where you can learn the language on your own and then flex your muscles with the big boys. That's real power. As *USA Today* wrote, "If you're a cyber whiz who is plugged into the pop culture world of sci-fi, fantasy, comic books and cult horror, maybe even the master of a Web shrine devoted to such once arcane matters, you don't just rule. You rock."

335 BC	287 BC	830	1284	1455	1543	1564	1632	1683	1746	1755	1811	1818	1821	1837	1847	1853	1865	1868	1876	1877	1879	1886	1889	1890	1893	1898	1899	1903	1905	1906	1907	1914	1921	1926	1929	1932	1934	1937	1938	1939	1941	1942	1945	1946	1947	1948	1949	1950	1951	1952

Food	Cars	Pop
Science + Technology	Sci-fi + Cyberpunk	Movies + TV + Robots
Miscellaneous	Gadgets	Games
Fashion	Comics	Computers + Hackers + Internet

FOOD

SCIENCE + TECHNOLOGY

MISCELLANEOUS

FASHION

CARS

SCI-FI + CYBERPUNK

GADGETS

COMICS

POP

MOVIES + TV + ROBOTS

GAMES

COMPUTERS + HACKERS + INTERNET

GEEK TIMELINE

How the Nerds became Geeks and got their Revenge.

When Nixon ruled America, his prime minister was Henry Kissinger. Now, even Henry's biggest fans would not call him good looking. But Henry was at all the right places with the most beautiful women, all hanging on him. No one could figure it out — this was, after all, the inspiration for Dr. Strangelove himself. Who would have thought Henry would get all the girls? Then a now-forgotten columnist figured it out. Henry was sexy because Henry was one of, if not the, most powerful men in the world. And power is sexy.

That might explain the rise of the geek as a sex symbol, an underground hero, and a self-confident synthesis of the hippie, punk, and yuppie eras. From taped-together glasses, T-shirts, and pocket protectors; from Revenge of the Nerds to The Matrix; from microwave pizza to overpriced but frothy cappuccinos and expensive vodka; from Kraftwerk to Moby, it has been a long and winding road. Honestly, we haven't a clue where the road is heading. For now, we're happy to look back and see just how it was we got here.

All articles written by Neil Feineman, Chelsea Kalberloh and Rob Davis. Except for: Neil Feineman (NF), Erwin van der Zande (EvdZ), Matt Sammons (MS).

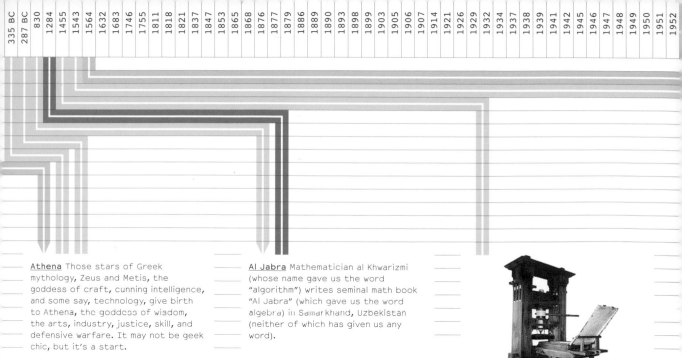

Athena Those stars of Greek mythology, Zeus and Metis, the goddess of craft, cunning intelligence, and some say, technology, give birth to Athena, the goddess of wisdom, the arts, industry, justice, skill, and defensive warfare. It may not be geek chic, but it's a start.

Al Jabra Mathematician al Khwarizmi (whose name gave us the word "algorithm") writes seminal math book "Al Jabra" (which gave us the word algebra) in Samarkhand, Uzbekistan (neither of which has given us any word).

Aristotle Aristotle coins the word "technology" and describes scholars who master technology as "technologizers" in his "Techne Rhetorike".
The meaning of the word has evolved over the centuries, but is rooted in the attributes of Metis. This is quite possibly the first tip of the hat to the geek in written language.

Printing Press The printing press makes copying a breeze, and is quickly put to work mass-producing Bibles. Who said pornography is always the first application for a new technology?

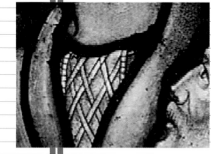

Archimedes Syracuse resident Archimedes carries out pioneering work in geometry, physics, mechanics, and hydrostatics. A friend of the royal family, he is asked to ascertain whether the king's crown is made of pure gold and famously shouts "Eureka" ("I've found it") while in his bath and runs down the street naked on discovering the solution. Geeks since then are reputed for their lack of

▼

▼

self-awareness and personal hygiene.

GEEK FASHION

Glasses Salvino D'Armate invents glasses in Italy. It would take over 600 years, though, to refine them into an iconic geek fashion accessory.

GEEK SCIENCE + TECHNOLOGY ICON

Nikolaus Copernicus This Polish cleric and gentleman theorized that the earth is a moving planet, birthed modern astronomy and propelled the single most revolutionary scientific idea in modern civilization until Darwin. For all that, he got labeled a heretic anyway. Born in Poland to a wealthy merchant who died when Nic was 11, he ▼

was then brought up by an uncle who was a noted scholar and bishop. The family left him set for life, so he didn't have to do anything more than study and later, when it was time for him to uphold the family honor, he became a canon of the Church of Poland. The title was more honorific than anything else, so even as a man of the cloth, he still had plenty of time to study and think. Following his muse, ▼

he became particularly interested in Ptolemy's idea that the earth was the center of the universe with everything in the universe revolving around us. If that were true, thought Copernicus, the earth would be a fixed center to the universe and an accurate predictor of the motion of the sun, the moon and the stars above. ▲

But try as he might, Copernicus could not find the formula that would prove the theory. He was not alone. As he read up on Ptolemy's contemporaries, he found several alternative theories of the universe, including a moving earth. The science behind these contrarians' suggestions seemed more sound than Ptolemy's, but the church, preferring the idea that the universe revolved around them, quickly squelched ▼

the work of these Godless "radicals". Even so, Copernicus used these theories to posit that the earth, moon and other planets revolve around the sun and that the earth spins on its axis every 24 hours. "In the center of all rests the sun. For who would place this lamp of a most beautiful temple in a better place", he wrote in his book On the Revolution of the Heavenly (or, depending upon the ▼

source, Celestial) Spheres. Although it was a simpler, more comprehensive, more empirical and more systematic explanation of the universe, Copernicus suspected that the work would come under attack from the religious community, so he privately floated his conclusions in a pamphlet called The Commentariolus, sometime around 1530. While not openly negative, the Pope and his henchmen suggested ▼

that accuracy notwithstanding, the earth-centered universe was far more theologically pleasing than his version. Not wanting a fight, Copernicus took their reaction as a signal to soft-pedal publication of the book. If rumor is to be believed, he postponed publication until he was ready to give up the ghost, and that the first copy, which was delivered to him on his deathbed, was one of the last things he saw. ▲

One reason for Copernicus' reluctance to take on the church may have been his inability to prove his theory. That would have to wait some 50 years, until Kepler and Galileo developed the physics necessary to support Copernicus' suspicions.
Once they did, the Church, which had reacted to Copernicus' book with a half century of benign neglect, banned it. The ban held until 1835, when the ▼

idea of a sun-centric universe was considered less blasphemous, and Copernicus dead enough to be non-threatening. NF

GEEK FOOD

Coffee
> see page 22

GEEK FOOD

Coffee
1615

Ever since the unsung death of
the three-martini lunch, coffee has
become the undisputed workplace
drink of choice. So here are a few
little tidbits to chew on while you sip
your latte:

a. The first people to consume coffee
were the Mufti of Aden, who stumbled
onto it in the early ninth century.

b. At first it was considered a food,
not a beverage. In East Africa,
warriors would grind the beans, mix in
some animal fat, roll it around, make
little balls out of it and pop one in
whenever they needed a boost.

c. The Dutch introduced coffee plants
to the rest of the world. They brought
the first plant to Holland from Mocha,
Yemen in 1616, and were cultivating it in
Ceylon (now Sri Lanka) by 1658.

d. Coffee first appeared in Europe in
1615, where was sold in pharmacies as
medicine. To this day, coffee has been
saddled with medicinal properties.
Depending on who you believe, it causes
or prevents cancer, enhances or impairs
brain activity and performance and
either weakens or strengthens the
effects of alcohol. The Japanese think
it soothes the skin, which explains their
habit of bathing in coffee grounds.

e. In the U.S. Civil War, Union soldiers
were given 100 pounds of food for
personal rations. Eight of those
pounds were ground or roasted
coffee beans. King Frederick, on the
other hand, thought that drinking
coffee was distracting soldiers from
their duty and established a task
force called the Kaffee Schnufflers
to sniff out illicit coffee roasters
and smugglers. The task force failed.

And in Turkey, women were allowed to
divorce husbands who failed to keep
the household stocked with sufficient
supplies of the bean.

f. Balzac drank forty cups of coffee a day, while Voltaire managed to down fifty. Frederick the Great wins Worst Coffee Drink for flavoring his with champagne and mustard.

g. The first English coffee house opened in Oxford in 1650. By 1700, more than 2000 of them dotted the English countryside. In one of these, either the Green Dragon or the Green Lion, depending upon who you believe, patriots (for some reason in England) sowed the seeds of the American Revolution. In Constantinople, the coffee shops were called schools of wisdom because they attracted men of arts and letters; and throughout Europe in the early 18th century they were called Penny Universities, generally because they were spawning grounds for the Enlightenment.

h. These days, coffee is the most widely consumed beverage in the world, and the second largest item on the international commerce board. More than 25 million people work in the industry; more than 4,800 cups are consumed per second in America alone; and one Starbucks tall mocha has more fat than three bags of M&Ms. More amazingly, one coffee tree produces about one pound of roasted ground coffee a year. (It is unclear where all these trees grow. Think about it – have you ever seen one?)

i. If you're going for the buzz, dark roasted is not your friend. The darker the coffee bean and the longer it's roasted, the more caffeine will be leached out of the bean. Espresso's even worse. It typically has less than one-third the kick of lighter, rotgut joe. NF

GEEK FOOD

Bagels Like pizza, the bagel has royal roots. In 1683 in Vienna, Austria, a local Jewish baker, wanting to thank the king of Poland for protecting Jews from Turkish invaders, made a special hard roll in the shape of a riding stirrup ('Bugel' in German), commemorating the king's favorite pastime and giving the bagel its distinct shape.

▼

From there, the bagel somehow became a gift for women in childbirth and the child's teething ring. They next popped up in Russia, where they were called "bubliki", sold on strings and thought to be good luck charms with magical powers. The bagel reached North America in the early 20th century, when the only magic associated with it was financial. Bagel Bakers Local #338 in New York, founded sometime between 1910 and 1915, for

▼

GEEK SCIENCE + TECHNOLOGY ICON

Galileo Galilei Galileo is made the first geek heretic after he studies pendulums, mechanics, and gravity, and invents the pump and the telescope. He proves Copernicus' theory that the earth revolves around the sun, and in true extreme-scientist fashion irritates the Catholic regime. When he refuses to stop writing about his

▼

▼

beliefs, he is exiled to Florence and put under house arrest for life. Ouch.

> see page 26

example, was a union of some 300 crafts-men with "bagels in their blood". At the time, historians report, "it was probably easier to get into medical school than to get an apprenticeship in one of the 36 union bagel shops in New York City and New Jersey".
Although primarily an urban, Jewish staple for years, bagels went suburban in the 1960s with the advent of the frozen bagel and became ubiquitous

▼

GEEK SCIENCE + TECHNOLOGY ICON

Benjamin Franklin Ben Franklin was America's first real rock star. Born poor, he managed to become one of America's best scientists, inventors, diplomats and writers. He treated the Atlantic like a pond, made a fortune without losing his touch with the middle class, and juggled pacifism and a revolutionary war without those values

▼

in the 1980s when they garnered a somewhat undeserved reputation as health food. And their popularity soared again during the dot-com boom when companies used Bagel Friday (free platters of bagels and cream cheese every Friday), to get their employees into work early, despite having gotten the jump on the weekend by going clubbing the night before. NF

seeming inconsistent. And he became a folk hero on both sides of the Atlantic Ocean at a time when those heroes were difficult to come by. Too poor to go to school, Franklin became a printer's apprentice instead. Naturally curious, he ended up reading every word that passed through the press. That was all the encouragement – and education – he needed to become a writer and an editor, penning such ▲

▶ early bestsellers as <u>Poor Richard's Almanac</u>, and catchy slogans like "early to bed, early to rise...". But, in a spirit of pragmatism that would distinguish Franklin throughout his life, he also realized that he need not stop at being a mere writer and editor. Wanting all the benefits of complete control of the process, he also opened a chain of print shops. If that weren't enough, on top of that, he was the postmaster
▼

of Philadelphia and owner of one of its most successful bookstores. By 1748, when he was 42, living proof of his own aphorism that hard work, thrift and honesty could catapult poor people out of poverty, he was rich enough to retire, secure that he now had the means to fund the next four decades he was planning on living. And so, finally, he turned his attention to science. For an opening act,
▼

he invented the Franklin Stove, a cleaner burning convector heater that generated twice the heat from a quarter of wood than had been possible before. After that, he developed the idea of positive and negative electricity (1746–47), put two different kinds of lenses together to create bifocals (1748) so he could see not just what he was eating at dinner but who was speaking to him, flew a kite
▼

in a thunderstorm to see if lightning was a form of electricity and built a rod to tame it (1752). Displaying the luck of the Irish (which he was not), he was not hurt during the experiment. Two other scientists were not so lucky, since they were killed by the "electric fire" that jumped from the key at the end of the kite to their fried knuckles trying to replicate Franklin's experiments.
▲

▶ Although Franklin continued to dabble in science after that, he became more involved with social and political issues. He began his political career in service to the Court of England as a loyal subject. As events unfolded, however, his loyalty shifted and he became an open advocate for independence and the only person to collaborate on all the key founding documents of the United States.
▼

Later he served as the ambassador to France, where he evidently was popular with the Parisian women, kings and nobles. Despite this courtyard attraction, though, he never lost his affinity for the "leather aprons", or working middle class, and maintained his "dislike of everything that tended to debase the spirit of the common people" to the end of his long and storied life. NF

Geek From humble beginnings. In his dictionary, Samuel Johnson defines geek as "to cheat" or "trick", citing its origins in the German word "geck", or 'fool'. In the 19th century, carnivals use the word geek to describe their sideshow spectacles (usually vagrants and hobos) who bite heads off chickens.

THE LEADER of the LUDDITES

Luddite Riot Angered by the Industrial Revolution and their subsequent job displacement, textile artisans in Nottingham, England, begin destroying their non-human counterparts during the Luddite Riot, so named after fellow machine-smasher Ned Ludd. The Luddites lose — especially the ones who get caught and executed. The resulting public relations nightmare causes them to shift tactics and merely render the Luddites obsolete.

GEEK SCI-FI

Jonathan Swift, Gulliver's Travels It can be pretty slow going but this four part satire of a ship surgeon's travels through lands with six-inch tall people, giants, illusions and talking horses remains the motherlode for literary fantasy dorks. NF

Galileo Galilei
1564–1642

You got to hand it to Galileo. He perfected the telescope, discovered sunspots, the sun's axis, the lunar terrain, Venus and the moons of Jupiter, the laws of falling bodies and the law of the pendulum. The father of modern experimental science, he wrote a book in 1610 called The Messenger Under the Stars (which, had he written it today, would have become a Barry Manilow love song). Then, thanks to a

handful of some seriously mean priests, became the ultimate couch potato. There was nothing, really, in his childhood to foreshadow all this drama. Born in Italy, he didn't dream about fame or fortune when he was growing up. Instead, he wanted to be a teacher – of mathematics, which was his favorite subject at Padua U. In fact, the only thing he liked more than his equations was his telescope, a recently

patented instrument that at the time had more potential than real use. That didn't stop Galileo, who started futzing around with the 'scope'. Before long, he had tweaked it enough for him to see spots on the sun. Ever since Aristotle, people were convinced that heavenly bodies were "incorruptible and unchanging," so Galileo was in for quite a surprise. Fully expecting to see the sunspots in

the same place from day to day, they moved. "Uh oh," he thought. "It's time to have a go at the old guy." By then, Galileo was also gaping at the lunar craters, Venus and Jupiter's four moons. His entire universe was expanding – at the same time the classroom walls seemed increasingly confining. In a somewhat transparent but inexplicably successful attempt to curry favor with the Medici family,

he renamed the Venetian moons the "Medicean Planets." Shortly thereafter, Cosimo de Medici, better known as the Grand Duke of Tuscany, made Galileo his personal mathematician. Before you could say "ciao," Galileo waved goodbye to Padua and moved into a fancy Florentine villa. Life was good, at least until those damn sunspots came back to haunt him. In 1614, both the Protestants and the

Catholic Church finally realized that Copernicus had upset the Ptolemian and scriptural applecart and closed ranks against all things Copernican, including Galileo, who was denounced from pulpits for blasphemy. These attacks culminated two years later in a command performance in front of the Inquisition. Proving more temperate than their Spanish counterparts, the inquisitors stopped short of calling

him a heretic. Instead, they slapped his wrists and officially warned him to back off and neither "hold nor defend" Copernican theory. Galileo shuffled, smiled and bided his time. Then, in 1632 (when he was almost 70 and losing his eyesight) he published The Dialogue Concerning the Two Chief World Systems. Like Salman Rushdie's The Satanic Verses, it was condemned by most people (without reading it)

and by the Inquisition. They invited him back for a second meeting, reminded him of their warning 16 years ago, found him guilty of heresy and placed him under house arrest – for life. Undaunted, in 1638, now fully blind, he published Dialogue's sequel, Discussion on Two New Sciences. Five years later, without losing his status as a heretic, he died. While Copernicus got his comeuppance

in the 19th century, the Church dragged its heels for another century and a half to exonerate Galileo. In 1979, Pope John Paul II was bothered enough by the charge to wonder if Galileo had gotten a raw deal and reopened the case against him. Even with the Pope behind him, Galileo had to wait another 13 years before the investigation was complete. In 1992, after an actual investigation, the Pope

admitted that the Church had made a mistake: Galileo was not a heretic after all. Galileo, unfortunately, could not be reached for comment. NF

GEEK SCI-FI ICON

Mary Shelley Wollstonecraft (1797–1851) Although remembered today because she wrote Frankenstein, Mary Shelley's life was as turbulent and tragic as a work of fiction. According to one account, "she entered the world (on August 30, 1797) like the heroine of a Gothic tale: conceived in a secret amour, her birth heralded by storms and portents". Her parents were both famous, left-wing and artistic. Mom, Mary Wollstonecraft, was a famous feminist and her father, William Godwin, was a philosopher and novelist. The two had been in a clandestine affair when Mary was conceived, and Godwin, who believed in omens, was convinced that the storm that raged while Mary was being born was an announcement that the child was going to be extraordinary.

In the first of the series of tragedies that would dog her throughout her life, Mary lost her mother when Mary (and her mother, for that matter) was still young. For the rest of her childhood, Godwin would insist on their spending hours each day at her mother's grave (a habit some family members thought was emotionally damaging). Then, when she was 16, Mary fell in love with Percy Shelley, then an unhappily married, radical heir to a wealthy baronetcy. Despite threats from her father that he would disown her, she took Shelley for a lover.

Mary's father wasn't the only one who was scandalized. Even their liberal friends shunned them. Feeling betrayed and isolated, they fled to Italy where infidelity didn't have the same stigma, and became part of a lively circle of talented expatriates. But tragedy soon interfered, with Mary's half sister and Shelley's first wife committing suicide within weeks of each other. To help deal with their grief the two decided to spend the summer in Lake Geneva, where friends like Lord Byron also resided. On June 16, 1816, they were partying at Byron's house when a horrible summer storm forced them to stay the night. In what sounds like a cliché for a bad horror movie, they decided to pass the time reading a collection of German ghost stories, The Fantasmagoriana, out loud. In one story, a group of travelers tell each other about supernatural experiences they had experienced. Thinking it would be fun, Byron dared his guests to write ghost stories and report back the next night to read them.

Mary didn't write one, and the rest weren't very good so the discussion turned to whether or not "the principle of life could be discovered and whether scientists could galvanize a corpse of manufactured humanoid". Then one of the guests read a poem of Coleridge that prompted Shelley, convinced Coleridge had written it to disparage Mary, to storm out of the room in a jealous rage.

The emotions of the two days, as well as the residual shock of the two suicides, caught up with Mary when she lay down to bed that night. Before she could fall asleep, however, she had a waking vision and saw the following words (later to be used verbatim in the novel) take form:

"I saw the pale student of unhallowed arts kneeling beside the thing he had put together. I saw the hideous phantasm of a man stretched out, then, on the working of some powerful engine, show signs of life... His success would terrify the artist; he would rush away... hope that... this thing... would subside into dead matter... he opens his eyes; behold the horrid thing stands at his bedside, opening his eyes".

That was all she needed to sit down and write Frankenstein. Eleven months later, she had finished the book, and on New Year's Day, 1818, it was published. The reviews were dismissive, calling it a disposable entertainment, but theater companies recognized its dramatic potential and kept interest in the book alive by adapting it for the stage.

In happier times, Mary might have spent more time worrying about the book's reception but she had far worse things to deal with. Two of her three children died, society continued to ignore the Shelley's even though they eventually had gotten married. Then, when she was

▶ only 24, Shelley drowned, leaving her and her last surviving child, then two years old, penniless. With no other option, she returned to England, where she wrote five more books that were barely enough to cover the bills. Angry, bitter and unforgiving, her health also deserted her. She was an invalid by 48; and died of a brain tumor in 1851, just as The Great Exhibition, a celebration of the technological progress she had warned

▼

about, opened. Sometimes, as in the case of Mary Shelley, truth isn't just stranger than fiction. It's sadder. NF

Difference Engine Charles Babbage, the man often referred to as the "father of computing" invents the first automatic calculator, the Difference Engine, which tabulates basic mathematical information. Babbage dreams of creating a more sophisticated machine, and in 1832 devises the Analytical Engine, a machine that would do any sort of calculation. Even with the assistance

▼

▼

of Ada Lovelace, a mathematician credited for being the first computer programmer, a lack of support technology prevents him from building this precursor to the modern computer (his drafts are proven solid when a working model is created in 1991). Babbage may not be chic, but he's Dad, God love 'em.

Telegraph Samuel Morse invents the telegraph. Words are replaced with a series of taps, and the mark of high geekdom — the code — is here to stay.

GEEK FOOD

<u>Doughnuts</u> No one knows exactly why, but the Dutch ate balls of sweetened dough fried in hog's fat on Shrove Tuesday (before Easter) for centuries, and brought the recipe with them when they came to America. The crossing did not solve the fried cake's basic problem: No matter how they were fried, the centers always were soggy.

▼

According to legend, a cook on a ship under the command of one Hanson Crocket Gregory of Rockport, Maine solved the problem. During a storm, he brought some freshly fried cake on deck to give the sailors some added energy. But he slipped, slamming the cake on the spoke of the ship's wheel. When Gregory went to eat what was left, he found that the remainder wasn't soggy. Knowing a good thing when

▼

he saw one, he told the cook to punch the centers out before serving them from then on.
Despite the holes in his story, including how the outer ring stayed crisp in the rain, Gregory's version seemed more logical than Chief High Eagle's, who swore his tribe invented it by shooting arrows at the immigrants and hitting the cakes dead center instead. So Gregory sailed into the history books

▼

and remained there for 90 years. Then, one of his relatives outed him, at a doughnut convention no less. Gregory, the relative pointed out, would have been 15 at the time of the storm. What really happened, he continued, was that one day Gregory simply told his mother to dump the soggy center of the cake before she put it on his plate. Being a good mother, she did just that. NF

GEEK FOOD

<u>Potato Chips</u> Sometimes the customer really is right. On an otherwise ordinary August 24, 1853, George Crum, chef of the Moon Lake Lodge in Saratoga Springs, New York, was in the middle of the dinner rush when a customer kept sending back his fried potatoes, saying that they were too thick. "I'll show him", thought the vastly irritated Crum,

▼

slicing a potato paper-thin, frying them and tossing them in a basket. Then he tasted them, and knew he had a signature dish on his hands.
The chips remained a handcrafted item until the 1920s, when a traveling sales-man named Herman Lay invented the mechanical potato peeler. That paved the way for the mass-market potato chip. Then, in the 1940s, a small Irish chip (or crisp, as they called it) com-

▼

pany named Tayto developed a tech-nology that produced flavored potato chips (Cheese and Onion and Salt and Vinegar). From there, the fat gates opened and the world was flooded with an array of fried, crispy potato chips, corn chips and radioactively bright orange Cheetos. Finger foods and waistlines would never be the same. NF

<u>MIT</u> William Barton Rogers founds the Massachusetts Institute of Technology (MIT), the world's premier university for tech. Any self-respecting geek will spend his lifetime dreaming of attending the ultimate geek academy.

GEEK SCI-FI

<u>Jules Verne, 20000 Leagues under the Sea</u> Considered the father of science fiction, Jules Verne gave us a tale of mad scientists, monsters, submarines and octopi, all centered around a hapless duo whose biggest mistake was finding Nemo. NF

<u>Typewriter</u> Basing his work on the prior inventions of Henry Mill and William Burt, American Christopher Latham Sholes develops the Remington, the first working model of the modern typewriter. It sets the stage for typing tools, and is the precursor of data processing departments.

GEEK SCIENCE + TECHNOLOGY ICON

<u>Alexander Graham Bell</u> (1847–1922) Like Galileo before him, all the young Alexander Graham Bell really wanted to do was teach. The scion of a distinguished Scottish family with a long-standing love of music and sound, he got his wish, started teaching elocution at 16 and was a happy guy. But two years later, he curled up with

▲

▶ the German scientist Herman Helmholte's book, <u>The Sensation of Tone</u>. Suitably inspired by its description of the fundamental principles of sound, he found a new calling: He would be the first person to figure out how to transmit sound electrically.

Just as he was hitting his groove, his family moved to London. In retrospect, it was a mistake since two of his brothers died of tuberculosis and

▼

Alexander showed symptoms of the disease. Not wanting to lose a third son, his father moved them again, this time to Ontario, Canada, where the dry, cold climate was supposed to keep the disease at bay.

At least on that level, the move achieved its purpose, because Bell made a full recovery. In 1873, as soon as the doctors said it was okay, he moved to Boston to become Boston

▼

University's Professor of Vocal Physiology. There, fortuitously, he fell in love with a wealthy deaf student. Even better, her father became Bell's patron, willingly underwriting several of Bell's experiments.

Dad didn't have to wait long for a payback. Several months after watching a long line of people waiting in the cold to send telegraphs, Bell got an idea that, within a year, would

▼

lead to his first major patent. Called the harmonic telegraph, it spelled out how to send multiple messages along a single wire, an innovation that would shorten, if not eliminate, those long lines at the telegraph pole.

The success of that rekindled his long-standing interest in the electric transmission of the human voice. Two years later, Bell held another patent in his hands, this time for the telephone. ▲

▶ Within several months, on March 10, he spilled battery acid on his pants and screamed to his assistant, "Liar, liar, pants on fire." (Actually, the message went more like "Mr. (Thomas A.) Watson," he cried, "come here. I want you."). The ever-faithful Watson heard him – through a receiver on another floor of the building.

By the time his pants had come back from the cleaners, the telephone had

▼

become a sensation. Within months, Bell Telephone Company had gone from a messy home operation to a full-fledged business. By the end of the year, they had installed long-distance connections between Boston and New York.

Had he wanted to, Bell, who was 29 at the time, could have lived off his royalties forever. But he was on a roll. Funded by a grant from France (why play with your own money, even if

▼

you're minting it?), he used selenium crystals and a beam of light to transmit sound waves, thus sending the first true radio transmission.

Then, he took on Thomas Edison. Edison had unsuccessfully sued Bell over the rights to the telephone, so Bell, figuring that turnabout was fair play, tackled Edison's phonograph with what he called the graphophone.

Other inventions were less successful,

▼

but more fanciful. A speed freak, Bell was determined to make a flying submarine, but settled merely on advancing the hydrofoil. In an attempt to save the life of President James Garfield, who was clinging to life after being shot by an assassin, he developed an electrical apparatus that could locate bullets in the body. (The President still died. As it turned out, the fault lay not with the ▲

▶ machine but with the doctors, who hadn't removed the steel springs in the hospital bed, thus rendering the machine impotent.) And try as he might, Bell failed to perfect a machine that would save people stranded at sea in open-air boats (how's that for a niche) by making fresh water out of vapor in the air.

Nonetheless, towards the end of his life, in 1915, he did manage to make

▼

the first transcontinental phone call. Fittingly, once again the person at the other end of the line was the long-suffering Thomas A. Watson. This time, Bell stayed far away from the battery acid and made the call without messing up his pants. NF

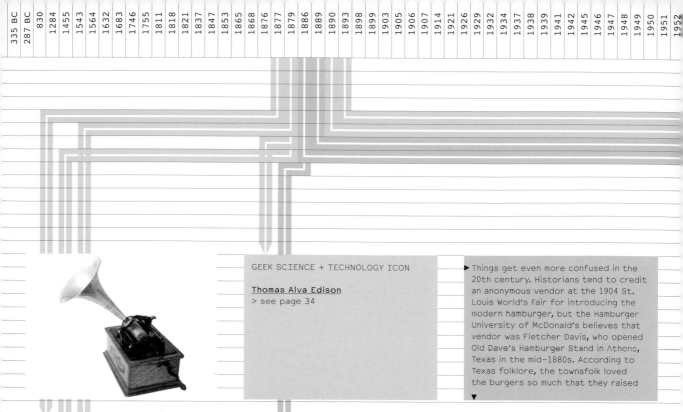

GEEK SCIENCE + TECHNOLOGY ICON

<u>Thomas Alva Edison</u>
> see page 34

Things get even more confused in the 20th century. Historians tend to credit an anonymous vendor at the 1904 St. Louis World's Fair for introducing the modern hamburger, but the Hamburger University of McDonald's believes that vendor was Fletcher Davis, who opened Old Dave's Hamburger Stand in Athens, Texas in the mid-1880s. According to Texas folklore, the townsfolk loved the burgers so much that they raised

<u>Phonograph</u> Thomas Edison invents the phonograph, which reproduces sound from rotating, foil-covered cylinders. Not suitable for playing big bass lines, it is left to Alexander Graham Bell to invent the gramophone, which plays one-off wax disks. It's not until 10 years later that Emile Berliner invents a method of mass-producing records and kicks off the record industry.

enough money to send Davis to St. Louis and present his invention to the world. (Davis also claimed to have been the first person to serve French Fries. According to an interview he gave to a New York reporter at the Fair, a friend of his from Paris, Texas, came up with the idea. The reporter thought Davis meant Paris, France and called the dish French Fries. (Given that the sitting president of the U.S. at the time

<u>Light Bulb</u> Edison goes on to invent the light bulb, which will inadvertently someday become the culprit of fluorescent lab tans. Say what you will, the guy's on a roll.

GEEK FOOD

<u>Burgers</u> Despite an almost universal bad press, about 60 percent of all sandwiches eaten these days are hamburgers. It's too bad, then, that its origins will be forever shrouded in mystery.
The first recorded antecedent of the burger was in Central Asia during Medieval times, when Tartars would

of this writing is both a Texan and no friend of France, it is odd that he renamed them Freedom Fries instead of Texas Fries.)
Some, however, think Davis is a liar. They insist that hamburgers were born in Seymour, Wisconsin in 1885 when 15-year-old Charlie Nagreen sold them from a stand at the Outgamie County Fair. They are so sure they're right that they've erected

<u>Ray Tube</u> German scientist Karl Ferdinand Braun invents the cathode ray tube (CRT), used in computers, ATMs, video game consoles, oscilloscopes, radar displays, and televisions. Errant yet predictable rock stars discover that the vacuum inside creates a satisfying implosion when these are thrown out of hotel room windows.

pack pieces of beef under their saddles and ride for days, secure in the knowledge that the leather tenderized the meat. Slightly more palatable was Hamburg style raw beef patties, thought to be the predecessor of steak tartare, and the lesser-known Hamburgian beef patty cooked in butter and topped with a fried egg conceived by Hamburgian cook Otto Kause in 1891.

a Hamburger Museum to honor old Charlie and his hamburger stand. Now that we are caught between a university and a museum, we say " pass the mustard please...". NF

GEEK FOOD

<u>Pizza</u> Thousands of years ago in the Middle East, everyone from the Israelites to the Babylonians baked unleavened bread in mud ovens and topped it with olive oil and spices. Then, in the 19th century, Italy threw in tomatoes. As a sign of support for King Umberto and Queen Margherita, who were making a swing through a

lower class neighborhood of Naples, a baker named Raffaele Esposito wanted to bake them something that would represent the Italian colors. He came up with a baked pie topped with red (tomatoes), white (mozzarella) and green (basil). The King and Queen were suitably impressed, and pizza became the rage. The Italians brought it across the globe in the early 20th century, but pizza warmers, cheap

GEEK SCIENCE + TECHNOLOGY ICON

<u>Nikola Tesla</u>
> see page 36

student labor and fleets of delivery cars in the late 1960 put, mixed metaphor notwithstanding, the icing on the cake.

GEEK FOOD

<u>Coca-Cola</u> Coca-Cola was invented in May 1886 by Dr. John S. Pemberton in Atlanta, Georgia, and first sold at Jacob's Pharmacy in Atlanta by one Willis Venable. There wasn't much business, about nine Cokes a day. That amounted to $50 at the end of the year, which was $20 less than they had spent on the product. But

familiar cursive logo. Despite media speculation that Coca-Cola had a major disaster on their hands, Diet Coke became the third most popular soft drink in the country within months and in the world by 1986. It also inspires rabid brand loyalty, and is commonly written into the riders of many powerful entertainers and politicians, including Nine Inch Nails, Cher, Elton John, Mariah Carey, Donald

small steps sometimes win the race; by the mid-1980s, Coke had become the most recognized trademark in the world, moving over a billion units a day. But that was just a warm up for Diet Coke, which was the biggest launch in soft drink history. Launched in July 1982 to capitalize on the aerobics craze to the tune of $100 million, it was the first product besides the original Coca-Cola that wore the

▶ Trump, both Clintons and Miramax heavy, Harvey Weinstein. NF

<u>Electric Chair</u> Capital punishment goes high-tech. William Kemmler, a convicted murderer, is executed by being exposed to 2000-volt blasts of electricity while strapped to a metal chair. It takes several attempts to kill him, after which the electric chair's inventor, Alfred Southwick, says, "There is the culmination of 10 years" work and study. We live in a higher civilization from this day". (See Luddite Riot.)

Thomas Alva Edison
1847–1931

Try to get this on one resume:
Inventor of practical electric
lighting (i.e., the light bulb) and the
phonograph, perfected the telephone
and telegraph, millionaire, power
broker in the motion picture industry,
owner of one of the first and most
important research laboratories in
the world. Then, squeeze in the name,
Thomas Alva Edison.
Born in Milan, Ohio, the son of an

expatriate Canadian shingle maker
and teacher, he grew up an example
of one of his most famous sayings,
"Genius is one percent inspiration and
99 percent perspiration". Inquisitive
to a fault, his teachers described
him as "addled" and expelled him from
school for asking too many questions.
His mother home schooled him, but
gave him plenty of free time, which
he put to good use, making intricate,

working steam-powered models of
saw mills and railroads, growing and
selling vegetables to the neighbors,
and newspapers, candy and sandwiches
to passengers on the train from Port
Huron and Detroit. Then he turned 13
– and, feeling the pressure of age,
decided to hire others so he could
move even more merchandise.
By 15, he was also printing and selling
a newspaper, The Weekly Herald, out

of one of the cars on the train and
starting to lose his hearing. He had
his hands full, but still managed to
rescue another kid, who had fallen
onto the tracks. The boy's grateful
father was a telegraph operator
who repaid Edison by hiring him as a
telegraph operator.
Edison was fascinated by every aspect
of the business and good enough to
be moved to Boston in 1868, where he

figured out, at least in theory, how
to send pictures over the wire. But
it was an electric vote recorder that
received the first of his record-set-
ting 1,093 U.S. patents. It increased
the speed with which legislatures could
operate, but the legislature had no
interest in becoming more efficient,
and the invention was never used. The
experience made a big impact on the
young inventor. In the future, he would

only invent things that could be used.
The first of these came one year
later, when he improved the stock
ticker mechanism. It was not just
successful, but established Edison's
M.O. Unlike inventors who create
something from nothing, Edison,
who had no background, interest or
particular affinity for theory or math,
liked to develop alternative solutions
to existing problems or objects.

Thus, in 1874, he crossed paths with
Alexander Graham Bell for the first
time, patenting the quadruplex,
a machine that let four telegraph
messages be sent along the same
wire. Two years later, with royalties
and financing from the stock market
and generous support from telegraph
companies, especially Western Union,
he moved to Menlo Park, New Jersey,
and built the first U.S.'s first great

research lab. The lab paid off a year
later, when he and his assistants
perfected the telephone transmitter,
allowing the person's voice to be
louder and clearer. (This also led to
a protracted and unsuccessful suit
against Alexander Graham Bell.) That
same year, he unveiled the phonograph
and the first record, which featured
him reciting "Mary Had a Little Lamb".
The invention immediately earned him

standard for power plants throughout the country, but his designs were less successful than those of competitor, Westinghouse. It was an irritant but not a crippling loss since he astutely had cornered the market on the auxiliary products necessary for both his and their power plants, including generators and cables and the like. By 1892, he had consolidated these products under the umbrella company,

the nickname, The Wizard of Menlo Park, but, curiously, the Wizard believed it would be used as a dictating machine, as well as a voice box for talking dolls, and was totally taken aback when people started using it to preserve and play music.

That says less about his ear than the cluttered state of his mind, which was also percolating with thoughts on incandescent light bulb (which created

light by passing electricity through a filament which then glowed). It was a revolutionary idea with a big problem: Only a handful of houses were wired for electricity. Realizing he had put the cart before the horse, Edison immediately went into the power plant business, constructing the Pearl St. Station in New York City, a stone's throw from Wall Street.

He hoped this plant would set the

The Edison Electric Company, which in short order mutated into General Electric.

Now that he was done with light, he turned his attention to moving pictures. "I can experiment upon an instrument which does for the Eye what the phonograph does for the Ear," he said. With money from his various inventions pouring in, he moved to another New Jersey ex-urb,

Llewellyn Park, and built a lab ten times the size of Menlo Park, introduced the kinetoscope, which let people view movies through a peephole, and designed the Black Maria, the first building designed specifically to make commercial movies. Then, for the next 30 years, until the US Supreme Court broke it up as a monopoly, he and his associates, operating under the moniker The Motion Picture Patents

Organization, controlled the way the motion picture industry produced and distributed movies.

Even so, he never went Hollywood. Throughout the early 20th century, he also found the time to pioneer cement manufacturing and construction, supplying the materials and know how for the construction of large scale projects such as Yankee Stadium and (unsuccessfully) promoting a line of

cement furniture. And, no doubt to spite his rival, Alexander Graham Bell, he developed [non-spillable] storage batteries that were used by the railroads to power switches and signals and by his best friend, Henry Ford, for the electric starters in gasoline-engine powered cars (Edison's idea, of course.)

About the only thing that he did not corner the market on was the Nobel

Prize, which he was denied due to lobbying from his archenemy Nicola Tesla. That was about the only honor that eluded Edison. When he died in1931, President Herbert Hoover had the country dim their electric lights for several minutes in memory of the 20th century's true lighting rod. NF

Nikola Tesla
1856–1943

Nikola Tesla is perhaps the best example of a geek gone haywire, someone so brilliant yet so off his rocker that you have to wonder: Was he was a victim or a hero?
Tesla was born in Croatia, and spent most of his childhood in Austria. While a student, he noticed that a dynamo operating on DC (direct current) was malfunctioning. Rather than wait for someone to fix it, he devised a

solution that involved implementing an AC (alternating current) system. It was an impressive demonstration of ingenuity, and helped Tesla land a job three years later (1882) at the Continental Edison Company, where he continued to develop AC systems. Tesla knew he was sitting on a gold mine, but couldn't convince Edison, who was myopically determined to stick with the DC format, to take

him seriously. Frustrated but hardly out of tricks, Tesla continued to work on his own and, under Edison's nose, patented polyphase AC dynamos, transformers and motors for himself. Adding insult to injury, he sold the system to Edison's biggest competitor, Westinghouse, giving Westinghouse an unexpected advantage in the electric wars against Edison and GE.

Although this would have been enough to secure Tesla a place in history, he was just warming up. In 1893, he invented the Tesla coil, which is a source of high voltage and high frequency currents and led him to predict the advent of radio two years before Marconi. Then, in 1899, proving that the earth is a conductor of electricity, he generated a giant flash of artificial lightning that had millions of volts and was 135 feet (41 meters) long.

He also found time to come up with neon and fluorescent lighting, no small feats in and of themselves. But there were darker elements to Tesla that undermined many of these accomplishments. Some disappointments, such as losing funding for his 200-foot tall radio tower in Long Island midway through

▶

the project, could be chalked up to the luck of the draw. But others, such as his announcement that he had been receiving signals from other planets or that he had discovered a new kind of death ray, were a bit more difficult to shake off.

Tesla, though, seemed surprised by his colleagues' skepticism, and became more withdrawn, paranoid and bitter. He especially resented Edison and

▲

Marconi. By now reduced to living in a series of New York flophouses, Tesla became a recluse, still churning out inventions but so disillusioned that he stopped getting patents for them. Why bother, he reasoned. Someone would steal them anyway. Ultimately, however, the system did not desert him entirely. First it allowed him the privilege of denying Edison the Nobel Peace Prize. Next it gave Tesla the

▶

head of Marconi, albeit posthumously, when the U.S. Supreme Court reversed most of the patents they had awarded to Marconi and officially gave Tesla credit for inventing the radio.

The honors did not stop there. Feeling guilty over their treatment of him, the scientific community agreed to call a unit of magnetic strength the Tesla. And, although this may well be a dubious distinction, a highly touted

▲

metal band called themselves Tesla in their attempt to unseat AC/DC. In a conceptually apt nod to their namesake, they had some great songs but self-destructed and disappeared, outlasted by people who may not have had more talent but played the game a hell of a lot better. NF

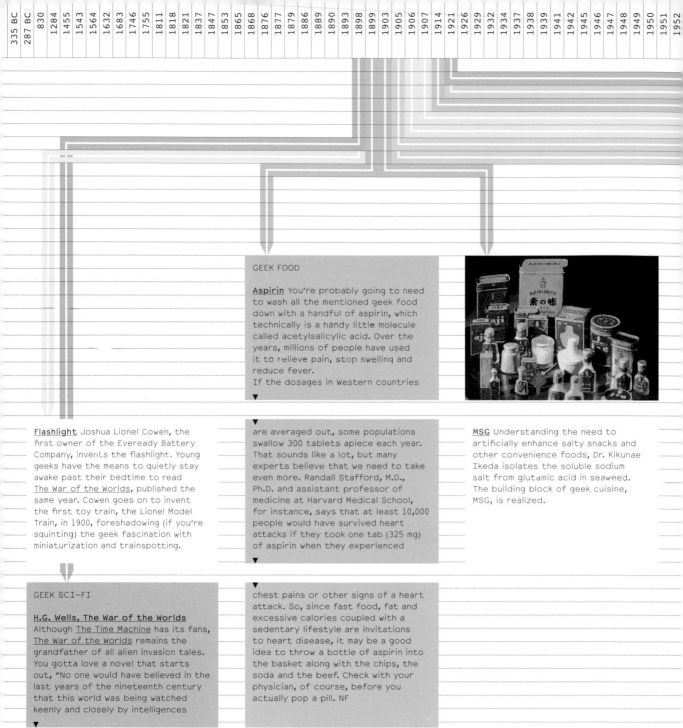

GEEK FOOD

Aspirin You're probably going to need to wash all the mentioned geek food down with a handful of aspirin, which technically is a handy little molecule called acetylsalicylic acid. Over the years, millions of people have used it to relieve pain, stop swelling and reduce fever.
If the dosages in Western countries

▼

Flashlight Joshua Lionel Cowen, the first owner of the Eveready Battery Company, invents the flashlight. Young geeks have the means to quietly stay awake past their bedtime to read <u>The War of the Worlds</u>, published the same year. Cowen goes on to invent the first toy train, the Lionel Model Train, in 1900, foreshadowing (if you're squinting) the geek fascination with miniaturization and trainspotting.

▼

are averaged out, some populations swallow 300 tablets apiece each year. That sounds like a lot, but many experts believe that we need to take even more. Randall Stafford, M.D., Ph.D. and assistant professor of medicine at Harvard Medical School, for instance, says that at least 10,000 people would have survived heart attacks if they took one tab (325 mg) of aspirin when they experienced

▼

MSG Understanding the need to artificially enhance salty snacks and other convenience foods, Dr. Kikunae Ikeda isolates the soluble sodium salt from glutamic acid in seaweed. The building block of geek cuisine, MSG, is realized.

GEEK SCI-FI

<u>H.G. Wells, The War of the Worlds</u> Although <u>The Time Machine</u> has its fans, <u>The War of the Worlds</u> remains the grandfather of all alien invasion tales. You gotta love a novel that starts out, "No one would have believed in the last years of the nineteenth century that this world was being watched keenly and closely by intelligences

▼

chest pains or other signs of a heart attack. So, since fast food, fat and excessive calories coupled with a sedentary lifestyle are invitations to heart disease, it may be a good idea to throw a bottle of aspirin into the basket along with the chips, the soda and the beef. Check with your physician, of course, before you actually pop a pill. NF

▼

greater than man". And yes, this is the one that Orson Wells read on the radio, causing a national panic in the States, and that Tom Cruise and Steven Spielberg are remaking. NF

Mechanical Pen Croat Eduard Penkala invents the mechanical pen. Can the pocket protector be far behind?

Pocket Protector After selling his patent for a fountain pen to pen manufacturing giant Waterman in 1900, Victor Ochoa patents a "pen clip" — the pocket protector. Geeks have a reason to accessorize. Interestingly, Ochoa is better known as a revolutionary than an inventor. Citing land ownership discrepancies, he spends the 1880s and 1890s trying

▼

RUR Czech playwright Karel Capek writes "Rossum's Universal Robots", introducing the term "robot" from the Czech word "robota," meaning "serf" or "forced labor", The word gets broadly adopted by '50s sci-fi ("Forbidden Planet" and Robbie The Robot) and by robot legends such as R2D2. By the 21st century, many children replace robot dogs with the real deal.

GEEK SCIENCE + TECHNOLOGY ICON

Albert Einstein
> see page 40

▼

to overthrow the Mexican government. When that doesn't work, he flees to Texas, is captured in the States, and in lieu of extradition (thanks to US President Grover Cleveland) spends three years in a US jail. There is, however, the small matter of a $50,000 bounty on his head, no questions asked, by the Mexican government. His solution: the faking of his own death.

Call Signs After over 20 years of radio operation — a history, like open-source computing, developed through valuable amateur contributions — the US government establishes call signs. Stations get their own abbreviated code names, and early HAM radio geeks devise clever personal call names and code phrases like "Roger/Wilco" and "MayDay". Working in the spirit of Morse Code, HAM morphs into a means of

▼

Theory of Relativity Einstein writes the "Theory Of Relativity", changing scientists' views of the world forever and confusing everyone else. He says that energy is equal to mass times the speed of light squared, meaning that the tiniest amount of matter can be converted into a huge amount of energy, and this is chillingly demonstrated in Hiroshima and Nagasaki in 1946.

MDMA Invention of MDMA, later known as "Ecstacy", by German chemical company Merk, supposedly to be sold as a diet pill. It is banned in 1985, but in 1993 becomes the first psychoactive drug approved for testing by the Food and Drug Administration (FDA). Not every geek's drug of choice (caffeine, surely is), but it's the one that will get the most attention.

▼

underground communication for social outcasts and is an early precursor to chat groups.

Albert Einstein
1879–1955

You may not understand a word of what he's saying, but no scientist does cool better than Albert Einstein. Born in southern Germany, he was the epitome of still waters running deep, and didn't talk until a relatively late age. He was also unpredictable in his passions. At five he developed his first great obsession, over a magnetic compass. At six it was the violin and the, at age 12, a pamphlet on Euclidean geometry he stumbled upon.

(The latter was, admittedly, an odd thing to fall for. But, as he later explained it, any system that enabled someone to deduce complex phenomena from a small number of self-evident statements about geometric figures was just fine by him.) These interests notwithstanding, he was a mediocre student who spent more time in the library reading physics than he did in his classes. His

high school attendance record and his brazen reliance on other people's notes made him unpopular with his advisor, who got his revenge by preventing or, more precisely, failing to encourage him from continuing with a university education. So rather than go to college, Einstein, who was then living in Bern, Switzerland, got a job as a patent clerk, where he was to read and evaluate patent applications.

The job suited him, because it gave him plenty of time to read about physics. All that reading paid off in 1905, his "year of marvels," during which he unleashed four bombshells into the scientific community.

The first of the papers detailed the photoelectric effect, essentially proving that light is composed of chunks of atoms. The second explained Brownian motion, and was instrumental in proving the existence of atoms. The third was his special theory of relativity, which showed that the velocity of light was a constant, and the fourth, perhaps the most pregnant of all, that Energy and mass are interchangeable, giving T-shirt designers their favorite equation, $E = MC$ squared.

It was a phenomenon – not one but four papers that turned the scientific establishment on its ears. Although it was only five years into the 20th century, Einstein had already secured his reputation as its greatest physicist. The ensuing torrent of attention swept away any lingering reservations about Einstein's worth as an intellect. The man without a degree soon found himself the object of a bidding war among academicians. By 1909, he was wearing professorial robes at the University of Zurich, and pounding out his general theory of relativity, published in 1916, which demonstrated the effects gravity had on time and light.

By then, Einstein, convinced that a scientist had a special moral and social responsibility, was a vocal human rights activist and pacifist. Being Jewish and German, he was also an early target of the Nazis, who vehemently attacked him and his theories. These attacks turned him into an ardent Zionist, and took him around the world campaigning for the creation of a Jewish state.

In 1933, in his third annual visit to the California Institute of Technology, where he would spend December lecturing, the Nazis seized power. That was all the proof Einstein needed to never set foot in Germany again. Initially he took refuge in Belgium under the protection of the royal family. Then he spent several months in England until becoming a professor at the prestigious Institute for Advanced Studies in Princeton, New Jersey, where he lived for the rest of his life. World War II put his pacifism in direct conflict with his views on social responsibility. When he got wind of the German efforts to build an atomic bomb, he wrote a now famous letter to U.S. President Franklin Delano Roosevelt, urging him to fund the Allies' effort to develop the bomb first. This letter prompted the government to underwrite the Manhattan Project, which led to the creation of the atomic bomb.

Like many who participated in the Manhattan Project, Einstein believed the bomb was a necessary evil but was haunted by its after-effects and spent the rest of his life arguing for tight controls on atomic energy. One week before his death, in fact, he and Edward Teller sent a letter to the world, begging all the countries that had atomic weapons to give them up. Needless to say, the letter was ignored and the arms race escalated, leaving Einstein and his ilk with the realization that they had gone Goethe one better and made the ultimate Faustian deal. NF

335 BC	287 BC	830	1284	1455	1543	1564	1632	1683	1746	1755	1811	1818	1821	1837	1847	1853	1865	1868	1876	1877	1879	1886	1889	1890	1893	1898	1899	1903	1905	1906	1907	1914	1921	1926	1929	1932	1934	1937	1938	1939	1941	1942	1945	1946	1947	1948	1949	1950	1951	1952

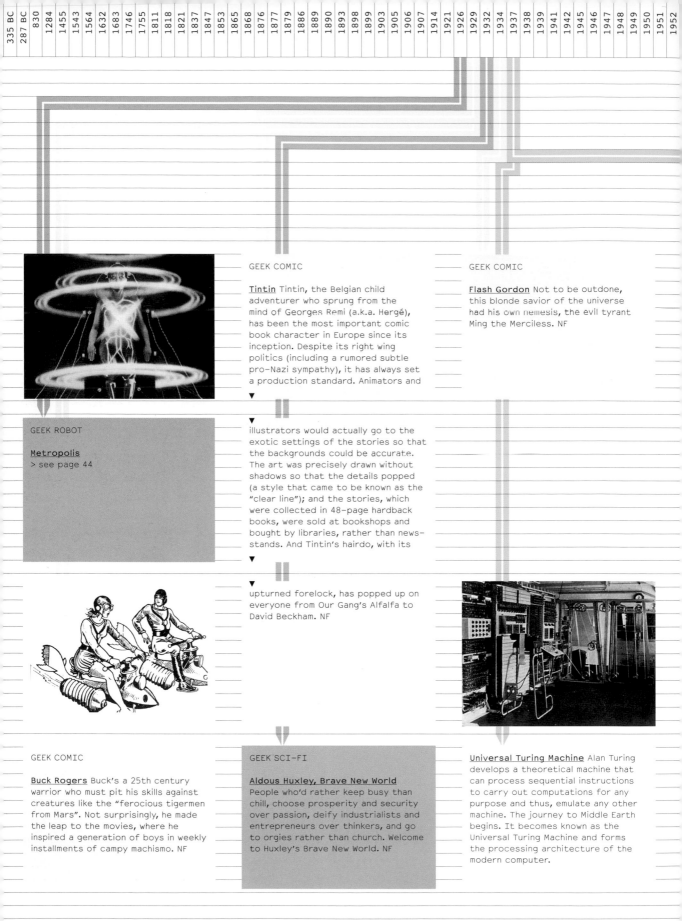

GEEK COMIC

Tintin Tintin, the Belgian child adventurer who sprung from the mind of Georges Remi (a.k.a. Hergé), has been the most important comic book character in Europe since its inception. Despite its right wing politics (including a rumored subtle pro-Nazi sympathy), it has always set a production standard. Animators and

▼

GEEK COMIC

Flash Gordon Not to be outdone, this blonde savior of the universe had his own nemesis, the evil tyrant Ming the Merciless. NF

GEEK ROBOT

Metropolis
> see page 44

illustrators would actually go to the exotic settings of the stories so that the backgrounds could be accurate. The art was precisely drawn without shadows so that the details popped (a style that came to be known as the "clear line"); and the stories, which were collected in 48-page hardback books, were sold at bookshops and bought by libraries, rather than news-stands. And Tintin's hairdo, with its

▼

upturned forelock, has popped up on everyone from Our Gang's Alfalfa to David Beckham. NF

GEEK COMIC

Buck Rogers Buck's a 25th century warrior who must pit his skills against creatures like the "ferocious tigermen from Mars". Not surprisingly, he made the leap to the movies, where he inspired a generation of boys in weekly installments of campy machismo. NF

GEEK SCI-FI

Aldous Huxley, Brave New World
People who'd rather keep busy than chill, choose prosperity and security over passion, deify industrialists and entrepreneurs over thinkers, and go to orgies rather than church. Welcome to Huxley's Brave New World. NF

Universal Turing Machine Alan Turing develops a theoretical machine that can process sequential instructions to carry out computations for any purpose and thus, emulate any other machine. The journey to Middle Earth begins. It becomes known as the Universal Turing Machine and forms the processing architecture of the modern computer.

GEEK SCIENCE + TECHNOLOGY ICON

Alan Mathison Turing (1912–1954)
Alan Turing was not just a product but, sadly, a victim of the times he lived in. Although he died only 60 years ago, his life story reads like a 19th century tragedy, full of secrecy, betrayal and hypocrisy.
Born into a comfortable, academically distinguished family of English

▶ War II forced a change in plans. His education, reputation and skills waltzed him into one of the most important assignments in the war effort: He was to crack the German "Enigma" codes. His efforts, as chronicled or alluded to in novels by, among others, Thomas Pynchon, Neal Stevenson and Richard Powers, and in plays such as <u>Breaking the Code</u> were instrumental in the Allied effort and

▶ better known for his private life. Turing was homosexual which today would be little more than a footnote but back then was a matter for the criminal court system. It wasn't just that he was homosexual, which would have been enough, either. He was powerful, successful, influential and, by all accounts, charming. Rather than help his case, those attributes and his accomplishments only served

mathematicians, Turing was a precocious mini logician and a model student. Educated at the best schools, including Cambridge and Princeton, he became fascinated with the notion of computability. He made his first impression on the scientific community in 1937 with a well-received philosophical treatise on the Turing Machine.
The machine remained a hypothetical

turned Turing into an underground war hero.
That war record made it easy for Turing to pick up his work with computers where he left off. This time he landed at the National Physical Laboratory in London, where they built the first British electric digital computer, ACE (Automatic Computing Engine), a forerunner of the modern computer.

to make the English government more determined to prosecute him both as a sexual deviant and as a security risk. Thus, in 1952, he was charged and convicted of homosexual activities. Rather than face prison, Turing chose the only other option offered him, estrogen therapy. Although it was thought (inaccurately) to cure homosexuality, it failed to "cure" Turing. Rather than endure continued

computing device that in principle could perform any calculation imaginable and also simulate all possible computing machines and programs. Although the machine itself was never built, its proposed structure became an important predictor for what could be programmed on a computer for years to come.
Turing had planned on spending all his time on the machine, but World

Few had as instinctive an understanding of computers' potential, as Turing proved in 1950 with his Turing test, which determined whether a machine could think.
The test began with a one-hour dialogue between a person and the computer. Then a transcript of the conversation was given to an outside observer. If that observer read the transcript without realizing one of

humiliation, Turing took matters into his own hands and on June 6, 1954, committed suicide. Apparently, you could be jolly and merry in ye olde England, just as long as you weren't gay. NF

the participants was a machine, the machine was said to "think". The test had too many holes to be of real use and the machines were still fairly primitive, but like the Turing Machine, the idea attracted attention, spurred discussion and helped lay the foundation for today's work with artificial intelligence.
Considerable as these achievements may be, though, he is probably

GEEK ROBOT

Metropolis
1927

One of Adolph Hitler's favorite films, Fritz Lang's depiction of the class struggle between the Workers and the Thinkers in a futuristic urban hell established the architecture for sci-fi movies. Not the least of Metropolis' legacy is the robot, a C3P0 prototype that is the centerpiece of the movie's famous poster. The robot also gets the best scene in the film when he mutates into

a flesh and blood imprint of the rebel hero – except for two "dead orbs" instead of eyes that tell the audience that no one's home. NF

335 BC	287 BC	830	1284	1455	1543	1564	1632	1683	1746	1755	1811	1818	1821	1837	1847	1853	1865	1868	1876	1877	1879	1886	1889	1890	1893	1898	1899	1903	1905	1906	1907	1914	1921	1926	1929	1932	1934	1937	1938	1939	1941	1942	1945	1946	1947	1948	1949	1950	1951	1952

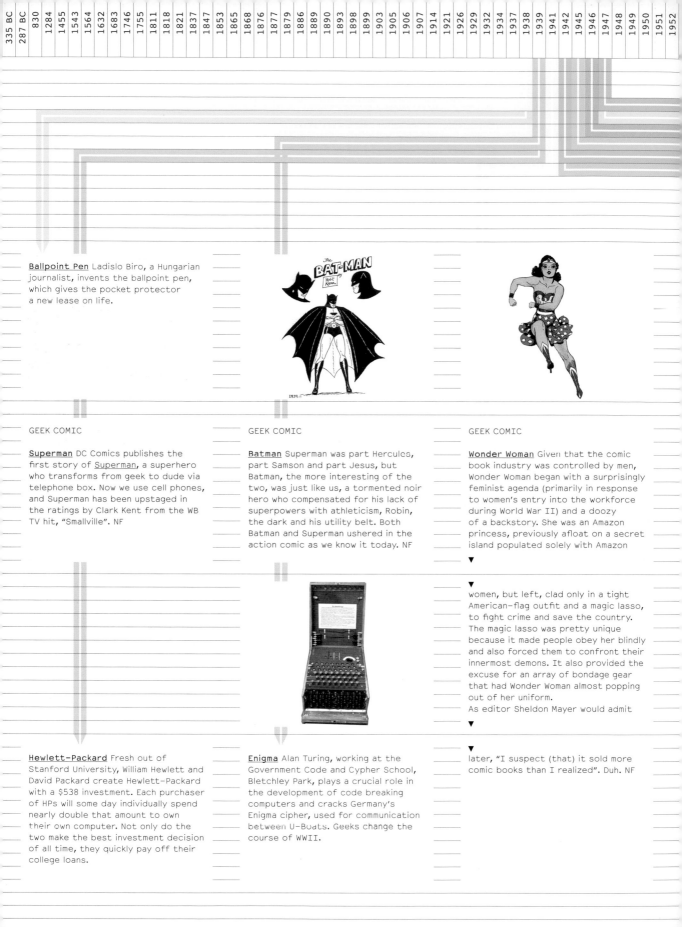

Ballpoint Pen Ladislo Biro, a Hungarian journalist, invents the ballpoint pen, which gives the pocket protector a new lease on life.

GEEK COMIC

Superman DC Comics publishes the first story of <u>Superman</u>, a superhero who transforms from geek to dude via telephone box. Now we use cell phones, and Superman has been upstaged in the ratings by Clark Kent from the WB TV hit, "Smallville". NF

GEEK COMIC

Batman Superman was part Hercules, part Samson and part Jesus, but Batman, the more interesting of the two, was just like us, a tormented noir hero who compensated for his lack of superpowers with athleticism, Robin, the dark and his utility belt. Both Batman and Superman ushered in the action comic as we know it today. NF

GEEK COMIC

Wonder Woman Given that the comic book industry was controlled by men, Wonder Woman began with a surprisingly feminist agenda (primarily in response to women's entry into the workforce during World War II) and a doozy of a backstory. She was an Amazon princess, previously afloat on a secret island populated solely with Amazon

▼

▼

women, but left, clad only in a tight American-flag outfit and a magic lasso, to fight crime and save the country. The magic lasso was pretty unique because it made people obey her blindly and also forced them to confront their innermost demons. It also provided the excuse for an array of bondage gear that had Wonder Woman almost popping out of her uniform.
As editor Sheldon Mayer would admit

▼

▼

Hewlett-Packard Fresh out of Stanford University, William Hewlett and David Packard create Hewlett-Packard with a $538 investment. Each purchaser of HPs will some day individually spend nearly double that amount to own their own computer. Not only do the two make the best investment decision of all time, they quickly pay off their college loans.

Enigma Alan Turing, working at the Government Code and Cypher School, Bletchley Park, plays a crucial role in the development of code breaking computers and cracks Germany's Enigma cipher, used for communication between U-Boats. Geeks change the course of WWII.

later, "I suspect (that) it sold more comic books than I realized". Duh. NF

Duct Tape Johnson & Johnson invents duct tape. Its original purpose is to keep moisture out of ammunition cases used during World War II. Eventually a better use is found: eyeglass adhesive.

Computer Bug Grace Murray Hopper, one of the first computer programmers and the inventor of the compiler, is working on the Harvard Mark II computer when she finds a moth beaten to death in the jaws of one of its relays; this becomes the first computer bug. Thereafter when the machine stops, they joke that they are "debugging" the computer. The moth still exists in the National Museum of American History of the Smithsonian Institution.

LSD Dr Albert Hofmann synthesizes LSD, changes the world (at least through the eyes of those who took it), and creates what will become the catalyst of the counter-culture. He uses himself as a test subject and has a dangerous cycle ride home as a result.

ABC ABC, the first electronic digital computer, is developed at the University of Iowa by John V. Atanasoff and Clifford Berry. The computer, which weighs 700 pounds, uses binary functions and has separate memory and computing capacities, among other key features. Based on the ABC prototype, Presper Eckert and John Mauchly go on to create the ENIAC between 1943 and

Transistor Radio Two scientists working for William Shockley at the Bell Telephone Laboratories make observations that lead to the discovery of the solid-state transistor, which supersedes the hot, unreliable, bulky vacuum tube in computers and other electronic devices. By 1955, kids all over the world are hiding under their covers, tuning their cool little portable

▼

1946, based on the early work on the ABC, and try to pass off their work as purely original. Is it the precursor to the Microsoft/Apple debate, or a minor geek clash? Either way, a patent infringement suit solves the case, and the ABC is dubbed the first.

Mountain Dew Named after the back-woods slang for moonshine, Mountain Dew is first bottled in Knoxville, Tennessee. In 1965, the potent, citrus-flavored, day-glow green soda is sold to Pepsi and distributed to the masses. Thanks to its 37mg of caffeine per 8-ounce serving (about the same as tea), Mountain Dew becomes the energizing elixir for young geeks, enabling them to solve algorithms at the speed of light.

▼

transistor radios into stations hundreds of miles away and getting a primitive taste of the virtual village.

335 BC	287 BC	830	1284	1455	1543	1564	1632	1683	1746	1755	1811	1818	1821	1837	1847	1853	1865	1868	1876	1877	1879	1886	1889	1890	1893	1898	1899	1903	1905	1906	1907	1914	1921	1926	1929	1932	1934	1937	1938	1939	1941	1942	1945	1946	1947	1948	1949	1950	1951	1952

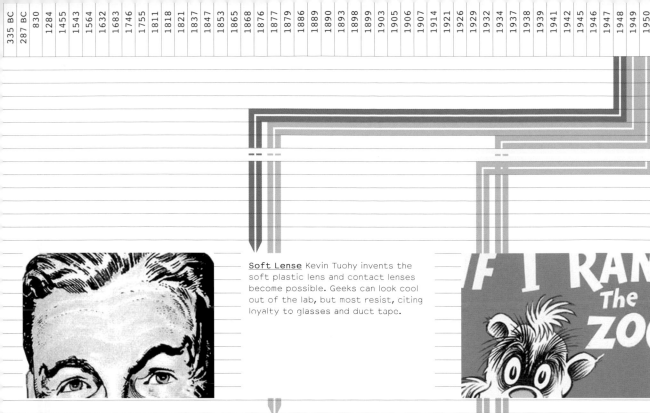

Soft Lense Kevin Tuohy invents the soft plastic lens and contact lenses become possible. Geeks can look cool out of the lab, but most resist, citing loyalty to glasses and duct tape.

GEEK SCI-FI

George Orwell, 1984 What can you say about a book with sentences like "Though the sun were shining and the sky a harsh blue, there seemed to be no color in anything but the posters that were plastered everywhere" and concepts like Big Brother, The Ministry of Truth and The Thought Police besides, "Read it". NF

If I Ran the Zoo Dr. Seuss writes "If I Ran the Zoo" and publishes the first use of the word nerd: "And then, just to show them, I'll sail to Ka-Too and bring back an It-Kutch, a Preep and a Proo, a Nerckle, a Nerd, and a Seersucker, too!".

GEEK COMIC

Dan Dare – Pilot of the Future An English character in the Eagle, a weekly British newspaper comic that was a response to the US actioncomics, Dan Dare became a national hero, selling more than a million copies an issue, starring in his own radio serial and inspiring a rash of Dan Dare merchandise. Roger Sabine in his invaluable history, Comics, Comix

▼

▼

& Graphic Novels, describes the series as "galaxy-hopping adventures of a stiff upper-lipped English spaceman. It was Dare's mission to speed through space and do battle with any alien who might have half a mind to colonize earth; a job which, give or take a few punch-ups and a few necessary acts of extermination, he performed with courtesy and charm". Sort of like Han Solo with a British accent. NF

GEEK SCI-FI

Dr. Seuss (1904–1991) Even the most cynical, post-modern cynic was once an innocent child, which is probably why Theodor Seuss Geisel, a.k.a. Dr. Seuss, has become the poet of the post-War generations. In addition to bringing the word "nerd" into the lexicon, he created a world that was vaguely familiar, enchantingly magical, irresistibly

▶ rhythmic and eccentrically logical. Born in 1904 into a family of prosperous Massachusetts brewmasters, Geisel had an idyllic childhood, punctuated by memories of his mother, Henrietta Seuss Geisel, lulling him to sleep with rhymes from her childhood. These rhymes, Geisel later said, inspired him to write his own, which drew heavily on scenes from his youth in Springfield, Massachusetts.
▼

▶ he got busted for throwing a "drinking party", the college administrators deemed him unfit to be the editor. Although he didn't fight the punishment, he refused to stop writing articles, sneaking them in under the pseudonym Seuss (his mother's maiden name). After he graduated, he bowed to parental pressure, agreed to become a respectable college professor and got himself shipped off to graduate school
▼

▶ book, which he both wrote and illustrated, called <u>And to Think That I Saw It on Mulberry Street</u>. The publishers liked working with him so they asked him to write a children's book using only 225 approved "new-reader" vocabulary words – not a single one more and not a single one less. Seuss lined up all the words, rolled them around a bit and somehow came up with <u>The Cat in the Hat</u>, the
▼

"Drawings of Horton the Elephant meandering along streams in the Jungle of Nool, for example, mirror the watercourses in Springfield's Forest Park from the period", his official web site (www.catinthehat.org) reports. "The fanciful truck driven by Sylvester McMonkey McBean in The Sneetches could well be the Knox tractor that young Ted saw on the streets of Springfield.".
▼

at Oxford. He loved England for the country, for its proximity to Europe and because it was there he met his future wife, classmate Helen Palmer. He did not love graduate school, dropping out and coming home, this time with Palmer in tow.
Since he wasn't qualified to be a professor, he fell back on his talent with words and pictures. At first he was a freelance cartoonist for magazines
▼

book that many still consider the defining book of his career.
Many more would question that honor because, with 41 more books to come, including <u>Green Eggs and Ham</u>, <u>Oh, the Places You'll Go</u>, <u>Fox in Socks</u>, and <u>How the Grinch Stole Christmas</u>, everyone has their own favorite. The books have been translated throughout the world and have inspired 11 television specials, a forgettable Broadway musical (the
▼

"In addition to its name, Ted's first children's book, <u>And to Think That I Saw It on Mulberry Street</u>, is filled with Springfield imagery, including a look-alike of Mayor Fordis Parker on the reviewing stand, and police officers riding red motorcycles, the traditional color of Springfield's famed Indian Motorcycles.".
While you might not be able to take Springfield out of the boy, you
▼

such as <u>The Saturday Evening Post</u> and. Although the work was satisfying and steady, it did not pay enough so he also became an advertising hack for Shell Oil, where he worked for 15 years, until the outbreak of World War II.
He wanted to fight, but was too old for combat. Instead, he joined director Frank Capra's Signal Corps, which made propaganda films aiding the war effort at home and abroad. It was here
▼

multi-million dollar bomb, Seussical) and the critically reviled feature film, The Cat in the Hat (soon to be followed by a sequel that may be even worse). Even without the sequel, the film proved, if any doubt, that no one does Seuss better than Seuss himself. Sure, as he said, "From there to here, from here to there, funny things are everywhere.". But it still takes someone like Dr. Seuss to make us laugh. NF

certainly could take the boy out of Springfield, as he proved when he went to college at Dartmouth. He got there during the height of prohibition (a period in the 1920s when America was officially "dry"), but that didn't deter him or anyone else from having a good time. Good times notwithstanding, he distinguished himself as the editor-in-chief of the school's famed humor magazine, the Jack-O-Lantern. But when ▲

that he became an animator and here that he developed the archetypical cartoon character, Private SNAFU (which technically means "a state of chaos or confusion" but in military slang stands for "Situation Normal All Fucked Up"). After the war, his cartoons for magazines such as Life and Vanity Fair got darker, and led to an offer to illustrate a children's book called <u>Boners</u>. That in turn led to a second ▲

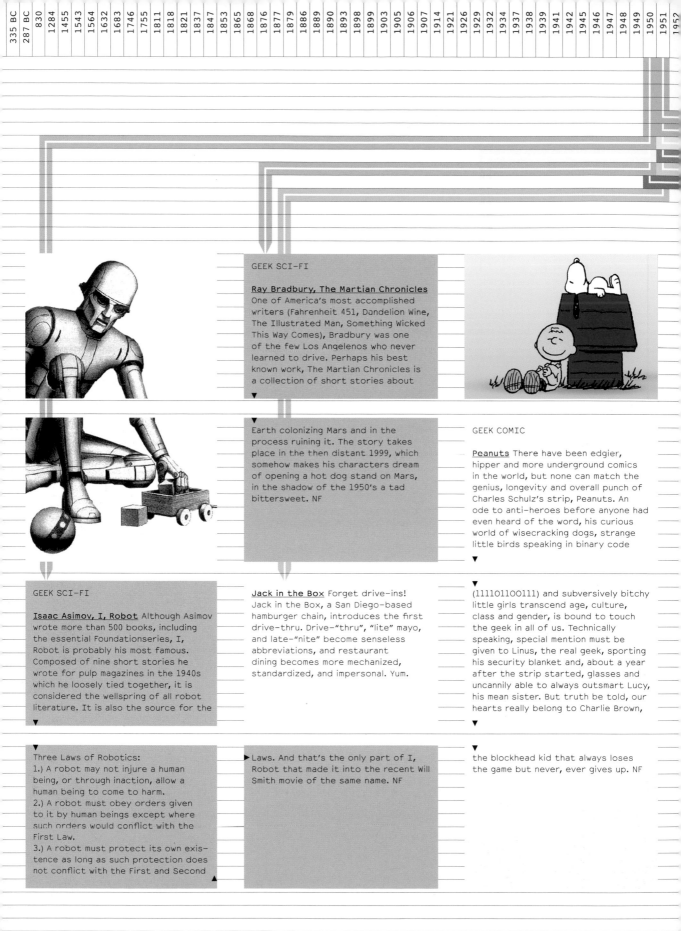

GEEK SCI-FI

Ray Bradbury, The Martian Chronicles
One of America's most accomplished
writers (Fahrenheit 451, Dandelion Wine,
The Illustrated Man, Something Wicked
This Way Comes), Bradbury was one
of the few Los Angelenos who never
learned to drive. Perhaps his best
known work, The Martian Chronicles is
a collection of short stories about
▼

Earth colonizing Mars and in the
process ruining it. The story takes
place in the then distant 1999, which
somehow makes his characters dream
of opening a hot dog stand on Mars,
in the shadow of the 1950's a tad
bittersweet. NF

GEEK COMIC

Peanuts There have been edgier,
hipper and more underground comics
in the world, but none can match the
genius, longevity and overall punch of
Charles Schulz's strip, Peanuts. An
ode to anti-heroes before anyone had
even heard of the word, his curious
world of wisecracking dogs, strange
little birds speaking in binary code
▼

GEEK SCI-FI

Isaac Asimov, I, Robot Although Asimov
wrote more than 500 books, including
the essential Foundationseries, I,
Robot is probably his most famous.
Composed of nine short stories he
wrote for pulp magazines in the 1940s
which he loosely tied together, it is
considered the wellspring of all robot
literature. It is also the source for the
▼

Jack in the Box Forget drive-ins!
Jack in the Box, a San Diego-based
hamburger chain, introduces the first
drive-thru. Drive-"thru", "lite" mayo,
and late-"nite" become senseless
abbreviations, and restaurant
dining becomes more mechanized,
standardized, and impersonal. Yum.

(111101100111) and subversively bitchy
little girls transcend age, culture,
class and gender, is bound to touch
the geek in all of us. Technically
speaking, special mention must be
given to Linus, the real geek, sporting
his security blanket and, about a year
after the strip started, glasses and
uncannily able to always outsmart Lucy,
his mean sister. But truth be told, our
hearts really belong to Charlie Brown,
▼

Three Laws of Robotics:
1.) A robot may not injure a human
being, or through inaction, allow a
human being to come to harm.
2.) A robot must obey orders given
to it by human beings except where
such orders would conflict with the
First Law.
3.) A robot must protect its own existence as long as such protection does
not conflict with the First and Second

► Laws. And that's the only part of I,
Robot that made it into the recent Will
Smith movie of the same name. NF

the blockhead kid that always loses
the game but never, ever gives up. NF

Buick le Sabre One of the new decade's most striking innovations was the Buick Le Sabre, designed by Harley Earl and immediately hailed as "a victory for automotive design". Described as a "rolling lab for new systems". the car combined racing and mainstream technology into an amalgam that sported performance features (such as an all aluminum radiator, a carburetor that could access either premium

or regular grade fuel depending on driving conditions) and radical design (such as tail fins, an automotive first, and marker lights at the ends of the bumper to give other drivers an idea of the car's dimensions). The whole thing took the country by storm: even if it was raining or snowing outside, customers literally lined up outside the showrooms for the chance of getting in and being driven around the block.

Jimmy Saville Jimmy Saville is playing records in a dancehall in Leeds, England, when he comes up with the idea of using two turntables and fading between them to create a continuous performance. He builds the equipment into a huge, heavy box that he lugs to the venue and becomes the first ever disk jockey (DJ). Surprisingly, he sustains no injuries in his exertions and it is not until 2002 that Judge Jules

becomes the first major DJ to complain of back problems.

Pill Vienna-born chemist Carl Djerassi invents the Pill in Mexico City. Technology liberates sex, undermines conventional morality, and makes everyone but condom manufacturers and the clergy happy.

GEEK FASHION

Clarks Desert Boot By 1950, Clarks, which had started as a sheepskin company in Somerset, England in 1825, had become synonymous with high quality, comfortable and somewhat stodgy shoes for English school kids and older people. So no one was surprised when the Desert Boot became a favorite of scientists,

naturalists and sporty executives. What was surprising was their emergence in the mid-'60s as part of the mod look (part of an ensemble that included sports jackets with narrow lapels, skinny ties and scooters). It has remained more or less a constant in geek wardrobes ever since. NF

GEEK SCI-FI

John Wyndham, Day of the Triffids Initially dismissed as a pulp sci-fi novel, this is the terrifying story of nature run amok. It begins as a comet shower which blinds all but a few humans, who not only have to rebuild society but fight mobile, flesh eating plants called Triffids. A "B" movie, a TV remake and a growing list of fans kept the book alive,

to the point that it was republished by Modern Library in 2003 and hailed as a bonafide sci-fi classic. NF

GEEK ROBOT

The Day the Earth Stood Still The only three words you need to know: Klaatu barada nikto. NF

GEEK COMIC

<u>Mad</u> With the advent of Mad, comics suddenly got dangerous. Creator and contributing editor Harvey Kurtzman explained its appeal by saying "Mad was necessarily thoughtful under the rowdy surface. Satire and parody work best when what you are talking about is accurately targeted; or, to put it another way, satire and parody work

▼

GEEK SCI-FI

<u>Arthur Clarke, Childhood's End</u> An article he wrote in the 1940s inspired the invention of satellite technology, but <u>Childhood's End</u>, who many prefer to his other masterpiece, <u>2001</u>, has a far more cautionary message. It begins with a visual later used in the film, <u>Independence Day</u>, but this time around the aliens usher in an era of

▼

GEEK FOOD

<u>PEZ</u> is an inbred acronym for "pfeffermintz", the German word for peppermint, and the 1927 invention of Austrian Edward Haas, who marketed it as a smoking substitute and/or breath-freshener. Initially, it was aimed at adults and sold in tins. In 1948, the tins were replaced by "easy, hygienic" (headless) plastic dispensers. Then,

▼

only when you reveal a fundamental flaw or untruth in your subject. The satirist/parodist tries not just to entertain his audience but remind it of what the real world is like". Which, in the end, is why they are so dangerous. NF

prosperity. But it ends with humans being bested by the universe's mysteries. Best line: "The stars are not meant for man". NF

▼

in 1952, targeting the burgeoning American youth market, the company put heads on the dispensers. Little did they dream that this admittedly weird idea (an early corollary of giving the hardware away so they'd buy the software) would snowball into a cult. Although many of the hundreds of dispensers can still be bought for peanuts, the most expensive, a Mr. Potato Head type nightmare that was

▼

GEEK SCI-FI

<u>Theodore Sturgeon, More Than Human</u> Like several other giants of the golden age, Sturgeon was best known for his short fiction, so it's not surprising that this book, one of his most famous, is a collection of three novellas tracing the evolution of the Gestalt, a superhuman who proves his whole is more than the sum of his parts. Where

▼

recalled because kids could swallow some of its body parts, recently sold for $5000 US. (Curiously, a much cooler LSD-inspired dispenser with an open eyeball can be had for less than $100.) Pez now has the requisite collectors, conventions and odd assorted merchandise, including Pez wall clocks, Pez flavored popcorn and a Pez museum, located on the outskirts of (where else?) Silicon Valley. NF

<u>T-Shirt</u> The American-style T-shirt is created, modeled, and named after the simple design worn by European troops in World War I. In 1955, James Dean glamorizes it as more than an undergarment in <u>Rebel Without a Cause</u>. Geeks would later adopt it less for fashion than out of laziness. Face it: T-shirts are cheap, don't have to be ironed, and can fit over thin and fat alike. NF

Sturgeon parts company from most of his peers is in his depiction of the superman not as a threat to humanity, but as its greatest fulfillment of human potential. Then again, what would you expect from someone who names his lead character Gestalt? NF

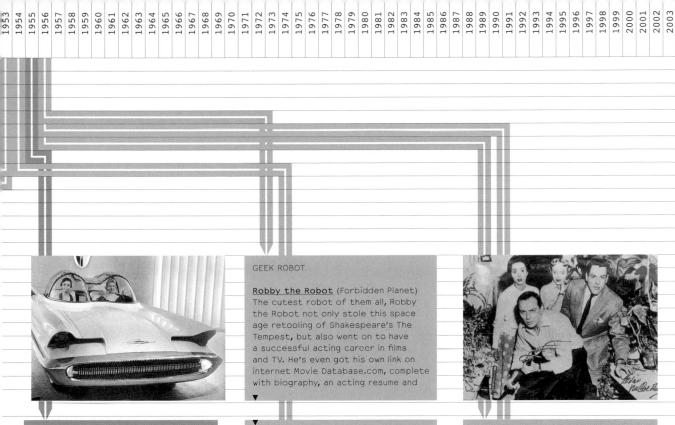

GEEK ROBOT

Robby the Robot (Forbidden Planet)
The cutest robot of them all, Robby
the Robot not only stole this space
age retooling of Shakespeare's The
Tempest, but also went on to have
a successful acting career in films
and TV. He's even got his own link on
internet Movie Database.com, complete
with biography, an acting resume and

GEEK CAR

Lincoln Futura The Lincoln Futura was a
custom/prototype car designed by an
Italian bodybuilding firm called Ghia for
Ford for a cool quarter mill. It made
its debut – under a specially designed
enclosure that kept all but the most
VIP VIPs at arms length. The car
itself was a beauty, with large chrome
bumpers and chrome trim, arched roof

a trivia page. For the record, he
was designed by Robert Kinoshita,
and built in 1955 by the MGM prop
department for $125,000.00.
He's 7'6" tall, weighs 300 pounds,
depending on what he ate the night
before, and beats Kraftwerk at their
own game, letting his clone do personal
appearances while he stays at home,
happily catching dustballs. NF

GEEK ROBOT

Invasion of the Body Snatchers
Okay. The pods aren't really robots.
But they're close. Besides, what's a
robot movie list without Don Siegel's
masterpiece of the Cold War? NF

rails, signature headlights, push button
turn signals, the speedometer in the
center of the wheel, and roll top
compartments to give the dashboard
that state-of-the-art look. It stayed
on the car show circuit for four
years and was then placed in storage,
save for an appearance in the 1959
comedy, It Started with a Kiss. The car
probably would have been relegated to
the scrap heap – a fate, unbelievably,

GEEK SCI-FI

**Alfred Bester, The Stars My
Destination** He won the first Hugo
Award in 1953 for Demolished Man and
wrote the Green Lantern Oath (in
addition to other comics, radio shows
and screenplays). But this cult novel,
also known as Tiger! Tiger!, is perhaps
his best work, anticipating cyberpunk
by 30 years with its depiction of

that befell most of these dream cars
– had it not been for George Barris's
need for a Batmobile for the 1960s
television series, Batman. He bought
it and, to the horror of many Futura
purists, modified it into the Batmobile
all the nonpurists now know and love.
NF

GEEK ROBOT

Gog The tagline's a classic: "Built to
serve man... It could think a thousand
times faster! Move a thousand times
faster! Kill a thousand times faster...
Then suddenly it became a Frankenstein
of steel!" But it's unavailable in video
or DVD so the only way you're going to
see it is by finding a bootleg version.
NF

evil megacorporations, cybernetic
enhancement and a flawed protagonist,
the aptly named Gulliver Foyle. NF

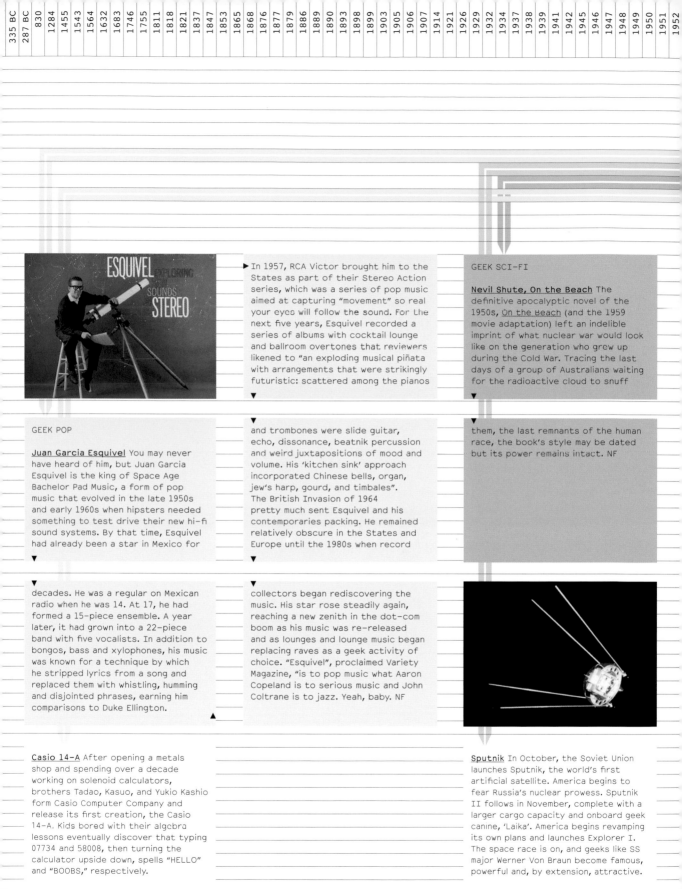

In 1957, RCA Victor brought him to the States as part of their Stereo Action series, which was a series of pop music aimed at capturing "movement" so real your eyes will follow the sound. For the next five years, Esquivel recorded a series of albums with cocktail lounge and ballroom overtones that reviewers likened to "an exploding musical piñata with arrangements that were strikingly futuristic: scattered among the pianos

GEEK SCI-FI

<u>Nevil Shute, On the Beach</u> The definitive apocalyptic novel of the 1950s, <u>On the Beach</u> (and the 1959 movie adaptation) left an indelible imprint of what nuclear war would look like on the generation who grew up during the Cold War. Tracing the last days of a group of Australians waiting for the radioactive cloud to snuff

GEEK POP

<u>Juan Garcia Esquivel</u> You may never have heard of him, but Juan Garcia Esquivel is the king of Space Age Bachelor Pad Music, a form of pop music that evolved in the late 1950s and early 1960s when hipsters needed something to test drive their new hi-fi sound systems. By that time, Esquivel had already been a star in Mexico for

and trombones were slide guitar, echo, dissonance, beatnik percussion and weird juxtapositions of mood and volume. His 'kitchen sink' approach incorporated Chinese bells, organ, jew's harp, gourd, and timbales". The British Invasion of 1964 pretty much sent Esquivel and his contemporaries packing. He remained relatively obscure in the States and Europe until the 1980s when record

them, the last remnants of the human race, the book's style may be dated but its power remains intact. NF

decades. He was a regular on Mexican radio when he was 14. At 17, he had formed a 15-piece ensemble. A year later, it had grown into a 22-piece band with five vocalists. In addition to bongos, bass and xylophones, his music was known for a technique by which he stripped lyrics from a song and replaced them with whistling, humming and disjointed phrases, earning him comparisons to Duke Ellington.

collectors began rediscovering the music. His star rose steadily again, reaching a new zenith in the dot-com boom as his music was re-released and as lounges and lounge music began replacing raves as a geek activity of choice. "Esquivel", proclaimed Variety Magazine, "is to pop music what Aaron Copeland is to serious music and John Coltrane is to jazz. Yeah, baby. NF

<u>Casio 14-A</u> After opening a metals shop and spending over a decade working on solenoid calculators, brothers Tadao, Kasuo, and Yukio Kashio form Casio Computer Company and release its first creation, the Casio 14-A. Kids bored with their algebra lessons eventually discover that typing 07734 and 58008, then turning the calculator upside down, spells "HELLO" and "BOOBS," respectively.

<u>Sputnik</u> In October, the Soviet Union launches Sputnik, the world's first artificial satellite. America begins to fear Russia's nuclear prowess. Sputnik II follows in November, complete with a larger cargo capacity and onboard geek canine, 'Laika'. America begins revamping its own plans and launches Explorer I. The space race is on, and geeks like SS major Werner Von Braun become famous, powerful and, by extension, attractive.

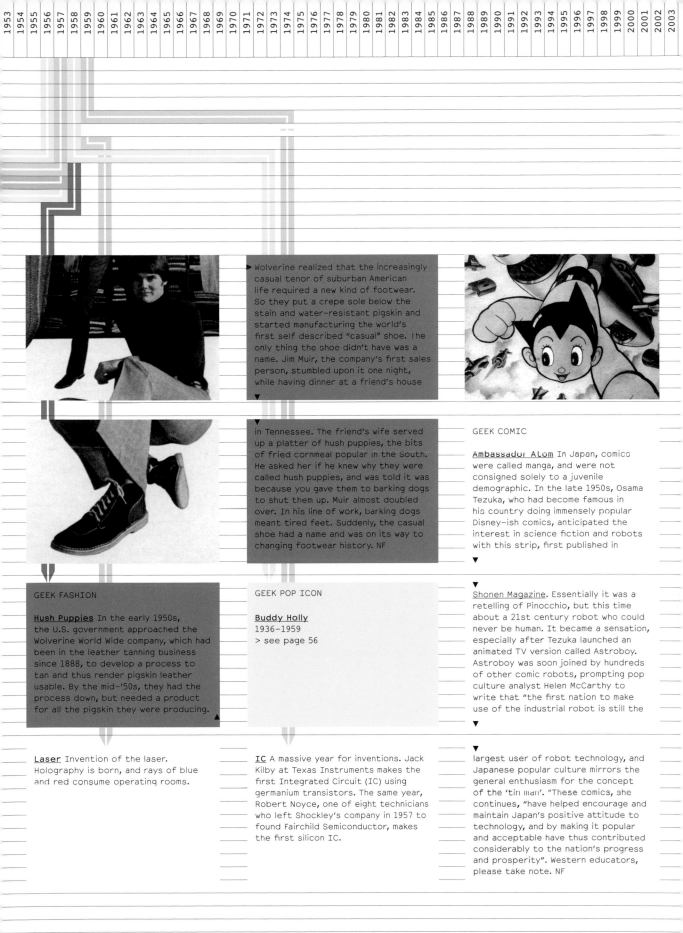

▶ Wolverine realized that the increasingly casual tenor of suburban American life required a new kind of footwear. So they put a crepe sole below the stain and water-resistant pigskin and started manufacturing the world's first self described "casual" shoe. The only thing the shoe didn't have was a name. Jim Muir, the company's first sales person, stumbled upon it one night, while having dinner at a friend's house ▼

▼ in Tennessee. The friend's wife served up a platter of hush puppies, the bits of fried cornmeal popular in the South. He asked her if he knew why they were called hush puppies, and was told it was because you gave them to barking dogs to shut them up. Muir almost doubled over. In his line of work, barking dogs meant tired feet. Suddenly, the casual shoe had a name and was on its way to changing footwear history. NF

GEEK COMIC

Ambassador Atom In Japan, comics were called manga, and were not consigned solely to a juvenile demographic. In the late 1950s, Osama Tezuka, who had become famous in his country doing immensely popular Disney-ish comics, anticipated the interest in science fiction and robots with this strip, first published in ▼

GEEK FASHION

Hush Puppies In the early 1950s, the U.S. government approached the Wolverine World Wide company, which had been in the leather tanning business since 1888, to develop a process to tan and thus render pigskin leather usable. By the mid-'50s, they had the process down, but needed a product for all the pigskin they were producing.

GEEK POP ICON

Buddy Holly
1936–1959
> see page 56

▼ Shonen Magazine. Essentially it was a retelling of Pinocchio, but this time about a 21st century robot who could never be human. It became a sensation, especially after Tezuka launched an animated TV version called Astroboy. Astroboy was soon joined by hundreds of other comic robots, prompting pop culture analyst Helen McCarthy to write that "the first nation to make use of the industrial robot is still the ▼

Laser Invention of the laser. Holography is born, and rays of blue and red consume operating rooms.

IC A massive year for inventions. Jack Kilby at Texas Instruments makes the first Integrated Circuit (IC) using germanium transistors. The same year, Robert Noyce, one of eight technicians who left Shockley's company in 1957 to found Fairchild Semiconductor, makes the first silicon IC.

▼ largest user of robot technology, and Japanese popular culture mirrors the general enthusiasm for the concept of the 'tin man'. "These comics, she continues, "have helped encourage and maintain Japan's positive attitude to technology, and by making it popular and acceptable have thus contributed considerably to the nation's progress and prosperity". Western educators, please take note. NF

GEEK POP ICON

Buddy Holly
1936-1959

O.G. Buddy Holly, he of the trademark extra-thick black horn-glasses (worn to correct his 20/800 vision) and skinny ties, unleashed the Geek look on the world. Again and again and again. He was just 13 when, along with mate Bob Montgomery, he was playing what he called "Western Bop" in clubs and bars in Lubbock, Texas, opening for acts like Bill Haley and the Comets. After getting wooed and then

rejected by a Decca Record scout, who had seen the youth perform with Haley, Holley (the "e" was dropped several years later, after a record company misspelled it) paid attention to the criticisms that he needed more seasoning, formed a band called The Crickets and, in no time, knocked out classics like "That Will Be the Day", "Maybe Baby", "Every Day", "Not Fade Away" and "Words of Love".

With songs like that, it didn't take long for Holly to become a sensation. None of the traditional media paid any attention to rock and roll, so there was a mystique about the music and the musicians. Holly, like Presley, infused his music with enough R&B that his race was obscured. Even bookers at the legendary (at the time all black) Apollo Theater in Harlem assumed he was black and were as surprised as the

audience when Holly and his southern white posse walked into the theater to begin their three-day engagement. To the Apollo's credit, despite the color bar, they let Holly perform. There were initial doubts about throwing lambs into a lion's den and, true to expectations, the audience booed Holly throughout the first night's sets. But then people got over the shock of the rock and, by the end of the third

day, Holly and the Crickets were being greeted like family.
The reaction was even more pronounced in England. As Keith Richards remembers it, "By about 1958, it was either Elvis or Buddy Holly. It was split into two camps. The Elvis fans were the heavy leather boys and the Buddy Holly ones all somehow looked like Buddy Holly". Future stars such as John Lennon fell firmly in the Holly camp. "He

made it easy to wear glasses. I was Buddy Holly". When it came time to name the band he was playing in, he and his bandmate, didn't look any farther than Holly's band, settling on the Beatles as a conscious homage to the Crickets. Holly did more, though, than just give the geeks his look. While Elvis was content to let his management control most of the creative output, Holly was a control freak. In addition to being

the first self-contained rock group to write and perform their own songs, Holly wanted to produce the records as well. At the height of the Cricket's success, he decided to leave producer Norman Petty, who had worked with the band from the beginning, and produce the music himself. The rest of the band, loyal to Petty and uneasy about Holly's ability as a producer, stayed with Petty. Wasting no time, Holly struck out on

his own, hitting number one with "Peggy Sue" and packing houses all across the States with a triple-threat bill of Holly, The Big Bopper and Richie Valens. One night, sick of dealing with a tour bus that kept breaking down, the three decided to fly to the next gig. All three were killed that night when the plane crashed (an event immortalized by Don McLean in the song, "American Pie (The Day the Music Died)." NF

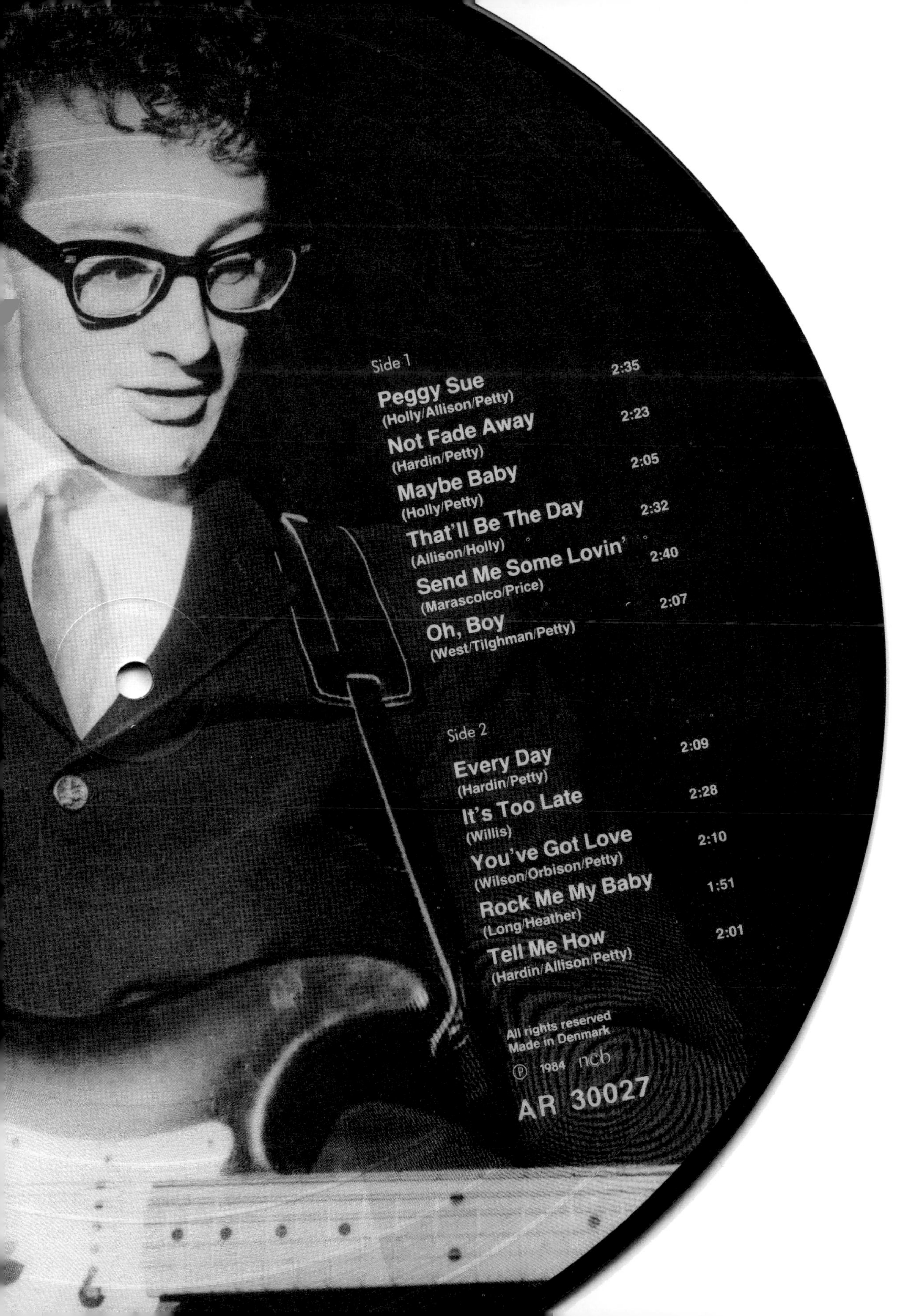

Side 1
Peggy Sue 2:35
(Holly/Allison/Petty)
Not Fade Away 2:23
(Hardin/Petty)
Maybe Baby 2:05
(Holly/Petty)
That'll Be The Day 2:32
(Allison/Holly)
Send Me Some Lovin' 2:40
(Marascolco/Price)
Oh, Boy 2:07
(West/Tilghman/Petty)
Side 2
Every Day 2:09
(Hardin/Petty)
It's Too Late 2:28
(Willis)
You've Got Love 2:10
(Wilson/Orbison/Petty)
Rock Me My Baby 1:51
(Long/Heather)
Tell Me How 2:01
(Hardin/Allison/Petty)
All rights reserved
Made in Denmark
℗ 1984 ncb
AR 30027

in negative figures. Each show is a carefully conceived and wrought piece of drama, cast with competent people, directed by creative, quality-conscious guys, and shot with an eye toward mood and reality. There will be nothing formula'd, nothing telegraphed, nothing so nostalgically familiar that an audience can join actors in duets. The exciting thing about our medium is its potential, the fact that it

doesn't have to be imitative. What it can produce in terms of novelty and ingenuity has barely been scratched. This is a medium that can spread out, delve deep, probe fully and reach out experimentally to whole new concepts. The horizons of what it can do and where it can go stretch out beyond vision. And that's what we're trying to do with The Twilight Zone. We want to tell stories that are different.

GEEK TV

The (Original) Twilight Zone If you were born in the early '50s, you were just hitting your stride when Rod Serling came up with The Twilight Zone. Forget the stories; the credits were enough to scare the be-jesus out of you. Since it became such a landmark in prestige programming, it is worth going back to November 7, 1959, and

revisit what he told TV Guide about the show: "Here's what The Twilight Zone is: it's an anthology series, half hour in length, that delves into the odd, the bizarre, the unexpected. Here's what The Twilight Zone isn't: it's not a monster rally or a spook show. It probes into the dimension of imagination but with a concern for taste and for an adult audience too long considered to have IQs

We want to prove that television, even in its half-hour form, can be both commercial and worthwhile. The half-hour film can probe effectively, dramatize and present a well-told and well-filmed story; at the same time, perhaps only as a side effect, a point can be made that the fresh and untried can carry more infinite appeal than a palpable imitation of the already proved. The Twilight Zone is a

wondrous land of the very different. No luggage is required for the trip. All that the audience need bring is imagination".
One can only guess what he would have to say about TV today when, it's safe to say, the last thing anyone needs to bring to the tube is imagination. NF

GEEK TV

The (Original) GE College Bowl Dubbed the Varsity Sport of the Mind, this game show pitted two teams of undergraduates against each other in an intellectual decathlon. Whoever answered the most science, literature and math questions won scholarships. The show, which had already been on the radio from 1953 – 1957, premiered

on CBS on January 4, 1959, became the first game show to win a Peabody award for broadcast excellence, and featured class-act quiz show host Allen Ludden as its moderator. It lasted until 1970 (changing networks to NBC in 1964), spawned an English version called University Challenge, and has been periodically revived on television with hosts such as Pat Sajak and Dick Cavett, himself a

self-promoted intellect. Despite its disappearance from the US network lineup years ago, the College Bowl is very much alive as a grass-roots international competition, awaiting a new life, one suspects, somewhere on cable television. NF

GEEK SCI-FI

Robert Heinlein, Stranger in a Strange Land Although some of his lighter works, such as Starship Troopers, are more fun, Stranger in a Strange Land was an essential component of every hippie's library. By today's standards, his story of an Earthling raised on Mars only to become a messiah spreading free

▼

love and psychic powers is a curious snapshot of a world gone by. It is also the source of the word, "grok", a buzzword for total understanding in the 1960s and '70s. NF

GEEK SCI-FI

Walter M. Miller Jr., Canticle for Liebowitz The intelligentsia's favorite and most literary post apocalyptic novel, Canticle, an examination of religious faith vs. scientific rationalism, begins with a group of Saints of the order of St. Liebowitz agog over the discovery of a holy relic, Liebowitz's (a long dead

▼

engineer) shopping list reminding him to bring pastrami and bagels home. The story behind the book is probably more interesting than the book itself: Miller, a pilot in World War II who never wrote another major book, was tortured by the fact that he had bombed a Benedictine Monastery during the war. This was seen by many to be his act of penance. Even so it was not enough: After grappling with

issues of faith for the rest of his life, he committed suicide in 1997. NF

GEEK COMIC

Fantastic Four By the early 1960s, superheroes seemed a bit tired and the Fantastic Four succeeded by playing to that perception. Developed by Stan Lee and Jack Kirby, it told the tale of a dysfunctional family of introspective, aging oddballs, Mr. Fantastic, the Human Torch, The Thing and Invisible Girl. In, again, Sabine's

▼

words, the four "spent as much time agonizing over beating up baddies than doing it". NF

GEEK SCI-FI

Stanislaw Lem, Solaris The most successful Polish writer in the world, Lem is not an easy read, tending more towards philosophy than plot. But this novel about a scientist's relationship with an alien, sentient ocean he's sent to study continues to captivate readers, including Stephen Soderbergh, who made it into a movie in 2003. (An

▼

earlier version by Russian film director Andrei Tarkovsky is considered superior, but its reputation is based on film critics from the 1970s who were, most probably, flying as high as the protagonists. On today's message boards, opinions on the Russian version are very divided.) NF

335 BC | 287 BC | 830 | 1284 | 1455 | 1543 | 1564 | 1632 | 1683 | 1746 | 1755 | 1811 | 1818 | 1821 | 1837 | 1847 | 1853 | 1865 | 1868 | 1876 | 1877 | 1879 | 1886 | 1889 | 1890 | 1893 | 1898 | 1899 | 1903 | 1905 | 1906 | 1907 | 1914 | 1921 | 1926 | 1929 | 1932 | 1934 | 1937 | 1938 | 1939 | 1941 | 1942 | 1945 | 1946 | 1947 | 1948 | 1949 | 1950 | 1951 | 1952

GEEK SCI-FI

Anthony Burgess, A Clockwork Orange
Frequently considered a companion piece to Brave New World and 1984, this futuristic vision of droogs afloat in an authoritarian, violent, high-tech world is best known for its use of slang, which was composed of a combination of Burgess's creation and Russian, and for Stanley Kubrick's movie. Pick your
▼

pleasure, because this is one of those rare instances where the two actually complement each other. NF

GEEK TV

The Jetsons Pre-Apollo America glimpses Hanna-Barbera's 21st century vision with the animated comedy "The Jetsons." George, Jane, Judy, and Elroy Jetson (and their robot housekeeper, Rosie) engage in space-age hi-jinx, proving that modern comforts (including George's computer RUDI, or referential universal digital indexer) are
▼

▼
neither modern nor comforts. Nevertheless, it's the inspiration, clearly, for the trendsetting Los Angeles "hip hotel," the Standard. Mercifully, "The Jetsons" is one of the few TV shows not to make its way onto the giant screen. NF

GEEK COMIC

The Incredible Hulk Fantastic Four creators Lee and Kirby upped the angst factor even more with this tale of Bob Banner, a tormented scientist who, in an experiment gone bad, gets a dose of radiation that turned him into a far-from-jolly green giant. It made a decent TV show, but it's also the source for perhaps the worst single
▼

▼
movie adaptation of a comic in history. That's saying something. NF

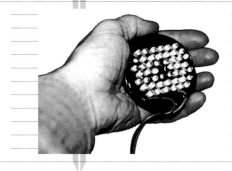

LED Invention of the light emitting diode (LED), used originally in scientific instruments, watches, calculators, and still used for bright information displays in supermarkets, streets, and sports stadiums. The 0-segment LED and its eerie red glow become a design classic.

GEEK TV

Astroboy How's this for a first episode? A scientist creates a boy robot in the likeness of his dead son, goes crazy and sells the robot to a circus owner who treats his robots like slaves. In the midst of a performance, the circus tent catches on fire; the robots save the people in the audience; are given their freedom and

sent out into the world. (Not to be outdone, some 200 episodes later, the show ends with the robot sacrificing himself to save the world from a renegade asteroid!)
The brainchild of Dr. Osama Tezuka, a legendary figure in Japanese comics, this series has been called the granddaddy of anime. A huge success in Japan from its first airing, it was equally well received in the States

GEEK COMIC

The Amazing Spider-Man The crowning glory of these early '60s efforts, Spider-Man is really bookworm Peter Parker, who gets bitten by a spider during a science exhibition and then gets to climb walls, spin webs and dangle from ceilings. Unlike the Hulk, he actually makes the transition to movie superhero without getting squished. NF

until citizen groups began complaining about its violent and mature content and got it yanked off the air in the States after 104 episodes. The series was remade in 1980 with Tezuka's full support, this time with director Noboru Ishiguro. NF

GEEK GAME

Space Wars Space Wars, designed by MIT student Steve Russell, is the first game that is played on a computer. Well, a big mainframe that is, the PDP 1. Two players fly their rocket ships around a sun trying to destroy each other. EVDZ

James Bond The first James Bond film, "Dr. No", is released, starting one of the most successful movie series ever — celebrating souped-up vehicles, geeky gadgetry, and suggestively named female characters — all based on the books by rakish ex-spy and journalist Ian Fleming. 007 proves that wit and charm are only enhanced by a grab bag of boy toys.

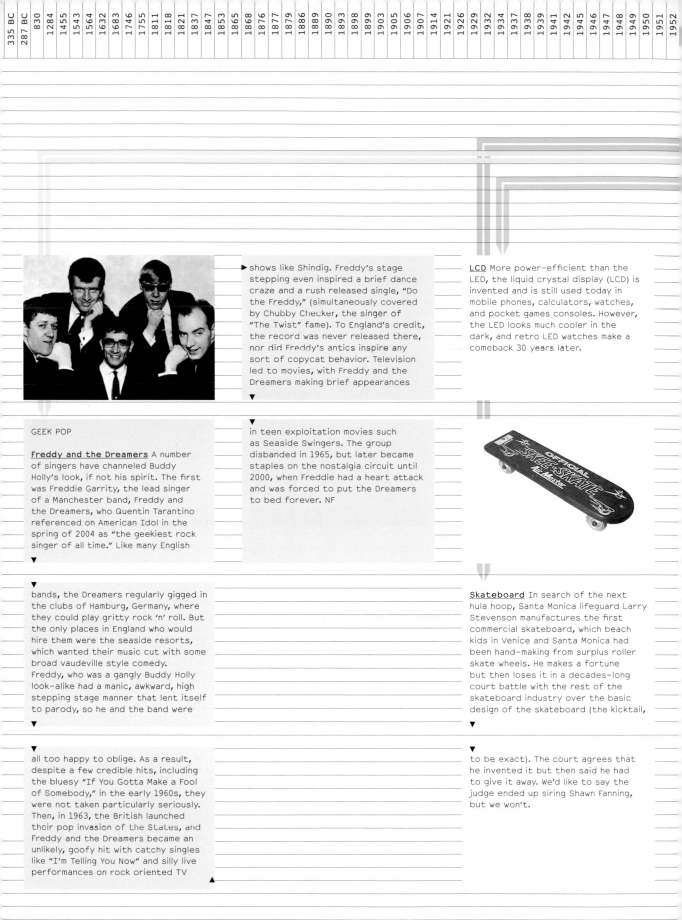

shows like Shindig. Freddy's stage stepping even inspired a brief dance craze and a rush released single, "Do the Freddy," (simultaneously covered by Chubby Checker, the singer of "The Twist" fame). To England's credit, the record was never released there, nor did Freddy's antics inspire any sort of copycat behavior. Television led to movies, with Freddy and the Dreamers making brief appearances

LCD More power-efficient than the LED, the liquid crystal display (LCD) is invented and is still used today in mobile phones, calculators, watches, and pocket games consoles. However, the LED looks much cooler in the dark, and retro LED watches make a comeback 30 years later.

GEEK POP

Freddy and the Dreamers A number of singers have channeled Buddy Holly's look, if not his spirit. The first was Freddie Garrity, the lead singer of a Manchester band, Freddy and the Dreamers, who Quentin Tarantino referenced on American Idol in the spring of 2004 as "the geekiest rock singer of all time." Like many English

in teen exploitation movies such as Seaside Swingers. The group disbanded in 1965, but later became staples on the nostalgia circuit until 2000, when Freddie had a heart attack and was forced to put the Dreamers to bed forever. NF

bands, the Dreamers regularly gigged in the clubs of Hamburg, Germany, where they could play gritty rock 'n' roll. But the only places in England who would hire them were the seaside resorts, which wanted their music cut with some broad vaudeville style comedy. Freddy, who was a gangly Buddy Holly look-alike had a manic, awkward, high stepping stage manner that lent itself to parody, so he and the band were

Skateboard In search of the next hula hoop, Santa Monica lifeguard Larry Stevenson manufactures the first commercial skateboard, which beach kids in Venice and Santa Monica had been hand-making from surplus roller skate wheels. He makes a fortune but then loses it in a decades-long court battle with the rest of the skateboard industry over the basic design of the skateboard (the kicktail,

all too happy to oblige. As a result, despite a few credible hits, including the bluesy "If You Gotta Make a Fool of Somebody," in the early 1960s, they were not taken particularly seriously. Then, in 1963, the British launched their pop invasion of the States, and Freddy and the Dreamers became an unlikely, goofy hit with catchy singles like "I'm Telling You Now" and silly live performances on rock oriented TV

to be exact). The court agrees that he invented it but then said he had to give it away. We'd like to say the judge ended up siring Shawn Fanning, but we won't.

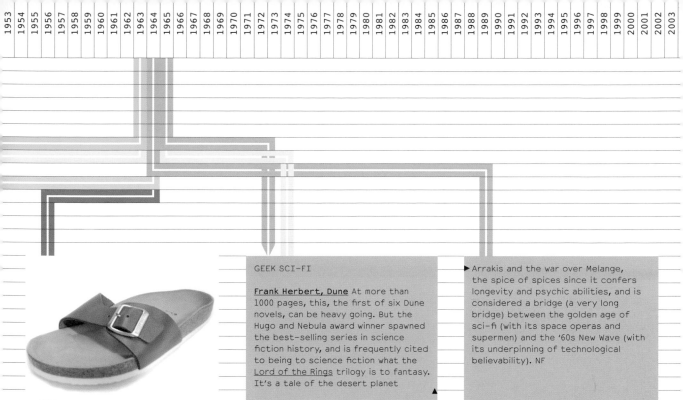

GEEK SCI-FI

<u>Frank Herbert, Dune</u> At more than 1000 pages, this, the first of six Dune novels, can be heavy going. But the Hugo and Nebula award winner spawned the best-selling series in science fiction history, and is frequently cited to being to science fiction what the <u>Lord of the Rings</u> trilogy is to fantasy. It's a tale of the desert planet

▶ Arrakis and the war over Melange, the spice of spices since it confers longevity and psychic abilities, and is considered a bridge (a very long bridge) between the golden age of sci-fi (with its space operas and supermen) and the '60s New Wave (with its underpinning of technological believability). NF

GEEK FASHION

<u>Birkenstocks</u> Way back in 1897, third generation German shoemaker Konrad Birkenstock designed the first shoes with compound insoles as a way of helping shoemakers produce custom footwear for their toeny customers. Then, five years later, he developed the first flexible arch support for factory-manufactured shoes, thus bringing his

innovation within reach of the masses. The company that bore his family's name built its identity around the insole, but it took Konrad's grandson, Karl, to make Birkenstock a household name, thanks to his introduction of the first contoured arch supported sandal in 1964. Two years later, Californian Margot Fraser stumbled across a pair in a European spa, flipped over how good they felt and

GEEK ROBOT

<u>Kiss Me Quick</u> This "nudie-cutie" features a seduction scene between dancing sex robots and an alien. It's working title was <u>Dr. Breedlove: Or How I Learned to Stop Worrying and Love</u>. Even more amazing – it was shot by Laslo Kovacs, who would go on to shoot <u>Close Encounters</u>, <u>Easy Rider</u> and four or five hundred other great films.

began importing them to the US. By 1973, millions of people were wearing the "stylish" Arizona model. "It's [sic] unique shape," crows Birkenstock, "pioneered the idea of form following function". It goes on to call the shoe a "steadfast old friend and a hip, on-trend style for the fashionable set." Substitute the word "geek" for "fashionable set", figure out what on-trend means and you've got it right. NF

<u>Moog</u> Inspired by his use of the first electronic-sound instrument, the Theremin (he once wrote a book about how to use the device, primarily used in early alien flicks), Robert Moog builds the Moog analogue synthesizer. The man who was regularly beat up as a kid for being the class brain, popularizes the synthesizer as an instrument primarily used and developed for music playing, and

▶ electronic beats are unleashed upon the world. The first hit to use a Moog comes in 1969 with "Switched on the Beach" by Walter (now Wendy) Carlos who also made the soundtrack to sci-fi thriller <u>A Clockwork Orange</u>. NF

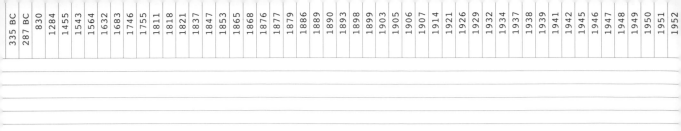

Doritos Nacho Flavour The curiously delicious scientific creation, nacho flavor, appears for the first time on Doritos. The burnt-orange corn triangles go on to kick-start a flood of new artificial-flavor creations that top crispy geek foods, not to mention guide America in its conquest to eradicate healthy local cuisine around the world (all while resurrecting the career of not-so-geeky, not-so-funny comedian, Jay Leno).

GEEK TV

Star Trek is the most unlikely phenomenon in television history. In fact, with its endless succession of spin-off series, films, books, cartoons, action figures, adventure rides and conventions, Star Trek is less a TV show than a lifestyle. And that can be a problem. Hit Google to get oriented and you'll get a

▼

GEEK ROBOT

Lost in Space Robby lite. In this sublimely dumb attempt to capitalize on Star Trek, the Robot, called Robert, has an aquarium head, flailing arms and an almost comical "Warning...Warning" vocal refrain. That didn't stop him from carrying the plot at times, most notably in the episode where he became a giant and ended up dwarfing the

▼

GEEK MOVIE

Fantastic Voyage Isaac Asimov's novel comes to life thanks to Richard Fleischer (20,000 Leagues under the Sea). Better known for putting its lead, Raquel Welch, in a wet suit than for its take on nanotechnology-sized computers, the movie begins with a miniaturized Welch and fellow explorer Stephen Boyd aboard a miniature

▼

staggering 3,500,000 home pages to sort through. One or two of those might admit to liking one of the sequels (Next Generation, Deep Space Nine, Voyager and Enterprise) or the ten movies, but for most, the real action happens under Captain Kirk's watch, in that first burst of glory. Although the episodes by now are old enough to have been watched originally by some of the younger

▼

humans. Like the rest of the crew, he made the transition to the big screen in 1998, but "Warning, Warning", avoid the big-budget remake at all costs. NF

▼

submarine. They are injected into a scientist's blood stream in a race against time to find the blood clot that ails him. NF

▼

viewers' grandparents, the fans still act as though the Starship Enterprise, whose ostensible purpose was to explore space and defend the United Federation of Planets, contains the secrets of the universe. Here's the hitch, though. If you're a fan, you already know these episodes by heart. If you're not, the only question you really have is, "Why?" NF

GEEK ROBOT

The Earth Dies Screaming The robots apparently look like lumbering oilcans or gas boilers. The title's just a plain old gas.

than the Thin White Duke. Way before Madonna, he reinvented himself so many times that no one knew who the "real" David Bowie was. Then, not content to be just a character gallery, he realized that his back catalogue was enough to keep him in trinkets for ages and he turned himself into a corporation, inviting people to invest in his songbook.
From there it was just a short jump

GEEK POP

David Bowie Back in the days when David Bowie was parading around in women's dresses, slinging his acoustic guitar in a plaintive Andy Warhol folk-rock kind of way, he seemed as unlike a geek as you could get. But, mercifully, that was just a passing phase, bracketed by songs like "Space Oddity" and "Rock 'n' Roll Suicide",

to the internet where Bowie, an early player, figured out how to sell not just merchandise, including limited edition prints of his art, but charge just to access the site. Then, although he hadn't released a profitable, let alone listenable, record in a long time – and despite his intelligent, candid and open pessimism about the future of the record album as an art form and the music business as a business, Sony

GEEK CAR

Volvo 1400/140 Volvo had already sold one million of its popular Amazon model and expanded production into Canada and Belgium when it announced its 1440 series (oddly, named numerically as models 144 and 145). The 1400 series had gotten its start in 1960, under the leadership of Jan Wilsgaard, when Volvo decided it

alien personae such as Ziggy Stardust, Aladdin Sane and Thomas Newton (his character in the Nicolas Roeg film, The Man Who Fell to Earth), not to mention his groundbreaking affair with electronic music in his great trilogy Low, Heroes and Lodger.
In addition to the futuristic themes in his music and stage shows, no one in glamland got the connection between technology, media and money faster

gave him his own record label. When asked if he didn't feel like a hypocrite for taking their money, he just laughed and said he would ride the wave as long as he could. Nor, despite "retiring" from the stage at least twice already and landing on Forbes' Rich Rock Star lists year after year, he is not above singing for his supper. (He's got a wife and a young kid and life in New York isn't cheap, ya' know). So every few

needed a more modern, roomier and safer car. The car, which was designed by 1962, rolled off the production line in 1966, and was universally praised for its energy absorbing crumple zones, all wheel disc brakes and dual circuit back up system, which prevented the car from careening out of control in an accident. Although no one was happy with the car's boxy looks, its safety record and reliability made the 1400

(and subsequent periodic retoolings in the '70s and '90s (as the 244 and 245) the vehicle of choice for safety freaks and geeks. NF

years, he dusts off his old red shoes, trots out the songs and works his hits for the faithful. In true geek fashion, though, he'll tell you that work's work but if he had his druthers, he'd be sitting at home with his wife and his kid, checking out his websites, curling up with a good book and sipping a cup of cocoa. NF

335 BC	287 BC	830	1284	1455	1543	1564	1632	1683	1746	1755	1811	1818	1821	1837	1847	1853	1865	1868	1876	1877	1879	1886	1889	1890	1893	1898	1899	1903	1905	1906	1907	1914	1921	1926	1929	1932	1934	1937	1938	1939	1941	1942	1945	1946	1947	1948	1949	1950	1951	1952

▶ programming for WQED in Pittsburgh, Pennsylvania, the U.S.'s first community sponsored educational television show straight from NBC headquarters in the mid-50s. There were no gaps in his employment; and thus no time for him to have been in a protracted legal battle. McFeeley was his middle name, which sort of blows the hoped-for double entendre. And the only reason he didn't want ▼

GEEK TV

Mr. Rogers Neighbourhood Λ Public Television institution, Mr. Rogers was a cardigan wearing nerd with a tinkling Neighborhood trolley who served as a voice of reason to 30 years of America's latchkey kids, teaching them how things worked and slipping in subtle life lessons wherever he could. To most people, Mr. Rogers was ▼

children on the set was because he thought they would undermine his ability to interact directly with the viewer at home.
The next two rumors were equally absurd. The first charged that Rogers had been a killing machine for the U.S. government during the Vietnam War; the second was that he wore cardigans to cover an armful of X-rated military tattoos. Again, the truth is more ▼

Microwave Raytheon's Amana division releases the first domestic microwave oven, the Radarange, based on its 1954 commercial model developed by Percy LeBaron Spencer. Food gets "zapped", dining becomes as easy as punching a few keys, and the TV dinner seems almost homemade by comparison.

▼ a beacon of morality, but towards the end of his career, a few pranksters on the web began spreading a number of rumors about Rogers that cast him in an entirely different light.
One of the most persistent, nastiest rumors had Rogers as child molester who had been forced into a career in children's television as community service for his conviction. That, according to the rumormongers ▼

▼ prosaic. He was born in 1928, making him too old to serve in Vietnam. And he liked cardigans because they reminded him of his mother. He had no tattoos – or piercings, for that matter.
The fourth rumor came complete with visual evidence – a photograph proving that Rogers' alleged long-simmering contempt for his audience expressed itself in his giving the audience the middle finger at the close of the show's ▼

Masters and Johnson carry out pioneering research in the field of human sexuality, measuring human sexual response of subjects in the lab. They go on to write what may be the driest bestseller in history. Technology once again helps liberate sex. Too bad it doesn't do the same for literature.

▼ explained why there were never any children on the set, and why one of his characters, a messenger, was called Mr.McFeeley.
Aside from the fact that the courts generally don't reward childmolesters with high profile kid's shows on public television, there was plenty of evidence debunking the charges. First, Rogers was a musical composer who went to work developing children's ▲

▼ final episode in December 2000. Despite being an obvious fake, the image flew across the web, showing that these days even in Mr. Rogers' hood, no one is safe from cyberslander. NF

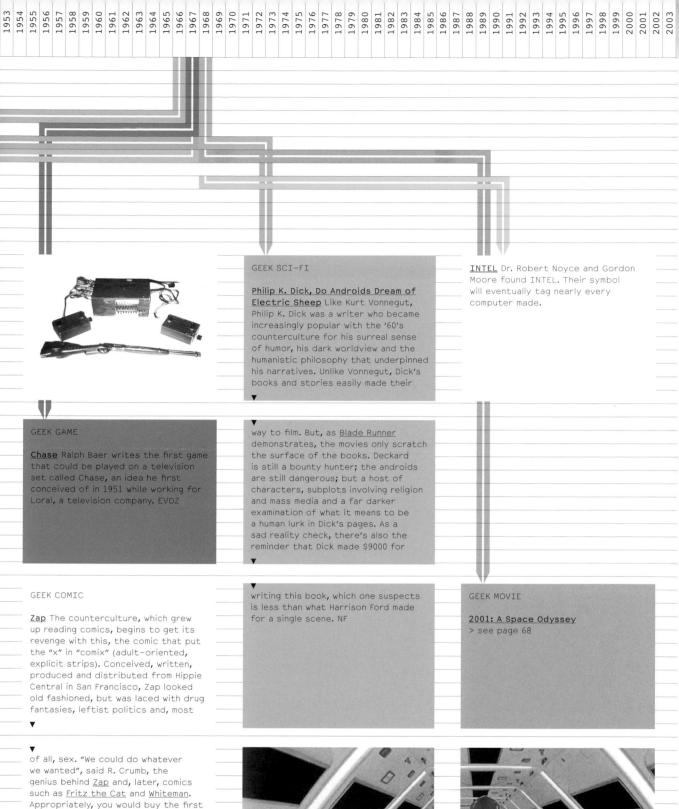

GEEK SCI-FI

Philip K. Dick, Do Androids Dream of Electric Sheep Like Kurt Vonnegut, Philip K. Dick was a writer who became increasingly popular with the '60's counterculture for his surreal sense of humor, his dark worldview and the humanistic philosophy that underpinned his narratives. Unlike Vonnegut, Dick's books and stories easily made their

▼

▼

way to film. But, as <u>Blade Runner</u> demonstrates, the movies only scratch the surface of the books. Deckard is still a bounty hunter; the androids are still dangerous; but a host of characters, subplots involving religion and mass media and a far darker examination of what it means to be a human lurk in Dick's pages. As a sad reality check, there's also the reminder that Dick made $9000 for

▼

▼

writing this book, which one suspects is less than what Harrison Ford made for a single scene. NF

INTEL Dr. Robert Noyce and Gordon Moore found INTEL. Their symbol will eventually tag nearly every computer made.

GEEK GAME

<u>Chase</u> Ralph Baer writes the first game that could be played on a television set called Chase, an idea he first conceived of in 1951 while working for Loral, a television company. EVDZ

GEEK COMIC

<u>Zap</u> The counterculture, which grew up reading comics, begins to get its revenge with this, the comic that put the "x" in "comix" (adult-oriented, explicit strips). Conceived, written, produced and distributed from Hippie Central in San Francisco, Zap looked old fashioned, but was laced with drug fantasies, leftist politics and, most

▼

▼

of all, sex. "We could do whatever we wanted", said R. Crumb, the genius behind <u>Zap</u> and, later, comics such as <u>Fritz the Cat</u> and <u>Whiteman</u>. Appropriately, you would buy the first few issues directly from Crumb, who sold them from a baby pram on the corner of Haight-Ashbury. Were those the days or what? NF

GEEK MOVIE

<u>2001: A Space Odyssey</u>
> see page 68

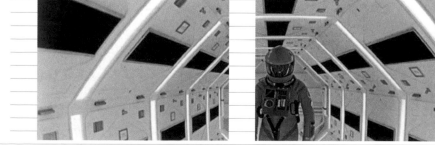

GEEK MOVIE

2001: A Space Odyssey

▼

After a string of masterpieces including <u>The Killing</u>, <u>Paths of Glory</u>, <u>Dr. Strangelove</u>, <u>Spartacus</u> and <u>Lolita</u>, the notorious director Stanley Kubrick decided he wanted to make "the proverbial good science-fiction movie." To get the ball rolling, he contacted top-of-the-pack sci-fi writer Arthur C. Clarke and asked him to develop the concept.
Clarke pulled <u>The Sentinel</u>, a short ▲

▶ story he wrote in 1948, out of his hat, suggesting it would make a great movie. Kubrick agreed that it was cinematic, but he wanted something bigger. Then he explained his plan: The two would collaborate on a screenplay and a novel, written simultaneously. Kubrick would focus on the screenplay; Clarke, on the novel, but that they would share material and ideas.

in the summer (before the book) with a massive drumroll of publicity, premiering in large theatters and sparking a heated debate as to its merits and meaning.

Part of the debate can be seen as a sign of the times. College-age kids in the States and Europe had discovered marijuana and LSD, and this big studio release, with its soaring visuals and booming, perfectly edited classical

by the response, Clarke took it as a compliment. "If you understand 2001 completely, we failed", he said. "We wanted to raise far more questions than we answered". On that note, they succeeded. The debate still rages across the internet. Advocates of the film defend the stately pace, obscure narrative and religious/metaphysical symbolism as part of a profound visual experience. Detractors laugh, saying

As the experiment progressed, scenes written for one would end up better suited to the other and the lines of who wrote what got a bit blurry. Curiously, they also abandoned their original plan of sharing the book's authorship, perhaps so Kubrick, who still had to approve the manuscript, could drag his hells and delay publication until the movie was released. In any event, the movie came out

music, seemed tailored to the drug experience. For this segment of the audience, 2001 was a mind-blowing light show. What more could you ask for? If you were lucid, considerably more. At a screening in Los Angeles, the film star Rock Hudson (never considered a great intellect) echoed the sentiments of many when he demanded that someone tell him "what the hell this is about". Rather than be perturbed

that's just a justification for a sloppy, stoney, empty film.

Regardless of which side you're on, it's impossible not to admire the apes, the light show, the deconstruction of HAL and the appearance of the Star Child. And since we have access to DVD players now, something Kubrick and Clarke did not anticipate, if you want, those are the only sequences you have to see. NF

335 BC | 287 BC | 830 | 1284 | 1455 | 1543 | 1564 | 1632 | 1683 | 1746 | 1755 | 1811 | 1818 | 1821 | 1837 | 1847 | 1853 | 1865 | 1868 | 1876 | 1877 | 1879 | 1886 | 1889 | 1890 | 1893 | 1898 | 1899 | 1903 | 1905 | 1906 | 1907 | 1914 | 1921 | 1926 | 1929 | 1932 | 1934 | 1937 | 1938 | 1939 | 1941 | 1942 | 1945 | 1946 | 1947 | 1948 | 1949 | 1950 | 1951 | 1952

ARPANET The first node of ARPANET, the US Defense Department's nuclear-bomb-proof communications network and the precursor of the internet, is installed at UCLA. Considering the alternative (which is death by bombing), sitting in a room in front of a computer screen doesn't seem so bad after all.

GEEK HACKERS

Dennis Ritchie and Ken Thompson (a.k.a. dmr and Ken) This dynamic duo created UNIX in 1969, which helped people operate computers, do word processing and network with each other. NF

Technics SP10 Technics launches the SP10, the first direct-drive turntable, and New York DJ Francis Grasso popularizes the cueing and mixing of records using a slipmat. They become the club DJ's favorite turntables until they are superceded by the SL1200-MK2 10 years later.

GEEK SCI-FI

Ursula Le Guin, Left Hand of Darkness This tale of a man sent to bring a genderless population of a rogue planet into the galactic fold was greeted with lavish acclaim when it came out, winning both the Hugo and Nebula awards. Since then, it is widely recognized as a groundbreaking excursion that helped pull sci-fi out

of pulp and into literature. Like many of the other books on this particular shelf, however, it has a slightly musty feel. As one young reviewer on Amazon posted, "Hopefully all the professors who grew up on this drivel in the 1960s will reread things like this before assigning them and realize that what made them great then does not make them great now". It makes us think we should retitle this section,

ALOHAnet ALOHAnet, an early version of a listserv created by Norm Abramson, helps surfers trade wave reports with other surfers via radio transmitters linked to computers.

"WARNING: YOU ARE ENTERING A HISTORICAL ZONE". NF

Floppy Disk IBM introduces an 8-inch flexible plastic disk, developed by Al Shugart, to store program code. It is the first floppy disk, with an initial capacity of 100 KB.

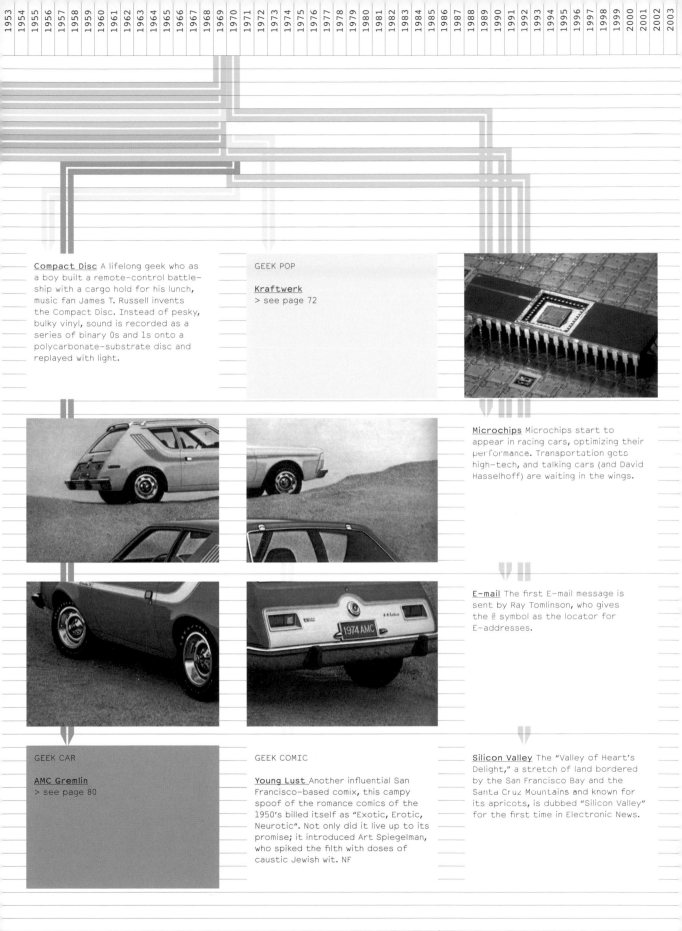

Compact Disc A lifelong geek who as a boy built a remote-control battle-ship with a cargo hold for his lunch, music fan James T. Russell invents the Compact Disc. Instead of pesky, bulky vinyl, sound is recorded as a series of binary 0s and 1s onto a polycarbonate-substrate disc and replayed with light.

GEEK POP

Kraftwerk
> see page 72

Microchips Microchips start to appear in racing cars, optimizing their performance. Transportation gets high-tech, and talking cars (and David Hasselhoff) are waiting in the wings.

E-mail The first E-mail message is sent by Ray Tomlinson, who gives the @ symbol as the locator for E-addresses.

GEEK CAR

AMC Gremlin
> see page 80

GEEK COMIC

Young Lust Another influential San Francisco-based comix, this campy spoof of the romance comics of the 1950's billed itself as "Exotic, Erotic, Neurotic". Not only did it live up to its promise; it introduced Art Spiegelman, who spiked the filth with doses of caustic Jewish wit. NF

Silicon Valley The "Valley of Heart's Delight," a stretch of land bordered by the San Francisco Bay and the Santa Cruz Mountains and known for its apricots, is dubbed "Silicon Valley" for the first time in Electronic News.

Kraftwerk

At a time when music was defined by Woodstock Nation, Kraftwerk and their robotic music, mechanical stage presence and conceptual take on music was the exception, not the rule. Founded by classical music students Ralf Hutter and Florian Schneider in Düsseldorf in 1970, the group became an international sensation with "Autobahn", a sparse twenty-two minute depiction of an uneventful trip down the German-

Austrian superhighway. This was followed several years later by "Trans-Europe Express" and "Showroom Dummies", both hits, and a tour of the States that is best remembered for their mannequin uniforms and their reliance on synthesizers rather than traditional instruments.

When asked if they didn't think their stage manner was a bit chilly, they seemed surprised. In a better world,

they said, they would send out cardboard cutouts and phone in the performance. (In this they were no doubt inspired by Andy Warhol, who had made it almost through his first college tour before someone figured out he had hired an imposter to give the lectures.)

For whatever reason, they have coasted on those early days for some time now. Their last hit album, "Man-Machine",

came out in 1981. The year later, in what is one of their most enduring claims to fame, Afrika Bambaataa, one of the forefathers of rap and a legendary Bronx DJ, released "Planet Rock," a record that laced hip-hop beats with Kraftwerk's futuristic techno-pop. The song became one of the most influential singles of all time, and helped herald the emergence of rap music. Kraftwerk's occasional releases since

show no signs of that energy, and certainly exhibit no obligation that they need return the favor. Regardless, they also go out on the road once in a while, knowing that no matter what, they will get headline status, rock-star treatment and a packed audience of first-time fans, eager to commune with one of the most provocative enigmas of modern music. NF

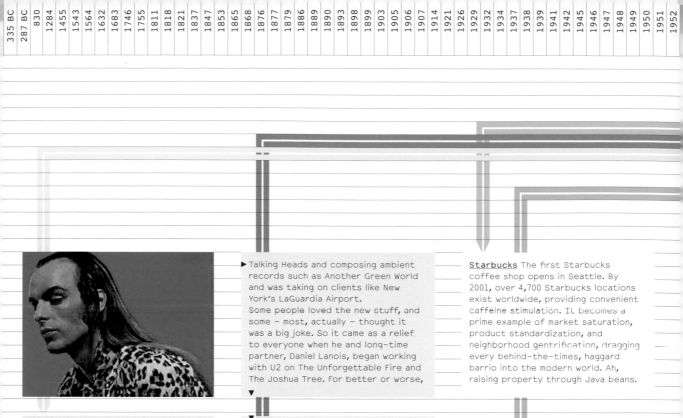

▶ Talking Heads and composing ambient records such as Another Green World and was taking on clients like New York's LaGuardia Airport.
Some people loved the new stuff, and some – most, actually – thought it was a big joke. So it came as a relief to everyone when he and long-time partner, Daniel Lanois, began working with U2 on The Unforgettable Fire and The Joshua Tree. For better or worse,
▼

Starbucks The first Starbucks coffee shop opens in Seattle. By 2001, over 4,700 Starbucks locations exist worldwide, providing convenient caffeine stimulation. It becomes a prime example of market saturation, product standardization, and neighborhood gentrification, dragging every behind-the-times, haggard barrio into the modern world. Ah, raising property through Java beans.

GEEK POP

Brian Eno If anyone was more outrageous in the 1970s than Bowie, it was Roxy Music's Brian Eno, who proved that a receding hairline could be sexy when tarted up with a lot of eyeliner and rouge and the right feather boa. But then, just as the band was becoming really famous, Eno, who played synthesizers and tapes
▼

those records changed the course of musical history, giving him the freedom to pursue his more abstract and experimental compositions in the lap of luxury. Now, if he'd bring back those feather boas... NF

▼ (whatever that meant) had a fight with suave lead singer Bryan Ferry and left the group.
Now, you'd think that you couldn't get much weirder than a drag queen that played the tape recorder but Eno was just warming up. For one, he loved Musak (light versions of pop songs, played in elevators) that everyone else ridiculed. For another, he liked using recording techniques
▼

GEEK ROBOT

Silent Running Shortly after he did the special effects for 2001, Douglas Trumbell directed this tale of a man on a spaceship keeping the earth's forests, which are afloat in the spaceship, alive. He is helped by three drones, named Huey, Dewey and Louie. As you could expect from a trio named after Donald Duck's nephews,
▼

▼ rather than instruments to compose music, developing a tape-delay system (Frippertronics, after guitarist Robert Fripp) that would later morph into sampling. And he created a deck of tarotlike cards called <u>Oblique Strategies</u>, which he used to make career decisions.
By 1975, he had started a label called Obscure, producing records for artists like Bowie, Devo, and the ▶

GEEK GAME

Computer Space Nolan Bushnell, 26 at the time, develops <u>Computer Space</u>, the first video arcade game based on <u>Space Wars</u>. The game wasn't a success but Bushnell didn't give up. He formed a little company called Atari, simplified his game concept even further and came up with <u>Pong</u> a year later. EVDZ

▼ the drones are beyond cute, whether they're waddling around, playing cards or performing minor surgery. The reason they were so lifelike? They were operated by four multiple amputees. NF

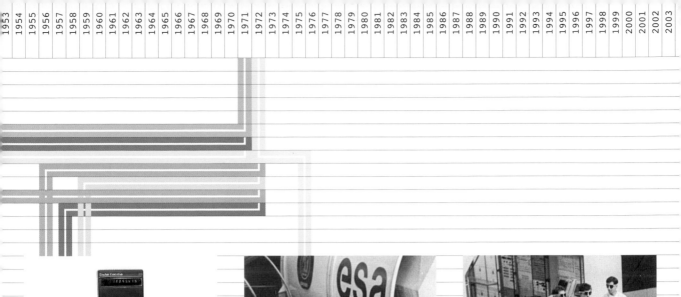

Sinclair Executive Clive Sinclair, eccentric geek inventor, launches the first electronic pocket calculator, the Sinclair Executive.

Futureworld Edwin Catmull creates the first computer-animated film called Futureworld. The subject is his own left hand.

GEEK GAME

Pong
> see page 76

GEEK POP

Devo Who else but a group of guys from Akron, Ohio called Devo could wear yellow reactor suits and hats made of upturned red flowerpots, sing about genetic and cultural devolution and get away with it? One of the first self-generated concept bands, Devo was the brainchild of two art students, Mark

▼

Mothersbaugh and Jerry Casale. Neither had musical backgrounds, so they recruited their brothers and a friend who did, made a 10-minute art film, The Truth About De-volution, which won a prize at the Ann Arbor Film Festival, invented a corporate mascot, a devolved robot called Booji, and, through a careful integration of art, marketing, irony and some music, packaged themselves into a cult band

▼

that the Rolling Stone Encyclopedia of Rock correctly identifies as a new-wave version of Kiss.
They were immediately given the royal treatment: David Bowie introducing them in their NY club debut and Brian Eno producing their debut album, "Q. Are We Not Men? A: We Are Devo!." The album was a huge hit, at least among the scenesters, and Devo looked like it would become big stars. ▲

▶ But, as it turned out, they were too smart for their own good. They scored well with "Whip It" and "Satisfaction", but the more interesting stuff – such as opening their shows in polyester leisure suits as Dove, the Band of Love, playing lounge versions of their songs – went way over most people's heads. Still, they remain extraordinarily influential, with many citing them as paving the way for shows like The

▼

Simpsons. Although their subsequent albums have been unsuccessful, they have a high nostalgia factor and can periodically be spotted on reunion road. NF

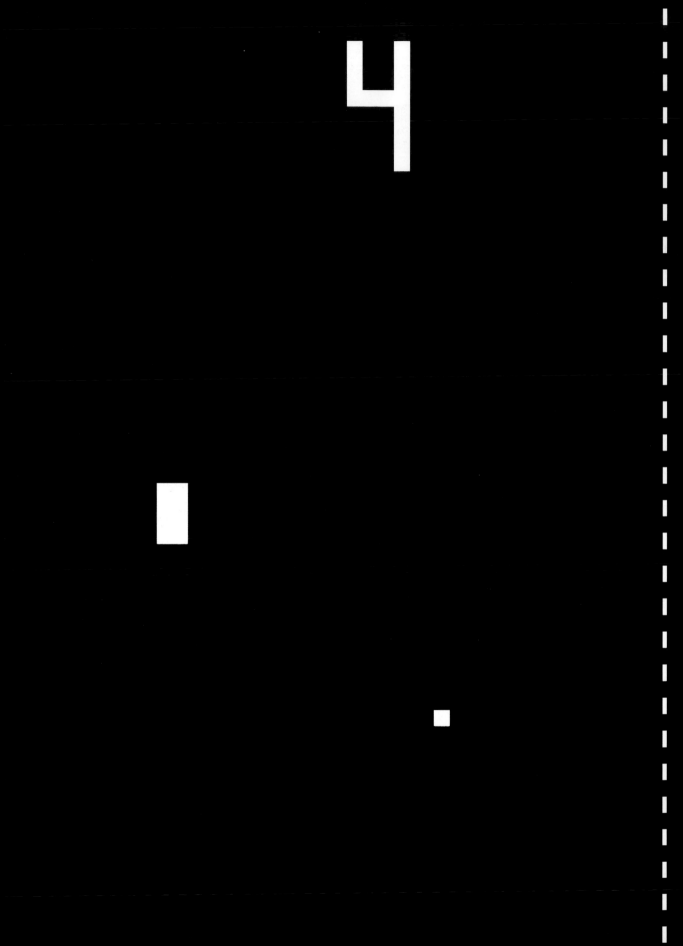

Pong/Atari After developing a fascination with computer games, Nolan Bushnell, a one-time HAM radio aficionado and amusement park manager, founds Atari. The same year he releases Pong, the first coin-operated video game system, which Bushnell developed in his daughter's bedroom-turned-lab. Pong's simple two-player game play, blocky monochrome graphics, and monotone bleeps make a surprisingly addictive combination. Mesmerized players discover that they have no choice but to plunk down one quarter after another in a quest to get their winning initials on the console. In 1976 Bushnell sells Atari to Warner Communications, which subsequently sells it to Hasbro after the company loses millions to knock-offs and falls short of managing itself as a key player in the next wave of tech: home computing. Bushnell goes on to found the popular (but not-so-tasty) children's pizza-slinging arcade chain, Chuck E. Cheese, which he also sells.

335 BC	287 BC	830	1284	1455	1543	1564	1632	1683	1746	1755	1811	1818	1821	1837	1847	1853	1865	1868	1876	1877	1879	1886	1889	1890	1893	1898	1899	1903	1905	1906	1907	1914	1921	1926	1929	1932	1934	1937	1938	1939	1941	1942	1945	1946	1947	1948	1949	1950	1951	1952

Dungeons & Dragons High school drop-out E Gary Gygax, who had been playing war games since the '60s, publishes <u>Dungeons & Dragons</u>, the first role-playing game (RPG), and sells 50,000 copies within a year. Players latch on to the strategy and mystery of being something else, and interactive Trekkies get a second extra-curricular activity.

Sleeper Woody Allen's "<u>Sleeper</u>" gets post-modern sex and drugs right. In the film, Allen rolls out the "Orgasmatron," a one-person sex booth, and a designer-drug silver ball that is passed around the living room. We don't think it's named in the film … if someone is offering it to us.

Hard-Disk Drive IBM develops the first hard-disk drive. With two 30-MB disk platters, it is named the "Winchester" drive after project manager Ken Haughten's 30-30 rifle.

GEEK ROBOT

Westworld Yul Brynner makes the debut film of Michael Crichton (Jurassic Park, The Lost World, ER) come alive as a gunslinging robot trying to terminate two pesky theme park guests. Although big-budgeted, the special effects often didn't cost much. To get the effect of his face burning from acid, for instance, ▶

▶ Brynner added ground Alka-Seltzer to the oil base of his makeup. When they threw water on it, the mixture fizzed, producing the desired visual. Hurray for Hollywood! NF

GEEK MOVIE

Soylent Green In a twisted view of the future, director Edward G. Robinson depicts 2022 New York City as a virtually post-apocalyptic wasteland where hungry, unemployed masses rely on government handouts — in this case, a foodstuff called Soylent Green — to survive. A video game makes a cameo (Nolan Bushnell's
▼

▼
<u>Computer Space</u>), Charlton Heston gives his typically Shakespearean performance ("It's made out of people!"), and sci-fi reminds us how scary things can get when the world grows out of control. NF

GEEK GADGET

Motorola Dyna-Tac Inventor Martin Cooper makes the first wireless cell phone call on April 3rd at Motorola with a Dyna-Tac prototype. He calls his rival at AT&T's Bell Labs, head of research Joel Engel. EVDZ

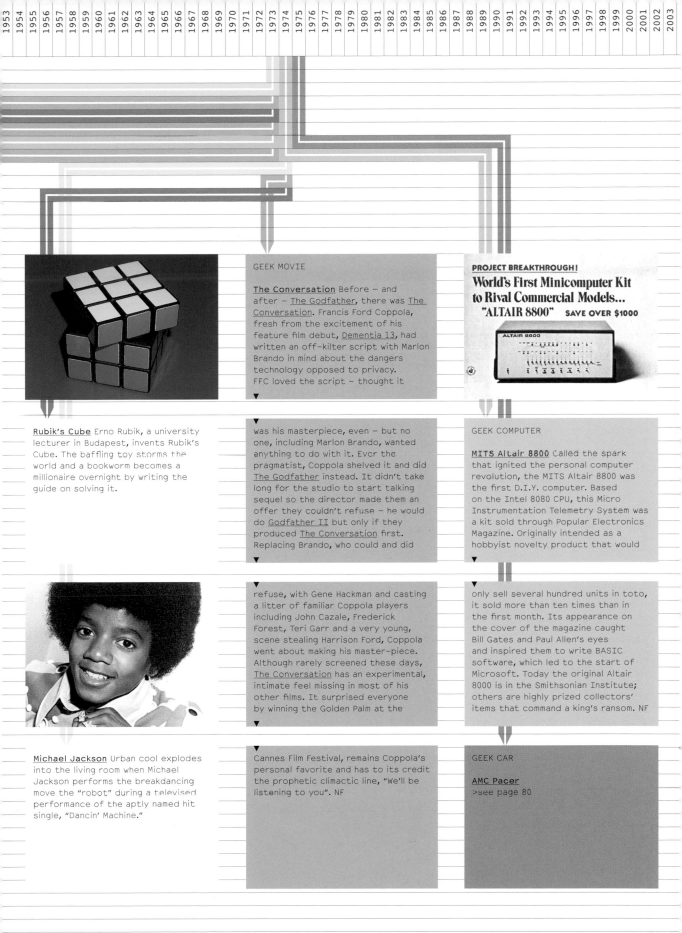

GEEK MOVIE

The Conversation Before — and after — The Godfather, there was The Conversation. Francis Ford Coppola, fresh from the excitement of his feature film debut, Dementia 13, had written an off-kilter script with Marlon Brando in mind about the dangers technology opposed to privacy. FFC loved the script — thought it

PROJECT BREAKTHROUGH!

World's First Minicomputer Kit to Rival Commercial Models... "ALTAIR 8800" SAVE OVER $1000

Rubik's Cube Erno Rubik, a university lecturer in Budapest, invents Rubik's Cube. The baffling toy storms the world and a bookworm becomes a millionaire overnight by writing the guide on solving it.

was his masterpiece, even — but no one, including Marlon Brando, wanted anything to do with it. Ever the pragmatist, Coppola shelved it and did The Godfather instead. It didn't take long for the studio to start talking sequel so the director made them an offer they couldn't refuse — he would do Godfather II but only if they produced The Conversation first. Replacing Brando, who could and did

GEEK COMPUTER

MITS Altair 8800 Called the spark that ignited the personal computer revolution, the MITS Altair 8800 was the first D.I.Y. computer. Based on the Intel 8080 CPU, this Micro Instrumentation Telemetry System was a kit sold through Popular Electronics Magazine. Originally intended as a hobbyist novelty product that would

refuse, with Gene Hackman and casting a litter of familiar Coppola players including John Cazale, Frederick Forest, Teri Garr and a very young, scene stealing Harrison Ford, Coppola went about making his master-piece. Although rarely screened these days, The Conversation has an experimental, intimate feel missing in most of his other films. It surprised everyone by winning the Golden Palm at the

only sell several hundred units in toto, it sold more than ten times than in the first month. Its appearance on the cover of the magazine caught Bill Gates and Paul Allen's eyes and inspired them to write BASIC software, which led to the start of Microsoft. Today the original Altair 8000 is in the Smithsonian Institute; others are highly prized collectors' items that command a king's ransom. NF

Michael Jackson Urban cool explodes into the living room when Michael Jackson performs the breakdancing move the "robot" during a televised performance of the aptly named hit single, "Dancin' Machine."

Cannes Film Festival, remains Coppola's personal favorite and has to its credit the prophetic climactic line, "We'll be listening to you". NF

GEEK CAR

AMC Pacer
>see page 80

Back when Austin Powers roamed the world, the Big Four – GM, Ford, Chrysler and AMC (the American Motor Corporation) ruled the road. Granted, the AMC was far enough behind the others that the company seemed as much a toy as the cars they made. But with the benefit of hindsight, models like the Gremlin and the Pacer were extremely cool and, to those idiosyncratic enough to appreciate them, totally beloved.

The story begins with the Nash Motor Company, a small company that was the only American small car company to stay afloat between World War II and 1960. Nash merged with Hudson, another small car company, in 1960 and changed its name to the AMC. They chugged along with models like the Hornet but by 1970, they knew they were in trouble. The Big Three had become

convinced that there was money in small cars; both Ford and Chevrolet were entering the market in 1971. Knowing they couldn't compete with the giants, AMC decided to beat them at their own game by unveiling a subcompact car six months before Ford and Chevy hit the shops with their small car. AMC's deadline was set, with no sense of occasion, it seems, for April 1, 1970. Or, in layman's terms, April Fool's Day.

The only problem: there was no subcompact car. So Vice President of Style [Design] Richard Teague came up with an ingenious solution. Rather than design a new car, which was impossible given the deadline, he and his crew simply chopped off the back end of their popular Hornet and added a glass hatch instead of a trunk. The result was, as critics noted, less a true subcompact and more a cut-

came complete with features like 8-tracks and CB radios and was unveiled in 1975 to mixed results. "An acquired taste for those with an open mind", said one critic. Others were more forthright, calling it a variety of names, including a hamstermobile, a fishbowl on wheels, a moonbuggy, an egg on wheels, a pregnant guppy and a jellybean. Others complained about the car's

demographic than it is today). The campaign worked. Despite all its flaws, the Gremlin became, if not hip, an object of pride to many of its owners and a cult favorite that still resonates today, as evidenced by a spate of Gremlin Clubs and restoration web sites and its use as a prop in period movies such as The Wedding Singer. In fact, it remained in production with minimal changes throughout the

weight and poor performance. But some people were thrilled by the chance to own a design classic (as evidenced by characters in Microserfs and in the Wayne's World movies, where the Pacer was called the Mirthmobile). As vocal as they were, however, it wasn't enough to save the line. After it was introduced in 1975, its sales steadily declined, until in 1980 manufacture stopped altogether.

down larger car. It was too wide and front-heavy to handle well, had a six cylinder engine which drank gas and was considered ugly. But that didn't stop AMC. They advertised their ugly duckling as "cute" and "different", added some cheap design options, such as a blackened grill, oversized tires, fancy wheels and racing stripes and marketed it to the under-35 market (which was a far less desired

decade, finally hanging up its hubcaps in 1979, when it was folded into a new model called The Spirit. The Pacer, AMC's next contribution to automotive history, had many of the same problems, and much of the same appeal. This time around, AMC had given Teague the directive to develop a car that was futuristic yet affordable. Designed with comfort and convenience as priorities, the car

And as with so many objects that get respect relatively late in their life cycles, only a few Pacers survive today. Chances are, however, the only way to get one now is to be rich and, most likely, famous. NF

GEEK COMIC

X-Men A revamped X-Men (with new characters such as Wolverine) sparked a new era of "fan" comics, which essentially were complicated ongoing story arcs that brought the child-like superhero genre into sync with their aging audience. After X-Men became the best-selling comic in Marvel's history, a slew of others

▼

▼

hit the stands. The best of the rest included Daredevil (1982) and Swamp Thing (1984), primarily because they introduced Frank Miller and Alan Moore to a larger audience. NF

GEEK POP

David Byrne The Talking Heads came out of the great New York punk explosion of the 1970s, cutting their teeth at CBGB's with future legends like Patti Smith, Tom Verlaine and Richard Hell. But while no one denied that the band's leader, David Byrne, was strange, he was more funky than punky. Even back then, it was obvious

▼

that he was one to watch. It started, as it so often did with rockers in the '60s and '70s, in art school. But Byrne, the son of an electrical engineer, wasn't comfortable with the affluent trappings of the Rhode Island School of Design and dropped out. From there it was a short ride to New York and stardom. Through it all, Byrne was the prototypical geek, with his ill-fitting clothes, awkward, jerky stage manner

▼

▶ Byrne and the other Talking Heads were not talking all that much to each other. The tension created a decade or so of great music, but at some point (some would say when the other three, as part of The Tom Tom Club, released their hit cover version of "Genius of Love") Byrne decided to go at it alone and told the Los Angeles Times that the band was finished. Lamely (at least according to the

▼

other band members), he hadn't yet told the band, who found out about it over Sunday breakfast.
The public nature of the breakup tarnished his image in terms of being a team player but he didn't waste a lot of time worrying about it, coming out with films, books, scores for highbrow dance and theater productions, a record label, Luaka Bop, and churning a definitive series of world beat

▼

albums. These have been greeted with persistent criticisms that Byrne has become a cultural imperialist, but Byrne shrugs off the charges. "I live in New York", he explains, going on to say that all he has to do to hear the musical sources is take a walk through his neighborhood and listen to what's on people's boom boxes. So say what you want. At the very least, the boy's got good ears. NF

Synthesizer The first digital synthesizer, the Synclavier, is developed at Dartmouth College in New Hampshire. The fundamental instrument behind New Wave and the subsequent dance-music explosion takes the ivories into the future.

▼

and nervous songs about psycho killers, buildings and food. One of the last bands to benefit from a patient record company, the Heads' reputation grew steadily with each release, culminating with the Stop Making Sense tour, filmed by Jonathan Demme in what remains one of the great filmed concerts of all time.
Although it was not immediately apparent to the casual observer,

▲

1953	1954	1955	1956	1957	1958	1959	1960	1961	1962	1963	1964	1965	1966	1967	1968	1969	1970	1971	1972	1973	1974	1975	1976	1977	1978	1979	1980	1981	1982	1983	1984	1985	1986	1987	1988	1989	1990	1991	1992	1993	1994	1995	1996	1997	1998	1999	2000	2001	2002	2003

mitzvah. The show had a small hard-core fan base but back then, there was no way to communicate with each other and the show met with a quick death – but evidently not before laying the seeds for The Revenge of the Nerds. It is also well remembered, mostly by girls who were teenagers then, on the web.

In the years since, Beatts continues to be a respected comedy writer and

GEEK COMPUTER ICONS

Bill Gates
Steve Jobs
Steve Wozniak
> see pages 84–87

GEEK TV ICON

Anne Beatts Anyone who has looked to geek angst and cluelessness as a source of humor in the past 25 years owes Anne Beatts, for she was the first writer to give the center of the stage to geeks as comic leads. She started trawling the subject in 1975 when Beatts, who had earlier been the first woman to become a contributing

comedic writing teacher in the Los Angeles area. But her biggest successes seem tied to Saturday Night Live, including her first and to date only Emmy for her work with Saturday Night Live: The 25th Anniversary show in 1999. NF

editor of the National Lampoon, joined the writing staff of Saturday Night Live. With her writing partner, Rosie Shuster, she introduced the broadly drawn, very geeky and very funny Todd and Lisa Lupner. These nerds, expertly played by Bill Murray, whose butt-crack seemed to get more play than his face in these sketches, and a whiney Gilda Radner, were a huge hit and led Beatts to develop a prime time sit-com called

Square Pegs in 1982. It was a fairly revolutionary show for its time, since it was the first show to cast actual teenagers to play teens, rather than baby-faced actors in their 20s. And it was well cast, featuring leads like Sarah Jessica Parker and Jamie Gertz as students who were obsessed with being popular, and guest stars such as Devo, who got to rock the joint when they played at Muffy Tepperman's bar

Microsoft Harvard dropout Bill Gates and Paul Allen create the first language for the PC (MS-DOS) and form Microsoft. The Uber-Geek arrives.

Apple I Former Atari employees Steven Wozniak and Steve Jobs, who had developed blue boxes that could scam free long-distance phone calls, found Apple I.

These three guys redefined the modern IPO and, in the process, ushered in the modern Gold Rush. Although Wozniak has opted over the years for a lower public profile, Gates and Jobs, who are in the news every five minutes, remain household names not just because of their enormous wealth, but because they are examples of a significant new paradigm of socio-political power.

It is that question, for instance, that motivates the unbylined writer of the Unofficial Bill Gates home page (www.zpub.com/un/bill). "As for why I created the 'unofficial' site'," he says, "I was intrigued with how Mr. Gates was becoming a symbol and mythic character. I was also interested in what he represented and how people reacted to him. Mr. Gates has the potential to become a major

is the richest person in the world and, according to Time Magazine's April 2004 list of the 100 most important people on the planet, wasted no time becoming the new face of philanthropy, dispensing billions of dollars to people and organizations he, his wife and their foundation, NAME, believe in. It seems impolite to mention that charity can be a very good thing, or it can be just another form of

philanthropist. What he does with his wealth can have a major impact on how philanthropy is done in the 21st century. What he does sets a model for how a person who has amassed far more wealth than he personally needs to live relates to others with his wealth. Will he give some of it away? How much and to whom?".
Interesting questions, to be sure. Gates still has an incredible work ethic,

imperialism. So political correctness aside, one has to wonder if Gates is behaving any different than the robber barons of yore. And there is a certain disconnect between Gates' lavish displays of generosity on the one hand and the creation of a ruthless corporate culture and strong-arm business conduct on the other. The issue is disturbing enough to undermine Gates' cool factor, because,

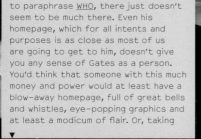

in court. Look all you want – there is no suggestion of a pulse. No humor, no outrage, no passion and no cool. Although he takes a completely different tack, you end up feeling much the same way about Steve Jobs. Back in the glory days, when he and Wozniak had become instant multi-millionaires (and celebrities), he was even more colorful than Gates: Books and miniseries couldn't get enough of

cyberspace once again, he can be found with singers like Sheryl Crow draped over his professional arm, determined to bring the music industry into the 21st Century as well. Like Gates, it would be foolish to question Jobs' influence, accomplishments and vision. But, again, does that make him cool? Not a chance. Here are three quick reasons why.

to paraphrase <u>WHO</u>, there just doesn't seem to be much there. Even his homepage, which for all intents and purposes is as close as most of us are going to get to him, doesn't give you any sense of Gates as a person. You'd think that someone with this much money and power would at least have a blow-away homepage, full of great bells and whistles, eye-popping graphics and at least a modicum of flair. Or, taking

Jobs as a tie-dyed, barefoot, b.o.-ridden, tripped out and erratic boy wonder throwing temper tantrums and, generally, behaving very badly. Most people in the media expected that Jobs would retreat to his castle and spend the rest of his days counting his money. But Jobs fooled everyone, first with Pixar and then with his dramatic come-from-behind save of Apple. Now, having conquered

1. Planned obsolence. Want to keep that "deluxe", iBook you bought a few years ago current by upgrading from OS9 to OS 10? Surprise. You can't.
2. The mini-iPod. It was designed to be a $99.00 US product, which is about what it's worth. But, if reports from Macworld 2004 are correct, Jobs surprised everyone, including the people working on the project, by upping the price to $249 (only $50

the other tack, to be so unimaginative as to be cool in spite of itself. But Gates takes a middle of the road approach with clean, formulaic design and low-key copy that boringly catalogues his speeches, achievements, and offers one pull quote – about how great reality is. Nary a mug shot from his 1977 bust in New Mexico, anecdotes about being pied, or nuggets from his myriad days

cheaper than the vastly superior "supersized" model). Is that what Jobs means by power to the people?
3. His homepage, which sets new standards for ingenuousness. It's low-tech and very Family Channel. In his chattiest tone, he'll let you see his resume, which is so self-satisfied that it practically winks at you. Once you've done that, you can watch an iMovie of his dog being watched, and

GEEK COMPUTER ICONS

Bill Gates
Steve Jobs (picture)
Steve Wozniak (picture)

read lots of postcards and postings from his kids, talking about their family vacations and after-school activities. It 's like a parody, a web version of Waiting for Guffman, only it's real. Don't know how you feel about it but from this vantage point, the idea of Jobs pimping his kids to sell himself seems way more creepy than cool. Which leaves us with Steve Wozniak, or Woz as he likes to be called. The

aggrandizing Jobs or the glacial Gates, Woz actually seems to inhabit his homepage, peppering it with geek-proud features like Dial-a-Joke, his favorite software of the moment, his experience buying a Sedgeway (or MacIntosh software) and, most tellingly, his shrine site to the US Festival, the mega-present he bought himself in 1983 after the first (really) big paycheck. While most of the other

designer of the Apple I and II computers, he, more than any of the others, seems to enjoy himself, whether it's devoting time and resources to the community he lives in (Los Gatos, perhaps the only redeeming 'hood in Silicon Valley) or to projects that promote his dream of "a free exchange of information/the way it should be". His website (www.woz.org) is also the most human. Unlike the self-

new multi-millionaires were content with mansions, Ferraris, personal trainers and supermodels, Woz threw a massive three-day pop festival, held in a dustbowl a few hours outside of Los Angeles. He celebrated with bands like LIST and unveiled an array of technological innovations, including a powerful demonstration of detente with the first two-way, live broadcast with a rock band from the Soviet Union

play. Officially, the band claimed to be appalled by the hypocrisy of the event, and remained backstage until Woz agreed to donate a substantial sum of money to the promotion of local bands. (Unofficially, as was evidenced by the performance that night and subsequent accounts of the band's history, they already were on the verge of breaking up and were looking for excuses to throw temper tantrums).

By the time The Clash took the stage, almost half the crowd had left. And when they finally stopped playing around 1 A.M., those who remained had yet another ordeal in front of them. Thousands of people were already in line for Day 2, which was heavy metal day. No one at the US Festival had anticipated the combustible reaction that would happen when you dangled thousands of exhausted punks down

a quarter mile or so gauntlet of angry, bored metalheads (apparently because no one at the US Festival even knew that the punk and metal scenes hated each other). It would have been funny had it not been so flat-out terrifying. By the end, though, all was forgiven. David Bowie, who had been MIA for several years, unveiled his red shoes in the debut of his Serious Moonlight ("Let's Dance") tour, and anointed Woz

in history that was to take place as the sun set on the festival's first day. Poor Woz – he introduced the live feed with fanfare appropriate to the occasion, exhorting the crowd to show their respect for Russia's finest. Russia's finest, however, turned out to be a bunch of aging, derivative and not very talented 40somethings playing (badly) in a Moscow basement. Woz wanted a warm and fuzzy

"hands-across-the-ocean" welcome but the crowd of Southern California punks booed, mooned the band and screamed insults at the "commies", telling them to shut up and go home. So much for detente.
Things continued to spiral out of control for the rest of the night. Just as the Clash, who were the first night headliners, were scheduled to take the stage, they decided not to

a pop hero. Even two decades later, with the only remnants of the US Festival Woz's timeworn shrine page, it doesn't get cooler than that. NF

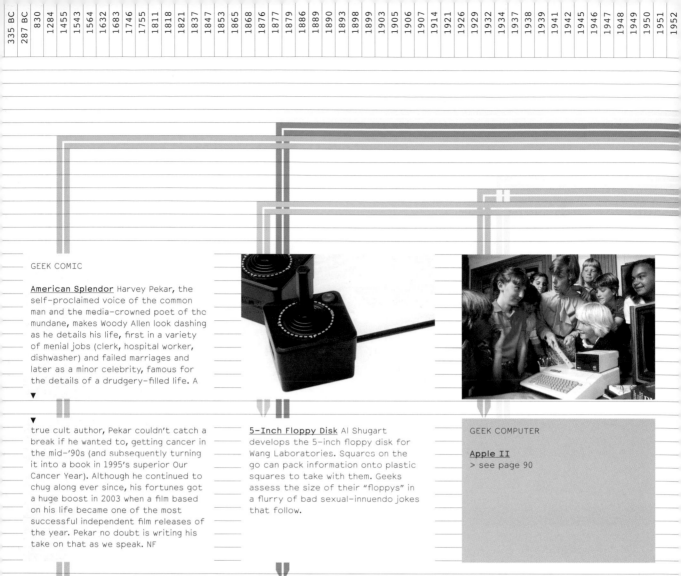

GEEK COMIC

American Splendor Harvey Pekar, the self-proclaimed voice of the common man and the media-crowned poet of the mundane, makes Woody Allen look dashing as he details his life, first in a variety of menial jobs (clerk, hospital worker, dishwasher) and failed marriages and later as a minor celebrity, famous for the details of a drudgery-filled life. A

true cult author, Pekar couldn't catch a break if he wanted to, getting cancer in the mid-'90s (and subsequently turning it into a book in 1995's superior Our Cancer Year). Although he continued to chug along ever since, his fortunes got a huge boost in 2003 when a film based on his life became one of the most successful independent film releases of the year. Pekar no doubt is writing his take on that as we speak. NF

5-Inch Floppy Disk Al Shugart develops the 5-inch floppy disk for Wang Laboratories. Squares on the go can pack information onto plastic squares to take with them. Geeks assess the size of their "floppys" in a flurry of bad sexual-innuendo jokes that follow.

Joystick Atari invents the joystick. Geeks assess the size of their own "joysticks" as another set of bad sexual-innuendo jokes follows.

GEEK COMPUTER

Apple II
> see page 90

GEEK COMIC

2000AD A hip British anthology that blended punk cynicism and science fiction and then brought it to the mainstream. Over the years, it introduced a galaxy of major talent, including Alan Moore, Alan Grant, Grant Morrison, Peter Milligan and Garth Ennis, as well as the comic book hero, Judge Dredd (who would get his own

GEEK MOVIE

Demon Seed After he co-directed Performance, Donald Cammell gave us the luckiest supercomputer of all: Proteus IV. If only because Proteus gets to impregnate the luminous Julie Christie. Granted, it is obsessed with her and finally ends up raping her. The movie just begs for a revenge-drenched sequel, but Cammell ended up

► committing suicide, taking all hopes of for a sequel with him. NF

comic, Judge Dredd: The Megazine, in 1990 and his own movie, starring Sylvester Stallone, in 1995). It was such an important cultural touchstone and so many bands cribbed names, ideas and looks from it that NME once said that "2000AD in the 1980s is to rock what Brylcreem was in the '50s, what drugs were in the '60s, and what hair gel was in the '70s". NF

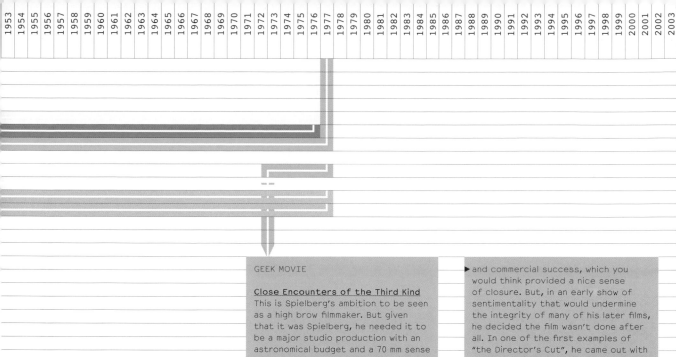

1953 1954 1955 1956 1957 1958 1959 1960 1961 1962 1963 1964 1965 1966 1967 1968 1969 1970 1971 1972 1973 1974 1975 1976 1977 1978 1979 1980 1981 1982 1983 1984 1985 1986 1987 1988 1989 1990 1991 1992 1993 1994 1995 1996 1997 1998 1999 2000 2001 2002 2003

GEEK MOVIE

Close Encounters of the Third Kind

This is Spielberg's ambition to be seen as a high brow filmmaker. But given that it was Spielberg, he needed it to be a major studio production with an astronomical budget and a 70 mm sense of scale. (The UFO landing site, for example, was the largest indoor set that had ever been constructed,

▼

▶ and commercial success, which you would think provided a nice sense of closure. But, in an early show of sentimentality that would undermine the integrity of many of his later films, he decided the film wasn't done after all. In one of the first examples of "the Director's Cut", he came out with a revised ending that made the film even more gooey than it was before. We're lucky he stopped there. Lately,

▼

measuring 27 meters high, 137 meters long and 76 meters wide, and requiring 6.4 kilometers of scaffolding, 1570 square meters of fiberglass and 2740 square meters of nylon canopy.) Given Spielberg's previous films (Duel, The Sugarland Express, Jaws) and the film's marketing campaign, which was based on the slogan "we are not alone", most people expected an Exorcist , but with aliens and UFOs.

▼

he's been feeling bad for poor Ray (Richard Dreyfuss) who became so obsessed with UFOs that he had to risk his family, his job and community opinion to go find them. Never mind that this is the critical source of drama in the film. Sure, Spielberg may feel bad for making Ray suffer. But as he should know, even in a Spielbergian universe, you can't make an omelete without breaking a few eggs. NF

GEEK COMIC

Heavy Metal A beautifully illustrated science fiction anthology, it mutated from the French original, Metal Hurlant. It brought a remarkable realism and sophistication to its painted art, and featured lots of naked women, Nubian and otherwise. In what may be its most lasting achievement, it also attracted an easy mix of top American

▼

What they got instead was a somewhat stately, thoughtful treatment of extra-terrestrials. Even worse, when the aliens got there, they weren't even evil or threatening but New-Agey warm and fuzzy (and not just metaphorically – the aliens were really children in rubber suits and only looked realistic when shot out of focus). Nice aliens??? How boring.
At least that's what screenwriter

▼

and European talent. Over 5000 animators in five different countries collaborated on the movie version (which still flopped). NF

▼

Paul Schrader, who hated the changes Spielberg was making enough to have his name removed from the credits, thought. The Motion Picture Association were happy to oblige him, but told Spielberg someone had to take the writing credit or the film could not be released. No problem, said Spielberg, taking the writing credit all for himself.
In any event, the film was a critical

GEEK COMPUTER

Apple II

The Apple II is launched. The world welcomes the first production home computer.

someone had scheduled an advance screening of the film just before they were ready to unload it. The test audience's over-the-top response to the film convinced them to hold off on the sale. It was a good call because the movie ended up making enough money to rescue the studio.

In a less astute move, the executives casually agreed to Lucas' request for the film merchandising rights. They were

Wizard of Oz, Robin Hood, Casablanca and High Noon all rolled into one. To them it's a classic story of good and evil, friendship and love, treachery and nobility with hyper speed space battles, exotic creatures and daring escapes. Coming at a time when great art tended to be dark and ugly, Star Wars reminded people that there was nothing bad about art that made you feel good. The ultimate film web site,

GEEK MOVIE

Star Wars A long time ago in a galaxy far, far away, George Lucas mattered. It had been about ten years since Kubrick's 2001 and when the dust had settled, neither Kubrick nor anyone else knew where to go next. With relatively little fanfare, Lucas hand-delivered a new mythology to a willing generation and a new business model to a shocked

so certain the rights were worthless that they actually gave him the rights for free. This made Lucas rich beyond comprehension, and made merchandising rights a critical contractual issue in any film or TV show.

The Director's Guild was not as easily swayed. After seeing a print, they told him that movies had to have opening credits and his had none. Lucas explained that the movie harkened

IMDb.com, has one bit of useless trivia that is worth recounting. "George Lucas and Brian De Palma held a joint audition for Carrie (1976) and Star Wars (1977). Originally, Sissy Spacek was casted as Princess Leia, and Carrie Fisher as Carrie. However, Fisher refused to appear in nude scenes, but Spacek was willing to do them. So, they switched parts". That'll teach you to keep your clothes on, Sissy. NF

industry. The film itself was a kitchen sink of cinematic homages. The credits came from a 1939 series, The Phantom Creeps, and were followed with shot-by-shot lifts from John Ford's The Searchers (the farm scenes), 1954's Dam Busters and 1964's 633 Squadron (the battle scenes) and 1934's Triumph des Willens (the medal scene), and references galore to films like Kurosawa's Hidden Fortress.

back to old-school serials, and that opening credits would ruin the mood he was trying to establish. The Guild pretended to be sympathetic but then ordered Lucas to pu the credits in or that they would fine him. Lucas remained unapologetic, paid the fine and, after Star Wars hit the theater, resigned from the DGA. Not that it mattered. By the end of the first week (as documented accurately in an

These days, the producers would be worried about plagiarism, but back then the executives at 20th Century Fox were simply concerned with staying afloat. And they saw Star Wars as one gigantic liability. Rather than risk further financial exposure, they decided to recycle the special effects in some of their TV shows and then sell their shares in the film and take it as a tax loss. Lucky for them,

episode of the TV series, That '70s Show), it was evident that Star Wars was a full-fledged phenomenon. That the force eventually deserted Lucas and was inherited by the Frodos and, to a lesser extent, Harry Potters in no way diminishes the magnitude of Lucas' achievement. To several generations, including the one that brought geek culture into the mainstream, Star Wars was The

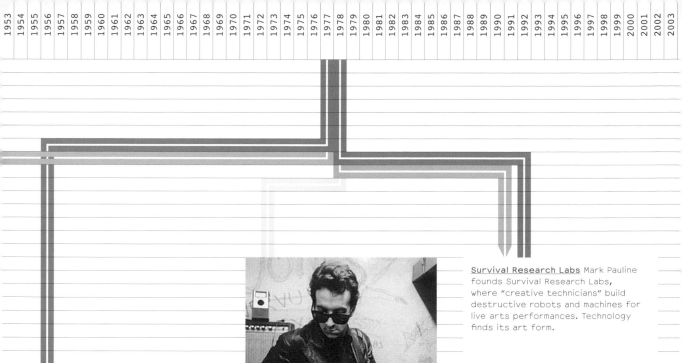

Survival Research Labs Mark Pauline founds Survival Research Labs, where "creative technicians" build destructive robots and machines for live arts performances. Technology finds its art form.

GEEK POP

Elvis Costello Punk goes New Wave with the release of the album "This Year's Model" by Elvis Costello. Only this year's model looks just like Buddy Holly. In 1975, computer operator and aspiring musician Decline Patrick McManus quit his day job to become a roadie with the legendary British bar band, Brinsley Steward. The band's

GEEK GAME

Atari VCS (or 2600) Atari founder and Pong inventor Nolan Bushnell introduces a game system that could be used at home. Games were sold separately on cartridges. Atari wasn't the first but would dominate the market for many years and sell over thirty million consoles. Releasing home versions of arcade hits like

bass player, Nick Lowe, introduced Decline to maverick manager Jake Riviera, who put the name Elvis together with McManus' mother's maiden name, Costello, and proclaimed him England's next angry young star. Unlike mild-mannered Freddy, the geek Elvis had vitriol, wit and talent to spare, and spewed it out in a torrent of albums revolving around themes of revenge and guilt. The live shows were

Space Invaders, Asteroids, Pac-Man, and the missus contributed to its success. EVDZ

as revelatory, causing critics to fawn and established rock stars to pout. David Lee Roth, then of Van Halen and never one to keep his thoughts to himself, echoed many of his peers' sentiments, for example, when he said that "critics like the bespectacled, nerdy Costello so much because they all looked like him". NF

GEEK GAME

Space Invaders Toshihiro Nishikado designs an arcade game for Taito with characters based on his nation's favorite foods: squid, crab, and octopus. Like Star Wars, Space Invaders moves the battlefield from the Wild West and WWII to the stratosphere. In Japan the game is so popular, it caused a shortage of 100 Yen coins. EVDZ&MS

GEEK POP

The Descendents The forefathers of geek core and one of Southern' California's most beloved seminal punk bands, the Descendents have been sporadically recording and playing for the past 25 years without once losing their trademark wry humor and angst-driven punk riffs. "Rejection, food, coffee, girls, fishing

▼

and food", is how the band's leader, Milo Aukerman described the band's interests. He wasn't kidding: Among early songs were odes to fast food like "Weinerschnitzel" and teen-age anti-authority complaints like "My Dad Sucks". In what fans hoped was a joke, they followed those songs with their first full-length record, "Milo Goes to College". There was no metaphor at work here. Milo was actually going

▼

to college to study biochemistry – and did, eventually getting a Ph.D. Like Bad Religion, the other SoCal band of the era that was fronted by a graduate student in the sciences, The Descendents have remained local heroes in Southern California and the punk community. Their most recent album, "Cool To Be You", makes no concession to age or political correctness. There's even a song

▼

called "Mass Nerder", about being a nerd and "kicking somebody's butt with good grades". As one fan put it, "this is the sound of a grown man realizing he is grown up and acting like a grown man". Heady stuff, and surprise evidence that punk is an attitude that gets better with age. NF

GEEK ROBOT

KISS Meets the Phantom of the Park In this TV movie the members of the band KISS are threatened by alter-ego robots. The band hated the movie. One band member, sensing a stinker, didn't even bother showing up to read his lines. But the Japanese video is currently going for $500 (about what it costs to make one of the robots) on eBay.

GEEK POP

Prince In a world where people are increasingly afraid of their own shadows, Prince rules because he does exactly what he wants to do.
Consider that:
a. He wrote, sang, played and produced all the songs on his first five albums.
b. In the early 1980s, when people didn't do these things, he ran around

▼

the stage in red bikini underwear, ate out his guitar, humped the bed and still got every woman in the stadium to "wish he were mine".
c. He filmed and delivered Purple Rain with no outside involvement. The studio wasn't even aware that it was good enough to release until an assistant phoned them in the middle of a San Diego screening, telling them they had struck gold.

▶ d. A studio virtuoso, he apparently has more than 800 full-length albums catalogued and waiting to be released.
e. He only does press when it suits him, and on his terms. Although he is a total exhibitionist on stage, he is pathologically shy and soft-spoken in private.
f. When he found out how the record industry worked, he wrote Slave on his cheek, changed his name to an

▼

unpronounceable symbol and went straight to the internet, where he continued to sell tons of records and stoke his fan base, again with no major label intervention.
g. Once he made his point, he took his name back, got into the Rock 'n' Roll Hall of Fame and launched a "good-bye" comeback tour that supposedly was going to retire his old catalogue (the second time he's made that decision)

▼

and then threw a blank-cover CD in with the price of a ticket, ensuring that Musicology, his first album for a new label, would enter the top 10 for weeks.
h. He's 5'2" (without his heels), but is still the sexiest person alive. What can you say other than that he's got the look and the magic. Paul Brownfield, trying to dissect his appeal in the Los Angeles Times after Prince had taken the city by storm in the

▼

spring of 2004, says it best. Calling him an unfathomable aphrodisiac in human form, Brownfield goes on to say, "Dismissing Prince as a geek is tantamount to not understanding what women want". NF

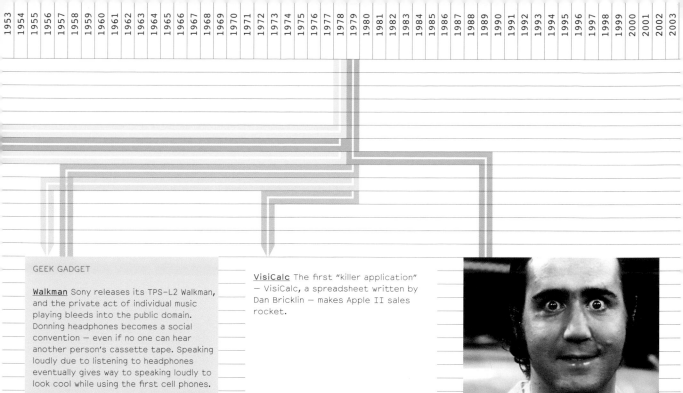

GEEK GADGET

Walkman Sony releases its TPS-L2 Walkman, and the private act of individual music playing bleeds into the public domain. Donning headphones becomes a social convention — even if no one can hear another person's cassette tape. Speaking loudly due to listening to headphones eventually gives way to speaking loudly to look cool while using the first cell phones.

VisiCalc The first "killer application" — VisiCalc, a spreadsheet written by Dan Bricklin — makes Apple II sales rocket.

Sinclair ZX80 Clive Sinclair launches the ZX80, the first cheap, mass-produced home computer. 70,000 are sold.

GEEK COMIC

Deadline Another hip British publication, Deadline was part conventional music magazine, part comic. Like 2000 AD, it was very good at discovering new talent. Its most famous discovery was Alan Martin and Jamie Hewlett's Tank Girl. A punked out version of Alien's Ripley, this female road warrior who wanders the outback

▼

looking for trouble was billed as "the girl that makes Superman want to take off his pants".
Dressed like a London club kid she became a mascot for feminists and riot grrls alike. Sadly, the movie was a disaster, and the critical fallout from it led Deadline's disillusioned publisher, Tom Astor, to pull the plug on the entire magazine. NF

GEEK TV

Andy Kaufman's Funhouse "I am not a comic", Andy Kaufman often said. "I just want to play with [people's] heads". In the summer of 1977, he set about fulfilling that goal with his very first network special, Andy's Funhouse. Enlisting longtime friend and writer Bob Zmuda as co-conspirator, Kaufman produced a brilliant, visionary satire

▼

that spoofed not only his own image, but the shallow, smug conventions of late '70s talk shows. The special opens cold with Andy, as Foreign Man, admitting that he has blown ABC's money on a lavish party for his friends, and then continues through a bewildering mélange of home movies, karaoke, ill-fated interviews, Elvis impersonations and even a conga rendition of Disney's "It's a Small World", before culminating in a

▼

sincere conversation with his childhood idol, Howdy Doody. Not surprisingly, such antics baffled network executives, and Andy's Funhouse was shelved for two years, eventually airing in a late-night, middle-of-summer slot. Outside a museum showing here and there, it hasn't been seen since. But as anyone who watched it that late summer night can tell you, television hasn't seen anything as twisted since. NF

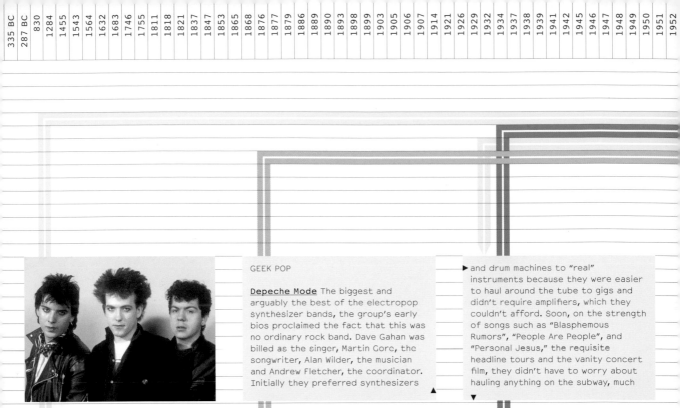

GEEK POP

Depeche Mode The biggest and arguably the best of the electropop synthesizer bands, the group's early bios proclaimed the fact that this was no ordinary rock band. Dave Gahan was billed as the singer, Martin Gore, the songwriter, Alan Wilder, the musician and Andrew Fletcher, the coordinator. Initially they preferred synthesizers

and drum machines to "real" instruments because they were easier to haul around the tube to gigs and didn't require amplifiers, which they couldn't afford. Soon, on the strength of songs such as "Blasphemous Rumors", "People Are People", and "Personal Jesus," the requisite headline tours and the vanity concert film, they didn't have to worry about hauling anything on the subway, much

GEEK POP

The Smiths/The Cure Given that they were militantly guitar oriented when synthesizer bands were all the rage, they may seem an odd choice for Geek adoration. But Morrissey did angst and gender bending better than any of his contemporaries (except, perhaps, Joy Division's Ian Curtis who, in an act that's difficult to top, did kill himself).

less the price of an amplifier. Still, heroin addiction, intragroup jealousies and feuds and suicide attempt took their toll and Depeche Mode became less a band than a rich source of remix materials for DJs who could afford the hefty licensing fee. Ironically, post-suicidal Gahan embarked on a comeback tour in 2003, playing the guitar, with nary a coordinator in sight. NF

And the band still inspires well-attended Smiths' conventions where fans can remember how miserable they were and pray that maybe next year in Jerusalem or elsewhere, the Smiths will make up and play again.
Then there's Robert Smith and his band, the Cure, who are every bit as self-absorbed, whiney, angst-ridden and jangly. Like The Smiths, they belong here less for who they are than for the

audience they attract: a melancholy, slightly glam, slightly Goth group of fans who grew up in the '80s. Then, as now, the appeal is in part based on Smith's teased hair and really bad makeup and in part to the rich melodies and quiver of hits. for whatever reason, it's prime nostalgia for the dot-com generation, pure and simple. NF

GEEK ROBOT

The Black Hole Disney's answer to Star Wars featured high-end actors like Roddy McDowall and Slim Pickens as voices for their robots, who infused them with more personality than many of the real characters. Cheesy production, bad science and the usual Disney agenda make this movie laughably wrong. NF

GEEK FASHION

Nike Air Nike develops its Air technology, which uses a gas-filled bag of air inserted in the sole of the shoe to cushion the impact of running. Sneakers go hi-tech.

GEEK COMIC

<u>Raw</u> Raw was the spawn of Art Spiegelman and Francois Mouly, a fine artist with ties to the European comic community. An avant-garde anthology, it was aimed at the intellectual community that loved graphic novels but had little interest in superheroes. The breakout piece was Maus, Spiegelman's rendering of his father's

▼

GEEK GAME

<u>Ms. Pac Man</u> The most popular quarter-munching arcade game of the 80's. Mr. Pac Man started the arcade craze, but look in the laundromat of the 00's – you'll find only his wife. Why? More mazes (Mr. had one, Ms. has 4), a cinematic story sequence rewarding the player for completing a maze, and point-awarding bonus fruit that runs away.

▼

▼

life during the Holocaust, with Jews cast as mice, Nazis as cats and Poles as pigs. Against all odds, the story, recast in such an unusual way, worked. Collected in a two-volume hardback to glowing reviews, it won the Pulitzer Prize for literature in 1992; marking the first time a comic or cartoon had won the prestigious award. NF

GEEK HACKER

<u>John Draper (a.k.a. Captain Crunch)</u> This is where hacking gets interesting. A true original, John Draper invented phone "phreaking" when he used the plastic prize that came with his breakfast cereal, Captain Crunch, to make free phone calls in the mid-1970s. Although many people were phreaking (an amalgam of free, phone,
▼

Ms. Thang also has a fashionable edge – she sports a bow and a sassy mole. MS

▼
freak), Draper took it to another level. Instead of just calling his friends, he would send calls around the world, bouncing them off satellites and, as one anecdote has it, asking someone walking by a pay phone in Victoria Station what the weather was like. He also wrote the first word processor program for the IBM PC, beating Bill Gates to the punch and out of the IBM contract. NF

ATARI 2600

MS. PAC-MAN

<u>3.5-Inch Floppy Disk</u> Sony launches the 3.5-inch floppy disk. It isn't actually floppy; the disk is encased in a protective plastic shell. As the size of geeks' hardware gets smaller, their portfolios get more compact and sturdy.

GEEK COMIC

<u>Eightball</u> Created by Daniel Clowes, blending confessional autobiography, literary ambition and social satire, Eightball launched several recurring characters and stories, including "Like a Velvet Glove Cast in Iron" (a mystery with vivid sexual overtones) and "I Hate You Deeply" (an unforgiving list of people and things he, well, hates). NF

GEEK HACKER

Ian Murphy (a.k.a. Captain Zap) In 1981, Ian Murphy became the first person to be arrested for computer crime. The crime? He and three others hacked into AT&T's computers and reset their internal clocks, wreaking havoc with the system's finances. After spending 1,000 hours in community service and two and a half years ▼

▼ probation, Murphy found himself on the big screen, the inspiration for the movie <u>Sneakers</u>. NF

GEEK POP

The Beastie Boys Modern day alchemists, this trio of cut-ups took silver spoons and turned them into platinum albums. All three, Adam Yauch, Adam Horovitz and Mike Diamond, grew up in rich, well-educated Jewish New York families, and were in the throes of adolescent rebellion when they recorded a prank call to Carvel Ice ▼

▶ quantum leap that established them as masters of the aural collage. In the years since, they embraced Buddhism and powered the successful concerts for Tibet, apologizing to gay people for the homophobia in some of their early lyrics and to everyone for writing "Fight for Your Right". They started, run and shut down their own magazine and record label, allowed people to customize their own Beastie ▼

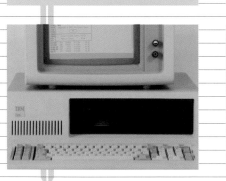

Cream and incorporated it into a rap satire called "Cookie Puss". Their friend Rick Rubin, who was about to start Def Jam Records, thought it was cool as hell, encouraged them to take their rap more seriously and booked them onto tours with Madonna and Run-D.M.C. Along the way, they recorded "Licensed to Ill", which included the anthemic "(You Gotta) Fight for Your Right (to Party)". To ▼

Boys Greatest Hits anthology on their website by choosing the tracks and sequencing before the album's release, and made so many innovative music videos that MTV gave them a lifetime achievement award.
Perhaps most importantly, they provided the soundtrack to the lives of the generation that was born between the late '60s and the mid-'70s. That gives them a life of street ▼

GEEK COMPUTER

IBM Personal Computer On August 12, IBM releases its Personal Computer built from off the shelf parts. It featured an Intel chip and the operating system MS-DOS to which Microsoft retained the rights. <u>Time</u> named the computer "man of the year". EVDZ

▼ almost everyone's surprise, the album sold 720,000 copies in the first six weeks, and catapulted the Beasties to instant stardom.
At that time, there was nothing terribly nerdy about them other than a smart sense of musical references and a bad wardrobe. Then they had a lengthy falling out with Rick Rubin, took a three-year hiatus and emerged with "Paul's Boutique", an artistic ▲

▼ credibility and the ability to continue to fight for the right, even though their party days are long gone. NF

GEEK COMPUTER

Osborne I The Osborne 1 is considered to be the first true portable computer, or laptop. Built by Adam Osborne, it weighed 24 pounds, had a five-inch screen, two floppy drives and cost $1795. EVDZ

GEEK COMPUTER

Sinclair ZX81 Clive Sinclair launches the ZX81, sparking the home-computer revolution. 300,000 are sold. As the stage for the home office is being set, traditional notions of the workplace become obsolete.

were better received in England and Europe than the States. May moved to Chicago, fell under the influence of the Chicago house scene and warmed up his music with elements of Chicago disco. Saunderson, in the meantime, made a move towards techno-pop, becoming the most commercial of the three with his group, Inner City. Through it all, they remained friends, co-founded the Music Institute, which

GEEK POP

The Belleville Three In the 1960s, Detroit gave the world Motown, and in the late 1990s, Eminem. But in the 1980s, Detroit belonged to three suburban kids from Belleville Jr. High, who stamped techno with a signature brand of urban grooves married to futuristic synthesizers, all before their voices changed.

moved the scene to downtown Detroit and ended up inspiring second-wave Detroit techno stars such as Stacey Pullen, Carl Craig, Kenny Larkin and Richie Hawtin. Atkins remained the most active in terms of recording, but to this day all three are in demand as DJs all over the world. And while they are still brilliant, how great would it have been to be there when they were 15, sitting in their Michigan suburban

Leading the charge was Juan Atkins, commonly referred to as the godfather of techno. He loved the loopiness of Parliament-Funkadelic but was equally taken by the synth pop of Kraftwerk, Prince, Gary Numan and the B-52's. It was a rarified set of references for the Motor City, but it was shared by his two best friends and schoolmates, Derrick May and Kevin Saunderson. While kids in

houses in a pile of synthesizers, putting off doing their homework so they could create sounds that would change the course of electronic music. NF

the inner city were bouncing around to hardcore hip hop, they started DJing dance music and throwing parties under the collective name, Deep Space Soundworks for other like-minded kids in their neighborhood.
Once they graduated high school, they maintained separate careers but still shared a similar vision. Atkins stayed in Detroit and put out records under the names Cybotron and Model 500 that

Internet Smiley Scott Fuhlman, a researcher at Carnegie Mellon University involved with early online newsgroups, creates the original internet smiley, :-). Fellow message-board users turn to emoticons in order to clarify ambiguous postings, and unnecessary flamings are averted thanks to the new geek-speak. Geeks around the world rejoice in this dehumanized form of expression.

GEEK COMIC

Love and Rockets One of the most interesting and most successful comics of the period came from two brothers in L.A., Jaimie and Gilbert Hernandez. The series intertwined two lengthy and complicated soap operas. Jaimie's took place in post-punk Los Angeles (a scene he belonged to), while Gilbert's concentrated on the

▼

▼

fictitious town of Palomar, Mexico, but drew primarily on anecdotes passed along by his extended family. Reflecting the emerging multi-cultural influences of Southern California, the book's whole was considerably more than the sum of its (two) parts. NF

GEEK COMPUTER

Commodore C64 Commodore launches the C64, the best-selling computer of all time. It sells up to 22 million units. Schoolboy geek Rob Davis develops the first text adventure game engine for it and gets to the top of the computer game charts. Now, in a shameless call for attention, Rob Davis embarrasses himself for bringing it up here.

GEEK MOVIE

Blade Runner Blade Runner gets its basic plot from the 1968 Phillip K. Dick novel, <u>Do Androids Dream of Electric Sheep</u>, but it's the film's look, not the plot, that makes <u>Blade Runner</u> so memorable. Inspired by the work of French artist Moebius (Jean Giraud), particularly on Dan O'Bannon's short story, <u>The Long Tomorrow</u> in <u>Heavy</u>

<u>Metal</u> magazine, it infused fantasy with 1940s Hollywood film noir so skillfully that it made the past look new again. William Gibson, who was also influenced by Heavy Metal, freaked when he saw the movie. <u>Neuromancer</u> hadn't been published yet and Gibson was convinced that Blade Runner had stolen Neuromancer's thunder. But the movie actually helped. "When Blade Runner works best," he says, "it influences a

lyrical sort of information sickness, that quintessentially postmodern cocktail of ecstasy and dread. It was what cyberpunk was supposed to be." Such results did not come smoothly. Lead Harrison Ford and director Ridley Scott fought over Deckard's character, with Ford reportedly coming to work even though he had been fired. And everyone fought with the producer, Bud Yorkin, who thought Scott's version was

way too dark. Once Scott was off the payroll, Yorkin commissioned a voiceover that would simplify the film. Ford, legally obligated to record ten takes of the voice over, read them all flat so they wouldn't be used. But Yorkin would not budge, used the voiceover and tacked on a happy ending.
Since Yorkin was the only one who liked the changes, purists were overjoyed when Scott finally released his director's

cut in 1992, sans voiceovers and happy endings. But it's stll Yorkin's opinion that counts. Scott has long wanted to do a sequel but it's Yorkin who owns the rights and he ain't sellin'. NF

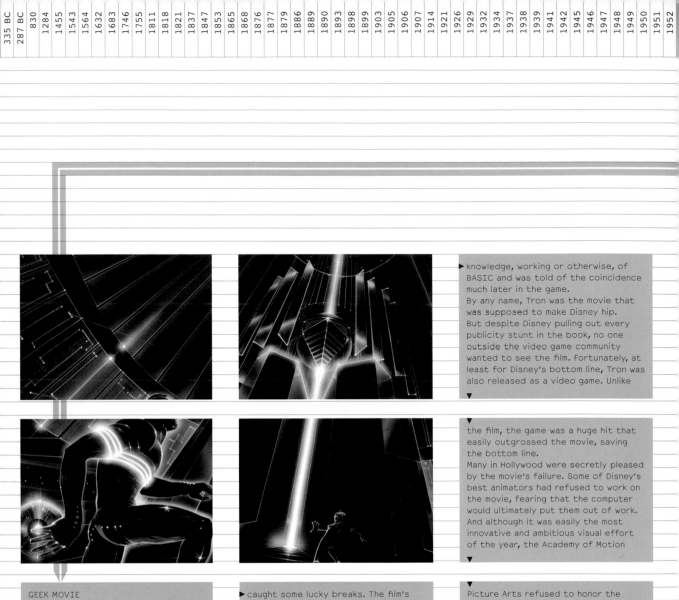

knowledge, working or otherwise, of BASIC and was told of the coincidence much later in the game.

By any name, Tron was the movie that was supposed to make Disney hip. But despite Disney pulling out every publicity stunt in the book, no one outside the video game community wanted to see the film. Fortunately, at least for Disney's bottom line, Tron was also released as a video game. Unlike

▼

the film, the game was a huge hit that easily outgrossed the movie, saving the bottom line.

Many in Hollywood were secretly pleased by the movie's failure. Some of Disney's best animators had refused to work on the movie, fearing that the computer would ultimately put them out of work. And although it was easily the most innovative and ambitious visual effort of the year, the Academy of Motion

▼

GEEK MOVIE

Tron Whether you think Steven Lisborger's Tron is a twisted religious allegory, a blatant attempt to capitalize on the video game craze or just a disposable slice of '80s Disney cheese, Tron's got a legitimate place in movie history. Generally considered the first movie to use computer generated special effects and, therefore, father

▼

► caught some lucky breaks. The film's name was assumed to be a reference to Tron, a BASIC command meaning "Trace On", especially since the Tron program in the movie behaved like the BASIC command, which uncovered and debugged the computer. At a retrospective for the film 21 years later, however, Lisborger admitted that he had come up with it as a nickname for "Electronics", had no

▲

Picture Arts refused to honor the film with an Oscar. Using computers to generate visual effects, it said, was cheating... NF

of films from <u>Toy Story</u> and <u>Finding Nemo</u> to <u>The Matrix</u>, Tron told its tale of a computer hacker who's abducted into a computer and absorbed into a battle for cyberspace with uncanny prescience. Although saddled with a fairly idiotic plot, the movie got the connection between politics, big business and computer operating systems right.

From the outset, Tron was a movie that

▲

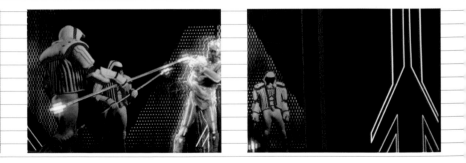

GEEK POP

William Orbit When asked why his novels were either popular or critical successes but not both, Graham Greene explained that he wrote the popular ones to subsidize the artistic ones. This "for love or money" strategy seems to be shared by William Orbit (real name, William Wainwright). An English ambient pioneer, he was one of

GEEK MOVIE

Sixteen Candles ignites an onslaught of 80s teen angst films. Self-professed former outcast, writer/director John Hughes, recalls his own traumatic, awkward adolescence via the fictitious scenery of Shermer, Illinois. Geeks get some on-screen redemption thanks to such actors as Anthony Michael-Hall and Jon Cryer. Even though real-life

▼

▼

geeks are still outcast, Hughes' geek characters get a second look from their peers and occasionally, nab the cute girl. In Hughes' best film, the 1983 hit Ferris Bueller's Day Off a witty, popular geek rules the school, his parents, and his meddling sister.

the first producers to remix songs for artists such as Sting, Madonna, the Human League, Erasure and Prince and then pour the proceeds into his own record label (Guerilla Records) and his own esoteric projects, such as the ambient series, Strange Cargo, and a classical crossover project called Pieces in a Modern Style. Although he completed the classical album in the mid-'90s, composers such

as Arvo Part and Henryk Gorecki, upset by the concept of remixing this music, blocked the album's release. It wasn't until Orbit co-wrote, produced and rode enormous international success with Madonna's Ray of Light in 1998 (winning several Grammy awards) that he got the clout to finally get the album released. Ironically, the album got a tepid response except for Ferry Corsten's trance remix of Adagio for

GEEK POP

Morrissey of The Smiths appears on chart program Top of the Pops wearing National Health spectacles and a hearing aid, and waving a bunch of gladioli. Awkward British teens have a reason to feel chic. NF

Strings, a track that's so reworked as to be unrecognizable with Orbit's reverential version. Sometimes, as it turns out, even remixers get beaten at their own game. NF

CD CDs debut. Databases of information can be stored on a small disc of efficiently compressed code. Ironically, it will take decidedly non-geek Bruce Springsteen to popularize the format with his three-CD concert set, "Live 1979-1985".

TCP/IP The internet exhibits signs of first growth. TCP/IP (transmission control protocol/internet protocol) networking takes over ARPANET, and remote file transfer, remote login, and data indexing make communication breezier.

GEEK TV

Inspector Gadget an animated, less swanky, libido-free contemporary of James Bond, fights the forces of Dr. Claw and along the way attracts children with his unassuming persona. Although he's got "go-go Gadget" retractable arms and a plethora of other robotic limbs and tools, he is clumsy and solves many crimes

▼

accidentally, while his niece Penny and dog Brain are the real heroes. In 1999, teen film fave Matthew Broderick plays Gadget in the film adaptation of the TV show. NF

GEEK MOVIE

Zelig Until they find their niche, many social outcasts will do whatever it takes to fit in. That's how it is for Leonard Zelig, played by Woody Allen in the movie he also directed. With 1920s documentary footage and a pre-Gump insertion of a character into historical footage, "Zelig" broke cinematic ground. But it's also the message,

▼

about an outcast who thrusts himself into a variety of personas until he find his own, that resonates. NF

GEEK CYBERPUNK

Steven Levy, Hackers: Heroes of the Computer Revolution
1989 Clifford Stoll, Cuckoo's Egg: Tracking a Spy through the Maze of Computer Espionage
1993 Bruce Sterling, The Hacker Crackdown: Law and Disorder on the Electronic Frontier
1996 Michelle Slatalla, Masters of

Deception: The Gang that Ruled Cyberspace

A handful of the more popular books written about hacking, Steven Levy's leads the pack, particularly for his depiction of the members of the MIT model railroad club, a group of brilliant and eccentric electrical engineers and computer innovators who banded together in the late 1950s

to, as they described it, "hack" or improve the systems that ran their intricate model railroad. They kept the tag as they graduated to improving computer systems, with only one eye on traditional letters of the law and, eventually it stuck.
Sterling's, which Publisher's Weekly cleverly tagged "Gunfight at the Cybernetic Corral", begins with a lengthy history of the phone and leads

up to the January 15, 1990 crash of AT&T as the entry point to what was then an eye-opening account of the hacker underworld, the government's cybercop response and the ethics underpinning civil liberties that have been thrown into a quagmire.
Slatalla's book is more focused and breezier, if considerably more sentimental, as she reduced the AT&T crash to an almost West Side Story

GEEK MOVIE

War Games In 1984, few people had given a lot of thought to how computers could have any direct impact on their lives. So when War Games, a film directed by respected commercial director, John Badham, starring Brat Packer Aly Sheedy and adorkable Matthew Broderick, came out, it plugged into every fear people had about

technology and the Cold War. The film, perhaps the first to feature a hacker in a lead role, imagined what would happen if a 14-year-old boy thinks he's playing a video game but really has slipped through the backdoor of the Pentagon's war program and is edging the world closer to a nuclear conflict. While the film iself soon slides into absurdity – Sheedy and Broderick avert World War III by using tic-tac-toe to

battle between two adolescent groups of nerds, the aptly named Legion of Doom. Either way, whether read singly or as a group, these books make it perfectly clear why journalists repeatedly used metaphors of the Wild West because back then, that's exactly what cyberspace felt like. NF

convince the computer that war is a no-win proposition. "[War] is a strange game," the computer intones. "The only winning move is not to play. How about a nice game of chess?" How about a new script? NF

GEEK MOVIE

Revenge of the Nerds Gilbert, Lewis, Booger, and Poindexter fight back against the heartless jocks who torment them at Adams College. Finally, the nerds win! Legions of outcast, first-generation home-computer geeks get hope: The Mother Lode.
"They've been laughed at, picked on and put down. But now it's time for the odd

to get even. Their time has come."
The movie that put faces on a movement. Director Jeff Kanew and a cast that mostly ended up on television (<u>Disney's</u> Robert Carradine, <u>E.R.</u>'s Anthony Edwards, <u>Thirtysomething</u>'s Ted Armstrong, <u>Roseanne</u>'s John Goodman and that ubiquitous third banana, Ted McGinley) give geek empowerment a rallying cry. Until his reverse <u>Animal House</u> frat

comedy came out, no one even knew that nerds had urges. But after watching them stage panty raids and string up hidden cameras to get a sneak peek at the sisters of Pi sorority, the world was put on notice: As one character put it: "Jocks only think about sports. Nerds only think about sex."
The press kit was even better than the movie. It came in a red binder,

stamped "nerd planner", with a photo of grandma, a loaded pocket protector, a pencil case with an eyeglass repair kit, a Nerd fashion guide and a Nerd manifesto that's worth repeating in its entirety: Nerds have always gotten a raw deal. But times are changing. Nerds are coming into their own, and 1984 is going to be the Year of the Nerd. The jocks and homecoming queens have had their

day. It's nerds who make the world go 'round, so it's time for the nerd in everyone to stand up, adjust those eyeglasses and proclaim "I'm a nerd... and I'm proud of it!"
For centuries, the nerd has been responsible for advancing the world's technologies, providing the trickle of brains in an ocean of brawn. Without the sharp mind of the analytical nerd, the great pyramids would have been

rockpiles, explorers would have come back empty handed and the boomerang would never have come back at all. And what thanks have the nerds received? None, unless being kicked in the shins by football players and thrown naked into the girl's shower room is your idea of a pat on the back. Well, nerds have had enough! It's time to fight back... And they want you to join them! No more glasses

shattered by bullies and mended with Mom's adhesive tape. And no more going steady with Dad's magazines because real women sneer at the mere mention of a simple library date. It's time for this oppressed minority to brandish their calculators, polish their penpacks and get set to take over the world! As mankind cowers before the advancing threat of the all-powerful computer, nerds are our first line of

defense. Who else knows the difference between "bie" and "byte?" Who else can conquer entire data systems with the flick of a well-chosen switch? Only nerds can understand such complexities. This year the new BMOC is not the star running back but the gold medalist at the Science Fair.
Women, being heretofore out of reach of the love-starved nerd, are now shifting their focus. They have realilzed

that nerd boyfriends can be invaluable in figuring out physics homework. More important, this kind of guy will not pass up an opportunity for steamy sexplay because the World Series is about to start. Even the nerd look is coming into style. Penpacks are replacing alligators on shirt pockets; white socks and black shoes have become a signature of high fasion, and hair grease has made a triumphant return to trendy scalps.

In short, nerds are "in". You won't have nerds to push around anymore, Mr. Fraternity President! You can't terrorize them on the gym floor again, Mr. Blockhead Coach! These outcasts have come together, realizing that there is strength in numbers – not to mention binomial coefficients. They're nerds, and their time has come! NF

▶ The show got glowing reviews for its intelligence, sophistication and weirdness. Max even got his own soda commercial out of it. But then, because it was just too good, the show got cancelled and Max disappeared. NF

GEEK TV

<u>Max Headroom</u> (1984, 1987)
Max Headroom, television's first foray into cyberpunk, was part <u>Network</u> in its anticipation of the increasing link between news and entertainment and part <u>Brazil</u> (the movie, not the country). Quirky, political and flat-out bizarre, it featured innovative computer generated effects

GEEK ROBOT

<u>Transformers</u> This hugely popular and influential cartoon was based on the Transformer toys, robots who could be rearranged into different machines. The plot line revolved around two armies of alien transforming robots fighting over Earth. It's a thinly veiled morality play of good vs. evil, with the forces of good, called the Autobots, led by one of the

(performed, if you care about such things, on Amiga 1000s) and a convoluted "us vs. them" plot that only made sense if you already were an "us". Max's saga began, appropriately, in 1984 when Britain's Channel Four got the idea of using a fake computer-generated host to supply the narrative between a set of music videos. The two elements never jelled, but the character and his story were compelling enough to hold

great father figures, Optimus Prime, getting all the character development, and the evil boys, called Decepticons, getting to have much of the fun. The complicated cast of characters led to numerous bloopers, including color shifts and identity problems. For all that, the animation was spectacular. And for a show about schizophrenic machines, a series whose heart, surprisingly, was in the right place. NF

a TV movie/pilot starring American actor Mat Frewer as Max. The pilot was, well, just too good, the show got cancelled and Max went away. It was well received in England but languished in limbo until U.S.-based Lorimar Productions rewrote and compressed the Channel Four project into a standard-length series pilot and filmed 14 episodes for American network television and subsequent global consumption.

GEEK ROBOT

<u>Challenge of the GoBots</u> A cheap attempt by Hanna-Barbera to cash in on the Transformer craze, this short-lived cartoon series featured a robot called Scooter that could turn into a kid's scooter. Can things get sillier? NF

335 BC	287 BC	830	1284	1455	1543	1564	1632	1683	1746	1755	1811	1818	1821	1837	1847	1853	1865	1868	1876	1877	1879	1886	1889	1890	1893	1898	1899	1903	1905	1906	1907	1914	1921	1926	1929	1932	1934	1937	1938	1939	1941	1942	1945	1946	1947	1948	1949	1950	1951	1952

GEEK COMPUTER

<u>Apple</u> introduces its MacIntosh computer. They also debut Chiat/Day's legendary MacIntosh commercial with its chilling futuristic vision in the most macho of venues: the US Super Bowl.

GEEK CYBERPUNK

<u>William Gibson's Neuromancer</u>
"The sky was the color of a television set turned to a black channel," said William Gibson in the opening line of Neuromancer, and everything about science fiction changed – at least according to acolytes such as Bruce Sterling. As Paul Brian points out in his study guide to Neuromancer (www.wsu.

edu8080/~brians/science_fiction/ neuromancer.html), Gibson tapped into "the amoral urban rage of the punk subculture and the developing human–machine interface created by the widespread use of computers and computer networks, set in the near future in decayed city landscapes" and handed it on a platter to "postmodern academics searching for the next trend."

GEEK ROBOT

<u>The Terminator</u> The first (certifiable) robot to hold an elected office in the history of the world. The credit or blame must go to James Cameron, who got the idea for the movie from a vision he had of a metal skeleton walking out of a fire. When he began to write it, he realized the movie needed to be set in the future (where flame-retardant

▶ endoskeletons lived), but that the movie's budget, which was surprisingly small, couldn't pull the future off. To compensate, he came up with the idea of time travel, and the rest of the script, not to mention Arnold's political career, fell into place. NF

Like Burgess' <u>Clockwork Orange</u>, the language was new, with terms such as cyberspace (first introduced in Gibson's story Burning Chrome two years earlier) and the Matrix, Gibson's name for the global information network. Although almost elementary by today's standard, the story of Case ("the hottest computer cowboy cruising the information superhighway – jacking his consciousness into cyberspace, soaring through tactile lattices of data and logic, rustling encoded secrets...burn[ing] the talent out of his brain, micron by micron. Banished from cyberspace, trapped in the meat of his physical body, Case courted death in the high-tech underworld. Until a shadowy conspiracy offered him a second chance—and a cure-for a price.") was hot stuff. As Brian details, the self-proclaimed

GEEK POP

The Stone Roses In the end, New Order may be more important and the Happy Mondays more mythologized, but it was the Stone Roses who first forged the link between rock and electronic music. Part psychedelia, part post-punk Smithy pop and 100 percent drugged, the band took acid house from the Hacienda in Manchester to

revolutionary attitude owes sizeable thematic and stylistic debts to the mid-'60s experimental new wave authors such as J.G. Ballard, Philip K.Dick, Harlan Ellison and Samuel R. Delany, and on noir writers such as Raymond Chandler. And for all the breast beating about something new under the sun, you can't help but note that the generation it was supposed to represent was slow jumping on the bandwagon. The punks

GEEK HACKER

<u>Richard Stallman</u> Geeks versus geeks! Prompted by AT&T's mass marketing of Unix, Richard Stallman develops the concept of "free software" and founds the <u>Free Software Foundation</u> and creates the operating system GNU (GNU's Not Unix). It is the precursor to the Open Source Initiative, the future anti-Microsoft collective rooted in the

stadiums in England and to Top 40 radio in the States. Their self-titled album, which included songs like <u>Fool's Gold</u> and <u>I Wanna Be Adored</u> remains perhaps the best single document of the period, and tales of their implosion, including the trashing of their former record company's office after the company released an unauthorized disc of old material, remain the stuff of legend. NF

that did read seemed to prefer more traditional writers such as Larry Niven, Frank Herbert and Robert Heinlein, leaving cyberpunk the province of eager academics.
Perhaps. But it didn't stop Neuromancer from becoming the first novel in history to win all three major science fiction awards, the <u>Hugo</u>, the <u>Nebula</u> and the <u>Philip K. Dick</u> prize, and from changing the way that we look at the world. There

concept of free swapping of source code and the building of programming through the free and public domain. Linux creator Linus Torvalds, Bruce Perens, and Eric Raymond become early leaders of the movement. NF

have long been rumors and false starts on a film version, most recently by Chris Cunningham. Some would say, though, that the movie's already come out – and it's called <u>The Matrix</u>. (Or, if you're really up on these things, 1995's Johnny Mnemonic, which at least was directly pulled from a Gibson short story and a Gibson screenplay.) NF

<u>Electric Car</u> Clive Sinclair launches the first cheap electric car, the C5, based on a washing machine motor. It's a total flop and forces him to sell his business, Sinclair Research Ltd., to Amstrad. NF

Microsoft 1.0 The era of numbers games begins as Microsoft unveils Version 1.0. From now on, the public is doomed to play catch-up.

Eventually, Stein walked away with a quarter of a million dollars, Maxwell died, the Soviet Union collapsed and the Academy gave comrade Pajitnov his own 286 PC. Thinking he could do better, Pajitnov migrated to the States in 1996, and finally started receiving some of his royalties. Nowadays he's still creating puzzle games; this time, for Microsoft. NF

GEEK GAME ICON

Alexei Pajitnov Tetris is proof that a good game is easily understood but difficult to master. Available on more than 60 platforms and 70 countries, it has sold more than 30 million cartridges for the Game Boy alone. The game is a puzzle in which various shapes, each made of four (or, in Greek, tetra) squares fall down a

shaft. Although players try to keep the shaft empty, the pieces fall with increasing speed. When the shaft is full, the game is over.

For a simple game, it's got a complicated back story full of nasty legal battles, thievery and betrayal. It begins in 1985, when Alexei Pajitnov created Tetris on an Eletronica 60 terminal computer at the Moscow Academy of Science's Computer Center and asked 16-year-

GEEK COMPUTER

The **Commodore Amiga** appears as the first computer with high-end graphics. Computers get snazzy.

old Vadim Gerasimov to port it to the IBM PC. It quickly spread across Moscow and Hungary, where it was ported to the Apple II and Commodore 64.

Soon thereafter, Tetris caught the eye of Robert Stein of the British software house Andromeda, who sold the rights, which were not his, to media czar Robert Maxwell. Three years later, the PC version, now a huge hit, was exposed as a fraud by CBS Evening News.

Nintendo Famicom The dawn of the age of Nintendo. Their first console, called Famicom in Japan and Nintendo Entertainment System (NES) elsewhere, would surpass Atari and was found in one of every three households in America and Japan. Super Mario Bros. 3 sold over 11 million copies, making it the best-selling game of all time. EVDZ

GEEK MOVIE

<u>Weird Science</u> The only thing better than having a hot babe is having a hot, smart babe. At least, that's how Gary (Anthony Michael Hall) sees it. With the help of his buddy – and no thanks to pesky jock Chet (Bill Paxton) – Gary uses networked computers to create the perfect woman. And what could be geekier than two nerds inventing a

woman to fulfill their desires? Naming her Lisa after the first Apple PC, saucy Kelly LeBrock is a modern-day Frankenstein, with the brain of Albert Einstein and the body of a Barbie Doll. In typical John Hughes fashion, the geeks win. NF

GEEK MOVIE

<u>Short Circuit</u> Okay, it isn't the most serious movie ever made, but kids love Short Circuit's lead character, the robot Number 5, who gets struck by lightening, goes haywire, gets a mind of its own, and escapes its lab run by its maker, Steve Guttenberg. No. 5 makes its way to the doorstep of Ally Sheedy, who takes it in just as she has

stray animals. Eventually Sheedy and Guttenberg fall in love, giving No. 5 the home he has always wanted. (No, we are not making this up!) NF

GEEK POP

<u>They Might Be Giants</u> Intellectual, lyrically sharp-witted band They Might Be Giants releases their first album, self-titled, and finds themselves playing to sold-out shows occupied by book-toting brainiacs.
<u>Rolling Stone</u> says: "Theirs is the revenge of the nerds: College radio play and videos that look more geared

for the Nickelodeon network than for MTV made them successful alternative artists and garnered them a major-label deal." The major label deal went the way of the dot-com IPO some time ago but MBG, under the influence of co-founders John Linnell and John Flansburgh, remain highly successful goofs, running a thriving career via the internet. Although they have become old enough to offer two

GEEK COMIC

1986 <u>Batman: The Dark Knight Returns</u>
1987 <u>Watchmen</u>
1989 <u>Arkham Asylum</u>
Batman and the comic industry comes of age. These three books, done respectively by Frank Miller, Alan Moore and Dave Gibbons, and Grant Morrison and Dave McKean turned myth and literature on their heads. Gorgeously

▶ drawn, noirish to a fault and seeped in angst, they featured characters that were past their prime, bone-weary and desperate. Thanks to some well-placed publicity, these books became critical darlings, prompting magazines such as Rolling Stone to announce the arrival of the graphic novel (which had in fact been around for almost 50 years at that point) as THE new medium for the new millennium. NF

different sets each night, one geared specifically to families, they've lost none of their edge. And they remain hackers at heart, once designing a track, <u>Fingertips</u>, which featured 21 refrains that would be activated when someone hit "random" or "shuffle" on their CD player, handily demonstrating that you can be really cool and really irritating at the same time. NF

335 BC | 287 BC | 830 | 1284 | 1455 | 1543 | 1564 | 1632 | 1683 | 1746 | 1755 | 1811 | 1818 | 1821 | 1837 | 1847 | 1853 | 1865 | 1868 | 1876 | 1877 | 1879 | 1886 | 1889 | 1890 | 1893 | 1898 | 1899 | 1903 | 1905 | 1906 | 1907 | 1914 | 1921 | 1926 | 1929 | 1932 | 1934 | 1937 | 1938 | 1939 | 1941 | 1942 | 1945 | 1946 | 1947 | 1948 | 1949 | 1950 | 1951 | 1952

Wealthy Uber-Geek Microsoft goes public. With an IPO of $21, and owning 11,142,000 shares of the company, Bill Gates is worth $233.98 million within seconds. Enter the era of the obscenely wealthy Uber-Geek.

Pixar Steve Jobs founds Pixar studios, the first studio dedicated solely to computer-generated animation.

GEEK MOVIE

Ferris Bueller's Day Off If you've not watched it before, you might wonder what the fuss is about, but back in the day, Ferris Bueller was the quintessential 80's teen comedy. Directed by John Hughes, who stuffed it full of references from his own films, and featuring Matthew Broderick in a career defining performance that

▼

blended geeky innocence and a con man's instincts, the film is loaded with buried in- jokes, including the use of the PacMan death knell soundbyte when the arcade girl spits on principal Ed Rooney, exhuberant feel-good fantasies, such as the parade scene, inept adults and great lines: "I do have a test today. That wasn't bullshit," he admits towards the end of the movie. But "It's on European socialism.

▼

PC Convertible IBM introduces its laptop, the PC Convertible. Without a hard drive but a 3.5" floppy disk that would become standard. Three years later Apple released the Macintosh Portable, which evolved into the Powerbook (1991). IBM scored big with its Thinkpad a year later, a laptop line that is still being sold today. EVDZ

GEEK FOOD

Pizza Delivery Pizza Hut introduces the pizza delivery service. Available all night, pizza looks like a floppy disk and can be eaten with one hand while the other is typing. Even more perfect as a food source than the egg, it now arrives at geeks' front doors with only the effort required to make a phone call. NF

▼

I mean, really, what's the point? I'm not European. I don't plan on being European. So who cares if they're socialists? They could be fascist anarchists. It still doesn't change the fact that I don't own a car." NF

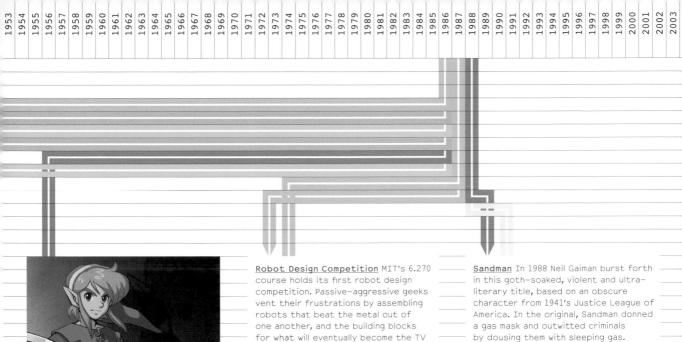

Robot Design Competition MIT's 6.270 course holds its first robot design competition. Passive-aggressive geeks vent their frustrations by assembling robots that beat the metal out of one another, and the building blocks for what will eventually become the TV show "Robot Wars" are set.

Sandman In 1988 Neil Gaiman burst forth in this goth-soaked, violent and ultra-literary title, based on an obscure character from 1941's Justice League of America. In the original, Sandman donned a gas mask and outwitted criminals by dousing them with sleeping gas. (Weird, huh?) In his more contemporary incarnation, he became "The Master of Dreams" who could inhabit the realm of the unconscious. Confusing? You bet.

▼

GEEK GAME

Legend of Zelda: A Link to the Past
Sprites and elves and anthropomorphic creatures of all types are great game fodder because they come from a place of abstraction and build a world subject to a compelling kind of poetic license. Enter Link. Link is the Peter Pan-ish hero of a long-running series set in the land of Hyrule, a kind

▼

As Gaiman says, "Sandman basically says that yes, every single theory about dreaming is true. This is a world created by the fact that people personify dreams; and so the Sandman exists in the same way that, because people personify death, death exists. Personal realities are all valid because they are based on perception, and agreement is reality." If you understand all that, you'll love Sandman. NF

of anime-medieval world filled with magic, monsters and danger. Link runs around Hyrule and through a series of increasingly challenging dungeons in an attempt to save the princess Zelda from evil pig-wizard Ganon. Gameplay is a mixture of simple combat, exploration and puzzle solving. The key to Zelda's success is that every inch of the game is packed with interactivity. Every screen contains a puzzle to solve, an

▼

GEEK FOOD

Red Bull Depending on your point of view, Red Bull and the other "energy" or "performance" drinks now crowding the market are either modern alchemy or old-fashioned quackery. Their strategy is admirably simple: take some obscure "minerals" and make some vague, unsubstantiated claims about their benefits, lace the mixture with

▼

item to collect, a person to talk to or a monster to defeat. The series' pinnacle – A Link to the Past – hit shelves in the Super Nintendo era of the mid-90s when games were made with good old hand-drawn 2D art. It's a beautiful game with a rich color palette, and it innovates on the Zelda formula by adding an "alternate world" which Link must travel to-and-from to navigate obstacles. MS

as much caffeine and caffeine-like stimulants you can find, doctor it up to look and taste like urine, charge four times as much as a comparable "dose" of Coke, get endorsements from a bunch of extreme athletes and rock stars. Then, in a touch of marketing genius, use it as a mixer with vodka and voila, you've got the taste sensation of a new generation. NF

Chime The gawky Hartnoll brothers record Chime onto a tape cassette at home and actually dub the low-fi cassette onto a DAT tape to impress the Positiva label with their professionalism. In doing so, they not only out-tech a generation of mixed-tape makers, they reveal one of the most important songs in modern dance music.

faster and more efficiently than he had thought. By the time he leaked instructions on how to kill the bug, it was too late. Computers at universities, military institutions and medical facilities were all affected, and cost between $200 and $53,000 apiece to debug. It was the first time the word "hacker" was introduced to the mainstream. Morris received a sentence of three years of probation, 400 hours

▼

GEEK COMIC

<u>Akira</u> was one of the first (and few) anime released in theaters outside of Japan and for many American and European geeks a first encounter with the popular culture of their Japanese counterparts called otaku. Set in post–WWIII Neo–Tokyo of 2019, Akira is the story of Tetsuo, a bike–gang member who acquires extraordinary

▼

▼

psychic powers when he becomes the victim of secret military experiments. Instead of turning into a superhero saving the world and all Tetsuo causes mayhem and releases his predecessor Akira. But it is not the plot what the movie is famous for. Katsuhiro Otomo's Akira is a cell–animation masterpiece. The two hour movie consists of 2,212 shots and 160,000 single pictures, two to three times more than usual. An

▼

▼

electrifying leap into the future it strengthened the link between manga (comics) and anime (animation). Between the film and the comic, Akira made the entire form hip, and set the stage for the next explosion of anime and manga in the houses of both the rising and setting suns. NF

GEEK HACKER

<u>Robert Morris (a.k.a. rtm)</u> While a graduate student in Computer Science at Cornell, Robert Morris, the son of the chief scientist of the National Computer Security Center, wrote a self replicating program called a worm and leaked it on the internet from MIT (to obscure its origin). To his surprise, the program infected machines much

▲

Prodigy Spotty teenager Liam Howitt produces the first Prodigy track on a home keyboard in his bedroom. The ultimate rave band is soon born.

▼

of community service and more than $10,000 in fines. Ironically, he now is a professor at MIT, the site from which he initially released his worm virus. NF

<u>CD vs Vinyl</u> CD sales exceed vinyl sales for the first time. In further irony, it's the digitally obsessed geeks who become vinyl junkies and revive the wax.

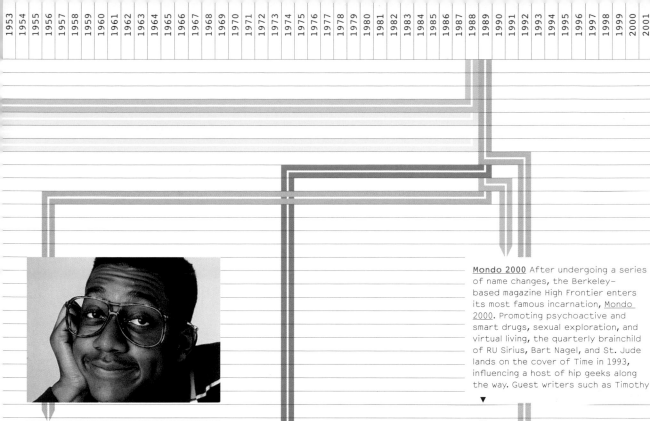

Mondo 2000 After undergoing a series of name changes, the Berkeley-based magazine High Frontier enters its most famous incarnation, Mondo 2000. Promoting psychoactive and smart drugs, sexual exploration, and virtual living, the quarterly brainchild of RU Sirius, Bart Nagel, and St. Jude lands on the cover of Time in 1993, influencing a host of hip geeks along the way. Guest writers such as Timothy

▼

Leary and Terence McKenna add fervor. The magazine eventually fizzles but paves the way for more commercially minded Wired. NF

GEEK TV

Family Matters When the American sit-com Family Matters debuts, it introduces one of the first geek stars, Steven Q. Urkel, who propels the show to the top of the Nielsen's, a computerized ratings poll used to determine a television show's popularity in the United States. Over the course of the show's 10-year history, Urkel

▼

invents a robot (the "Urkel-bot") and a jet-pack — and gets a few girls along the way. Family Matters final episode has Urkel going into space, a true Hollywood ending for any honorable geek. NF

GEEK GAME

Game Boy Nintendo apparently likes records. Its handheld Game Boy is the best-selling game system of all time. The original model had an eleven-year life cycle selling 120 million units. In the same year Sega introduced the Genesis (or Megadrive) console and their answer to Mario, a blue hedgehog called Sonic. Nintendo responds two years later

▼

with the Super Nintendo Entertain-ment System (SNES), Super Mario World, the Legend of Zelda, and Donkey Kong Country. EVDZ

GEEK TV

Saved by the Bell Saturday morning television goes geek. Real-life chess fanatic Dustin Diamond plays the awkward Screech opposite quick-witted blonde hunk Zack on the kids' show Saved by the Bell. Typically, Screech is far from a ladies man, but has a certain knack with inventions (he even concocts a zit-zapping cream)

▼

and eventually snags equally geeky love interest Violet. Diamond goes on to play Screech in various unfortunate incarnations of Saved by the Bell. NF

335 BC	287 BC	830	1284	1455	1543	1564	1632	1683	1746	1755	1811	1818	1821	1837	1847	1853	1865	1868	1876	1877	1879	1886	1889	1890	1893	1898	1899	1903	1905	1906	1907	1914	1921	1926	1929	1932	1934	1937	1938	1939	1941	1942	1945	1946	1947	1948	1949	1950	1951	1952

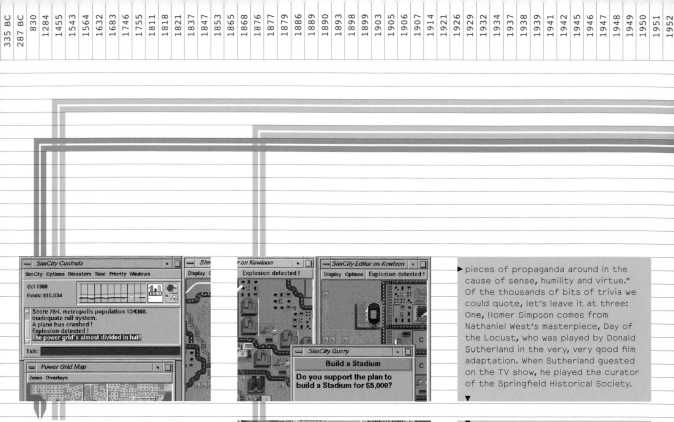

▶ pieces of propaganda around in the cause of sense, humility and virtue." Of the thousands of bits of trivia we could quote, let's leave it at three: One, Homer Simpson comes from Nathaniel West's masterpiece, Day of the Locust, who was played by Donald Sutherland in the very, very good film adaptation. When Sutherland guested on the TV show, he played the curator of the Springfield Historical Society. ▼

SimCity Game designer Will Wright of Maxis creates SimCity. The game sparked off a new paradigm in computer gaming by creating a game that could neither be won nor lost. EVDZ

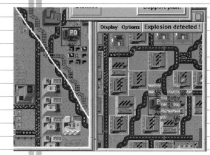

▼ Two, Lisa, ever the geek, is at constant odds with Homer. So when Stephen Hawking pays her a visit, Homer asks her if she had fun with her "robot buddy". And when she desparately wanted to win the math fair and take home a "brand new protractor" as the prize, Homer was unimpressed. "Too bad we don't live on a farm" he said.
Three, the producers turned down Al Gore, who had turned them down ▼

GEEK TV

The Simpsons As the English newspaper, The Observer, pointed out in its article celebrating the 300th episode of The Simpsons, there was no better reason to love the Simpsons, the most popular family of all time, than to recap George Bush Sr.'s 1992 (unsuccessful) promise to "keep trying to strengthen the American family; to ▼

▼ early in the show's run, when Gore later approached them about being a guest. Surprisingly, they also turned down David Beckham, for no apparent reason in the world. NF

GEEK MOVIE

Tetsuo I One of the earliest movies to explores the boundaries of the organic and the electronic, it's followed by "Tetsou 2" (1991). Can Mother Nature and science coexist? Animation shall decide. NF

make them more like the Waltons and less like the Simpsons."
Fat chance. As The Observer went on to say, The Simpsons is "proof to TV executives that dumbing up, rather than down, has nothing to recommend it except awards, integrity, ratings, laughter and profits. Even the Archbishop of Canterbury, Dr Rowan Williams, agrees, saying "It's one of the most subtle ▲

GEEK HACKER

Mark Abene (a.k.a. Phiber Optik)
Another nemesis of the phone company: Abene. A founding member of the Masters of Deception, a legendary New York group of crackers, he got a year in federal prison for his "study" of the phone system in 1990. Included in the "curriculum" were the secret credit histories of celebrities such as

▼

Geraldo Rivera and Julia Roberts and a cache of credit card numbers. The attempt at rehabilitation backfired when Abene became a cult hero and media celebrity. NF

GEEK HACKER

John Perry Barlow More an activist than a hacker, John Perry Barlow, ex-cattle rancher and songwriter for the Grateful Dead, is the co-founder of the Electronic Frontier Foundation, a nonprofit organization dedicated to the preservation of free speech on the internet. A self-described techno-hippie, he is waging war against the

▼

"evil conglomerate", including Microsoft, AOL and the large entertainment corporations. Echoing the sentiments of hackers everywhere, he proclaims that: "we will create a civilization in the mind of cyberspace. May it be more humane and fair than your governments have created...I place a great deal of faith in what's going to happen when more people are online and fewer people are watching television." Amen. NF

GEEK HACKER

Eric Steven Raymond An old school great, Raymond is not just a legendary programmer and defender of the Open Source Movement, but an outspoken defender of the hacker's image. Annoyed by what he felt was a lack of context, he wrote the books, The Hacker's Dictionary and How to Be a Hacker, and apparently is the source

▼

of the definitive line, "hackers build things, crackers break them." NF

Halloween Documents Microsoft gets outed. On November 1, an internal Microsoft memo detailing the viability and threat of open-source software to the computer giant is leaked to the press by OSS advocate Eric Raymond, who obtained the confidential memo from Microsoft insiders. Raymond dubs them the Halloween Documents and says they are proof of Microsoft's unethical business practices and

▶ market manipulation. In the Halloween Documents Microsoft's authors suggest that OSS must be stopped, while also vilifying that "recent case studies (the internet) provide very dramatic evidence ... that commercial quality can be achieved / exceeded by OSS projects." Microsoft scrambles to respond, dismissing the memo as an engineering study.

335 BC | 287 BC | 830 | 1284 | 1455 | 1543 | 1564 | 1632 | 1683 | 1746 | 1755 | 1811 | 1818 | 1821 | 1837 | 1847 | 1853 | 1865 | 1868 | 1876 | 1877 | 1879 | 1886 | 1889 | 1890 | 1893 | 1898 | 1899 | 1903 | 1905 | 1906 | 1907 | 1914 | 1921 | 1926 | 1929 | 1932 | 1934 | 1937 | 1938 | 1939 | 1941 | 1942 | 1945 | 1946 | 1947 | 1948 | 1949 | 1950 | 1951 | 1952

GEEK HACKER

Kevin Poulsen (a.k.a. Dark Dante)
One of the coolest pranksters, Poulsen seized control over all the telephone lines to popular Los Angeles radio station <u>KIIS-FM</u> during a contest in the early 1990s where the 102nd caller would win a Porsche 944 S2. He made all 102 calls, winning the car. Later on, he broke into computers to out

undercover businesses run by the FBI. He got busted in 1994 for breaking into phone-company properties after the television show <u>Unsolved Mysteries</u> ran an episode about his exploits and snapshots his friend took as souvenirs during the robbery surfaced (right after the episode aired, the show's 800 numbers all crashed). Poulsen received the harshest sentence ever given to a hacker: 51 months in prison

and a fine of more than $56,000. After serving three years in jail, he was released but was ordered to stay away from computers for another three years. These days, Poulsen is a "reformed and penitent" journalist. NF

GEEK HACKER

Linus Torvalds Like Steve Wozniak, Linus Torvalds is a hacker's hacker. While a computer science student at the University of Helsinki in 1991, he wrote the operating system, <u>Linux</u> ("Linus's Minix"), and provided it free to anyone who wanted it. NF

The World Wide Web, designed single-handedly by Tim Berners-Lee, is launched, based on his work with linking various computer networks. Having polished the project since 1980, he designs a uniform format for Web documents (HTML, hypertext mark-up language), a system for giving the documents unique addresses (the URL, universal resource locator), a set of rules for transferring the documents

between computers (HTTP, hypertext transfer protocol), and the first Web browser. Compared to Bill Gates, he's a no-name who never directly profits from his invention. He goes on to direct the World Wide Web Consortium, an outfit that oversees Web development, and serve as the chair of the 3Com Founders at MIT.

MP3 The Fraunhofer Institute invents MP3 compression.

▶ characteristics of Generation X because, as he said, the point was "that there never was or will be a definition. I think it started out being pejorative, and now it's like Kleenex or Jell-O. Semiotically blank. I've always thought the kerfuffle was pretty silly and have consistently shied away from this sort of phone-sex-type explicitness of X-definition mania since there's nothing to describe. I guess

▼

GEEK CYBERPUNK

<u>Douglas Coupland, Generation X: Tales for an Accelerated Culture.</u> When <u>Generation X</u> came out, most people assumed it was a reference to the punk band that Billy Idol fronted in the late 1970s, but soft-spoken author Douglas Coupland remained cagey about the term. Then, in an interview in 1995, he claimed that it was taken from the ▶

▶ final chapter of a book on pop culture called Class by writer Paul Fussell, who argued that there was "an 'X' category of people who wanted to hop off the merry-go-round of status, money and social climbing that so often frames modern existence."
Because he had waited four years to credit Fussell, not everyone was convinced. There was more agreement with his refusal to pin down the exact ▶

▼

if you identified with the characters or the themes in that book you might be "X," but even that's corny." "Back in 1991," Coupland continues, "some guy in Orange County named Warren kept hounding me to sell/make/produce Generation X T-shirts, and I said, "Warren, keep your money, because nothing could be less X than wearing a T-shirt saying 'Generation X.'" NF

▶ were being passed around the East Coast. Sonic Youth, who loved his skate stuff, booked him as an A.D. in one of their videos, and Peter Care, then a director for Satellite Films, hired him to shoot rave footage for an expensive commercial.

Tt was an auspicious debut. Under Satellite's wing, Jonze turned out one great video after another for bands such as the Breeders, P. Diddy, the ▼

NCSA Mosaic ™ for Microsoft Windows

MOSAIC

NCSA Mosaic ™ for Microsoft Windows

Welcome to the Mosaic for Microsoft Windows Home Page. Mosaic is a World Wide Web client that was developed at the National Center for Supercomputing Applications on the campus of The University of Illinois at Urbana-Champaign.

Search Our Space
News and Announcements
○ Version 2.0.0
○ Next Win32s Information

GEEK MOVIE ICON

Spike Jonze "The guys with the shades? Some of the Beastie Boys. The other guy? He took the picture, and did the video ["Sabotage"]. Now, after making some of the greatest pop clips ever, he's directed his first film. It's great. He's a pretty nifty actor, photographer, skateboarder and prankster, too. Spike Jonze: We salute you." ▼

▼ Pharcyde, Wax, the Beastie Boys, Weezer, FatBoy Slim and Jack Black, becoming the most popular video director of the era.

Movies came next. After a few false starts, he won an Academy Award nomination for his first feature film, Being John Malkovitch, deserved one for his acting role in The Three Kings, and cleaned up as the executive producer of Jackass. He also owns a thriving

MOSAIC Marc Andreesen, Yahoo developer, creates MOSAIC, the first graphics Web browser.

> see page 134, Dorm Digirati

▼ So began The Face's 2000 cover story on Spike Jonze. It was the first time a music video director had made the cover of an international magazine. He was raised a latch-key kid in Baltimore, is part of the Spiegel (as in Spiegel Catalogue) family, was a BMX rider and later a skateboarder, kissed his first girl when he was 14, started photographing skating and riding for small 'zines and with ▼

▼ skateboard company with old friend Rick Howard, was married and unmarried to Sofia Coppola, and won MTV's Best Video of All Time for Praise You, the Fatboy Slim video he made for only a thousand bucks. He also got to direct Meryl Streep in Adaptation; and spearheaded the first ever music video director's cut DVD series for Palm Pictures. But there are some things that remain beyond his grasp. After losing the ▼

▼ friends Andy Jenkins and Mark Lewman started a magazine called Homeboy when most kids his age were still in high school. Later, the trio convinced Jane Pratt, editor of Sassy, to launch Dirt, a "brother" magazine the girl subscribers were supposed to pass along to their boyfriends.

Soon Jonze was shooting idiosyncratic fashion for Interview magazine and directing skateboard videos that ▲

Presidency in 2000, Al Gore decided to become more cool and hired Spike and Co. to hang with the family and come up with a 30 minute "documentary" that would hip up Gore's image. Sad to say, even Jonze can't work that kind of miracle. NF

GEEK POP ICON

Moby
> see page 122

Teledildonic Sex Toys In a humorous article, <u>Future Sex</u> magazine envisions the sexual experience of the new millennium: "teledildonic" sex toys linked together via the internet. By 2000, several companies are selling basic models.

journalist called. Rather than follow up one album with another that build upon the same themes, thereby maximizing commercial exposure, he shifted genres from one record to the next with no warning or apparent reason. And, most of all, rather than craft his records so you knew there was an artist at work, some of his records were minimal enough to cause widespread wondering over whether or not he

was goofing on the fans and releasing drivel. In retrospect, though, it seems like James knew exactly what he was doing. Throughout his career, James has weaved his way through acid house, jungle, ambient and hard-core industrial drum and bass with equal aplomb. As a result, his most famous records careen from the sublime ambient techno of <u>Selected Ambient Works, 1985 – 1992</u> to the harsh, disturbing sonic assault of

GEEK POP

Aphex Twin Richard James is the anti-Moby. While his bald "twin" gets caught talking through a Shins set in New York, stumps tirelessly for animal rights and the Democratic Party and opens up cozy Zen tearooms in NY, Richard James, a.k.a. Aphex Twin, in true electronic, crazed genius fashion, holes up in his bedroom with a bunch of computers and

<u>Come to Daddy</u> immortalized by Chris Cunningham's startling video. Like many great artists, James leaves a twisted trial of motivations and intent records like <u>Selected Ambient Works, v. 2</u>, tours that are performed underneath giant bunny suits or satirical yet off "lounge-porn" tracks like <u>Windowlicker</u> seem laced with contempt. So you can Play with Moby without worrying, but if you're going

MiniDisc Sony begins selling the MiniDisc (MD). An attempt to out-do the then non-burnable CD bombs commercially.

tape recorders creating music that will go around the world.
What's more, he became the most highly praised electronic artist of the 1990s, at least according to the encyclopedic <u>All Music Guide to Electronica</u>, without making any concessions to the fame game. Rather than court press, he frequently didn't bother to show up for live interviews or pick up the phone when the

to hang with James, you'd better bring along your Ventolin just in case. NF

Moby

As Jack Black's character in the film
<u>School of Rock</u> says, "you could be the
ugliest sad sack on the planet, but if
you're in a rocking band, you're the
cat's pajamas, man." If he's right, Moby,
the face of techno, the arch-enemy of
Eminem, the distant relative of Herman
Melville and the self-described "Little
Idiot" (a reference that does not refer
to his I.Q.), would not jus be wearing
the p.j.s. He'd own the company.

▼

By any standards, he's not much to
look at. He's as self-effacing, nerdy,
tortured and "sensitive" a New Yorker
as Woody Allen, who he often compares
himself to. It's a fitting comparison
for like Allen, he's inarguably literate,
impossible to pigeonhole, filthy but
tastefully rich. And like Allen, Moby's
probably going to walk in and/or
leave with the most beautiful woman
in the room. That's what you get for

▼

single-handedly rewriting the book
on rock stardom.
No one would have predicted that level
of success when Moby, born Richard
Melville Hall, was wandering around the
streets of New York in the late 1980s,
peddling his techno tapes to anyone
who would listen. By then he was DJing
around New York, developing a following
and selling several thousand copies
of singles like <u>Voodoo Child</u> he was

▲

▶ releasing. Then, in 1991, he released a single called Go. The right single for the right time, it became a club anthem, went on to sell more than one million copies and was recently honored by Rolling Stone Magazine as one of the best singles of all time.
The rave scene was exploding, and Moby was on his way to becoming America's top techno artist. He toured with groups such as the Shamen and

▼

▼ Prodigy, got signed to a major record label and, by 1995, was walking away with honors such as Spin Magazine's Album (Everything is Wrong) and single (Every time You Touch Me) of the year.
Feelin' sort of punky about the success, he next released an album, Animal Rights, that confused and alienated many of his fans. They treated him like he had done a "Dylan goes electric at Newport", abandoned

▼

his club roots for rock, replaced the synthesizers with guitars and actually seemed to be singing about something. It's failure took Moby by surprise but, to his credit, he didn't back down. After licking his wounds with some soundtrack music, he re-emerged several albums later with Play, a hook-rich record that dipped even deeper into non-electronic sources, including gospel and blues. Rather than rely on

▼

his mercurial fan base, he and his camp invented a new business model, pre-selling every track of the record to commercials or TV shows for millions of dollars before the album even hit the record stores.
In days of yore, that strategy would have been attacked as soulless commercialism, but in reality it ended up fueling the public's interest in the record, which ended up selling 10

▲

▶ million copies and catapulting him into superstar status. Within months of its release, Moby had become a staple on MTV, a model for Calvin Klein and a posterboy for the geek as a modern-day sex symbol.
Even better, Moby navigated the pitfalls of mega-celebrity beautifully. Like Wozniak and Perry Farrell before him, he bought himself a pop festival, Area 1 and its less successful follow–

▼

up, Area 2, which allowed him to hobnob with his personal heroes like David Bowie. And although he was obviously enjoying the glitz and glamour, he wasn't afraid to speak his mind. He was the only artist at the Grammies willing to go on record saying that Eminem played to negative, racist, homophobic and misogynistic elements of his audience. A militant vegan, he opened up a trendy vegetarian

▼

cafe, Teany. And venting his disappointment in the electronic community's continuing apathy, he became an increasingly vocal advocate for left-wing causes and the John Kerry political campaign.
Finally, realizing that he is his own best spokesperson, he has raised blogging on his website (www.moby.com) to a model of cybercommunication. When he introduced the site in 2000,

▼

he did so with an apology, saying that: "The site isn't as flashy as some of the other artist sites, but I specifically wanted something that loaded quickly and was nice and simple. I personally get annoyed at sites that take forever to load and have all sorts of fancy graphics but don't actually have any content. Maybe when everyone in the world has superfast internet access we will restructure

▲

▶ the site so that it's a bit more high tech, but in the meantime I'd rather just present something that loads quickly and has an easy to use and logical infrastructure. So thanks for visiting and please let us know what you think, Moby".
It turns out he was right. He still hasn't added the bells and whistles, but the dialogue between him and his acolytes remains as fresh as ever.

▼

Which just goes to show that this little idiot is in fact nobody's fool. NF

became committed to gender equality and social justice and began to think of myself as a liberal feminist. I'm so proud of the label that I'm thinking of getting two new tattoos: 'liberal' here" (right bicep) "and 'feminist' here (left)." After college she worked the usual day jobs, bike messenger, waitress and office temp, before being inspired by a David Letterman show to try her hand at standup. Her scathing wit and

unflinching look at her life made her a favorite of hipsters like Ben Stiller and venues like MTV. Without really suffering all too much, she had worked her way into cult status.
Everything was picture perfect for a while. Then the polarities began. A stint at Saturday Night Live went haywire. Garofalo was openly unhappy with the quality of the writing and the sexist nature of the show and, violating

with it." Garofalo did not seem to be mollified but some time later, after Fiona Apple complained that Garofalo's constant harping on Apple's emaciated appearance was unnecessary, Garofalo, with no apparent irony, snapped, "It's comedy. Deal with it."
Also, for a woman who has had numerous bouts with weight and beauty in an industry that values beauty more than intelligence, she resorted to

surprising low blows when it came to Monica Lewinsky. Rather than apply feminist ideals to her analysis, she went on record has having trouble believing Clinton would have done what he did because Lewinsky was so "ugly."
If those remarks raised hackles – and speculation in places like The Iconophile that Garofalo had become bitter over her failure to make more of an impact in Hollywood – the right

GEEK MOVIE ICON

Janeane Garofalo She's been in movies like Reality Bites, Dogma and The Truth About Cats and Dogs and a regular on landmark TV shows like The Ben Stiller Show, Larry Saunders and (Michael Moore's) TV Nation. She's the hip, cute counter-culture girl next door and the sometimes-strident anti-war activist. She's the woman you can see

the unwritten law that you keep your complaints to yourself, frequently complained to the press about it. Then, anticipating her friend Ben Stiller by a good five years, she chose roles poorly. As one reviewer remarked, "it's easy to get good reviews for your performance when the rest of the movie is terrible." Besides that, she was so smart and opinionated that some people got tired by what they say is her holier-than-thou

was about to go rabid. In the early days of the Iraq War, Artists United to Win Without War, concerned that the anti-war movement was getting so little coverage in the mainstream media, asked Garofalo to represent the organization and the peace activists. "I also believed that the media had simply become cheerleaders for the Bush doctrine," she said. "They had abdicated their responsibility to

taking home to Mom or, since she has 12 tattoos, to a biker bar as an icebreaker. Perhaps no one better encapsulates the ambivalence we have towards geek women than Janeane Garofalo, the mistress of "Shock and Jaw."
"I spent a lot of time at Wheaton College, where there were incredibly intelligent and interesting women, and we read and discussed feminist issues," she told Ms. Magazine. That's when I

attitude. According to The Iconophile, a website devoted to actresses who've achieved iconic status, Garofalo also was something of a diva who worked with a bit of a double standard.
Garofalo was so upset by Joan Rivers' remarks about her lack of a fashion sense, for instance, that she cried and talked about it during interviews so often that Joan Rivers, to no avail, told the press, "It's comedy. Deal

be watchdogs of the government. I wanted the anti-war position heard, and so I agreed to represent those views". The backlash against her (as well as similarly outspoken celebrities such as Susan Sarandon and Tim Robbins) was immediate and hostile. When it was suggested the projects she had in development would proceed more smoothly if she kept quiet, she went on the offensive.

▶ "Why should I apologize? We have more
looting than liberation. We protected
the Ministry of Oil but not the
treasures of the National Museum. We
have photographs of a statue brought
down and an Iraqi kissing a soldier, but
meanwhile where are the weapons of
mass destruction, where is democracy?
So, no, I'm not apologizing, and I'm not
letting them shut me up."
"I'm not wealthy, and I don't live in
▼

Hollywood," she continued. "I can
take the slams and I don't care
about the hate mail and the threats
of boycotts that are posted on the
websites either. They only make me more
committed to expressing the anti-war
views that millions of people around
the world share."
After several months, just as her
friend, Michael Moore, had predicted,
the furor had died down. She may not
▼

Wolfenstein 3D The definite rise of PC
games. Id Software creates <u>Wolfenstein
3D</u>, starting the first person shooter
genre (killing Nazi's, which prompted
Germany to confiscate the game).
One year later, id Software develops
<u>Doom</u>. It further defines the genre,
introduces the BFG9000 (Big Fucking
Gun), deathmatch and god mode, and
gives a tremendous boost to LAN
gaming and user-made expansions. EVDZ

be everybody's favorite girl next door
anymore, but her projects were back on
track. There is no blacklist," she said.
"In the entertainment business, money
talks, bullshit walks. So Susan Sarandon
and Tim Robbins won't be blacklisted
because they are bankable stars.
[Besides,] if you are a woman, the only
things you're going to be blacklisted for
in Hollywood are body fat and aging." NF

GEEK TV

<u>X-Men</u> In this popular addition to the
parade of Saturday cartoons, the
Sentinels were a group of genocidal
robots intent on giving the mutants
a run for their money. They were bad
enough to be persistent, but, in the
end, not bad enough to upset the new
world order or make it into the Bryan
Singer films.

335 BC	287 BC	830	1284	1455	1543	1564	1632	1683	1746	1755	1811	1818	1821	1837	1847	1853	1865	1868	1876	1879	1886	1889	1890	1893	1898	1899	1903	1905	1906	1907	1914	1921	1926	1929	1932	1934	1937	1938	1939	1941	1942	1945	1946	1947	1948	1949	1950	1951	1952

Intelligent Dance Music (IDM) Aphex Twin (a.k.a. Richard D. James), an English producer with a penchant for scary noises and computer manipulation, releases "Selected Ambient Works 85–92." And with that, the experimental genre for dance-music gearheads, intelligent dance music (IDM), is born.

GEEK CYBERPUNK

William Gibson/Bruce Sterling, The Difference Engine Two giants of cyberpunk, William Gibson and Bruce Sterling (who was more impressive as a journalist, especially in his book The Hacker Crackdown) joined forces for this long, winding trip through alternative history.
They began with the premise that

▶ continual problems with rebellious Luddites and clackers (the alternative version of hackers). Dubbed the first "steampunk" novel, The Difference Engine tends to be more admired than loved. Perhaps that's why it's also the last we've heard of steampunk. NF

GEEK GAME

Street Fighter 2 a classic arcade game from Japanese game giant Capcom, single-handedly defined the fighting game, and was primarily responsible for the second wave of arcade fanaticism of the mid-90's. The game pits two players controlling animated opponents, against each other against a backdrop of cheering spectators. SF2 goes

▼

▼ Charles Babbage built his Analytical Engine, which was a mechanical, steam-powered computer with numerous practical applications, in 1885. This ushered the Information Age in a century early and, in the book's world, put England firmly in the hands of technocrats and scientists, who our duo call savants, under the leadership of Lord Byron (don't ask). The savants have it pretty good, except for their ▲

over the top – it's all about flaming uppercuts, fireballs thrown across the screen, 720 degree spinning pile drivers, and elastic limbs which stretch to ridiculous lengths. SF2 attracted the most competitive of gamers to the arcades of its day. MS

"FAST-FORWARD FREE-STYLE MALL MYTHOLOGY FOR THE EARLY 21ST CENTURY"
—WILLIAM GIBSON

SNOW CRASH

A NOVEL BY

NEAL STEPHENSON

GEEK CYBERPUNK

Neal Stephenson, Snow Crash Eight years before <u>Cryptonomicron</u>, his 900-page-plus best-selling opus on code breaking in World War II, Neal Stephenson publishes <u>Snow Crash</u> and joins William Gibson as a cyberpunk god. This novel, which details the adventures of hacker/pizza delivery man Hiro Protagonist, has been a steady seller

▼

but, oddly, has never been made into a movie or a video game. NF

GEEK TV

The X-Files In the early 1990s, Chris Carter, a former editor at Surfer Magazine, had an idea. "I wanted to make a show that will scare people the way <u>Night Stalker</u> [a popular TV movie from the 1960s about a reluctant skeptic turned vampire killer] scared me back when I was a teenager." It was not an idea many noticed right

▼

away. The X-Files' first season ended up 102 out of 118 in the annual ratings, but the handful of people who watched it included some influential critics. By the second season, it was the 64th most-watched show (out of 141) and a critical darling, winning <u>Entertainment Weekly</u>'s Show of the Year, the Golden Globe for best drama and five Emmys. By season five it was ready for the big screen. The feature, aired as a bridge

▼

between seasons, cost $66 million, but grossed more than $200,000 worldwide, reaffirming the value of the brand. Despite this, the show's star David Duchovney was unhappy. The series was costing him movie roles; he was bored by the character; and, by his estimates, he was being robbed of millions of dollars in royalties he felt he was owed.
In retrospect, they should have folded then and there. But instead, they lured

▲

GEEK POP

Richie Hawtin After three years of releasing underground techno singles and throwing highly controlled, sensory-warping illegal raves, Canada's Richie Hawtin, under the guise of Plastikman, releases his first album. The classic single <u>Spastik</u> appears within, and geeky electronic-music fans emulate the nerdy producer by shaving

▼

their heads, donning black-rimmed glasses, and raiding their local Guitar Centers in search of 909s. NF

► him back. Three years later, it lumbered to an awkward close with the whimper of a guest that had stayed too long. Still, despite the clunkers, confusing plot twists and conventional finale, The X-Files was exceptional television. And now, thanks to syndication, DVDs and video, the truth is still out there, several times a day. NF

GEEK MOVIE ICON

Quentin Tarantino No one does geek better than Quentin Tarantino. A former video store clerk who became the most important film director of his generation, he's a. loud, brash, walking encyclopedia of pop culture who has taken to the world of celebrity with a vengeance equal to those his characters bring to mayhem.

For one thing, he does exactly what he wants to do, be it going onto The (Jay Leno) Tonight Show drunk, dropping Ecstasy in Beijing, or indulging in his love for the series, American Idol, by being a celebrity judge on what seemed to be a massive amphetamine high, spewing love, praise and advice to the hapless contestants. He lives in what Entertainment Weekly dubbed "a geek paradise," with the entire house,

enviably situated in the Hollywood Hills, "filled to the rafters with movie posters, books, CDs, DVDs, videos, comic books and memorabilia (including a shelf packed with Barbie and Madge lunch boxes and thermoses)." Somehow it's reassuring to know that he's still true to the Simpsons and rock 'n' roll, and not off indulging a newfound collector's lust for Limoge. And, best of all, he has as much control as

anyone can have over his career. Not bad for someone born on the wrong side of the Knoxville, Tennessee tracks. His single mother named him after Quint, a character from the old television series Gunsmoke that was played by Burt Reynolds. When he was two, they moved to South Central Los Angeles, the impoverished black ghetto. By the time he was in his early 20s, he was working in an independent

video store in Manhattan Beach called the Video Archives, with a bunch of other geeks in their early 20s, spending his day watching and arguing about all sorts of movies. When he wasn't working at the store, he was writing screenplays or going off to acting classes in Hollywood. Although nothing was coming of it, you wouldn't know it from his resume, which was peppered with fake credits such

as George Romero's original Dawn of the Dead — because he looked like one of the bikers — and Goddard's King Lear — because he was sure no one in Hollywood would have heard, much less seen, the movie. It didn't get him any jobs but it did earn him a footnote in film history. In early editions of his guide to the movies, none other than Leonard Maltin listed Tarantino as an actor in King Lear.

His first real score came as a screenwriter, when he sold his script for True Romance to Tony Scott and Natural Born Killers to Oliver Stone. After seeing both mutate (in Natural Born Killers' case, to something he wanted no part of), he vowed that he would use the money from True Romance, some $50,000, to direct his third, Reservoir Dogs, himself, in 16mm black and white if need be.

It never came to that, thanks to Harvey Keitel, who loved the script, kicked in some of his own cash and brought along a number of other name actors. The film, whose name is a mash-up from Au Revoir Les Enfants, a film Tarantino loved but couldn't pronounce and called the "reservoir" movie, and Sam Peckinpah's ultra-violent Straw Dogs, took the film community by surprise with its offbeat structure,

speed-fire dialogue and unsparing blend of humor and violence. Critical opinion was divided, but word of mouth was phenomenal, drawing steadily growing crowds to the small indie theaters the film had settled into. His second film, Pulp Fiction, didn't need the slow build. By the time it opened, Tarantino was already the toast of Hollywood and Pulp Fiction had already won the Palme D'Or at the 1994

Cannes Festival. Sensing they could make a killing, Miramax threw the indie rulebook out the window and opened the movie in a national blitz, as if it were a major studio release. The gamble paid off. Pulp Fiction became the first independent film in history to take in more than $100 million; was nominated for numerous Academy Awards won for best original screenplay, and made Tarantino a bona-fide cult hero...

Making the most of it, Tarantino traveled all over the world partying and promoting his film. Using his new clout, he distributed a number of obscure horror and kung-fu movies; helped finance and co-direct Robert Rodriguez's film Four Rooms (not to mention the inexorable From Dusk to Dawn); directed an episode of the TV show, ER (just because he could), and acted on Broadway in the much-

▶ ridiculed revival of <u>Wait Until Dark</u>. He finally got back down to serious work in 1997 with the unexpectedly subdued and very long Jackie Brown. Adapted from an Elmore Leonard book, this ostensible homage to blacksploitation films of the '70s ended up with more detractors than admirers. Some were disappointed by the film itself, but others, including Spike Lee, were outraged by what they considered

▼

Tarantino's wigger (white boy posing as a ghetto black) posturing and, in particular, his fascination with and use of the word, "nigger." Tarantino, true to form, remained unrepentant. After noting that "nigger" was one of the most volatile words in the English language, he observed that. "Any time anyone gives a word that much power, I think everybody should be shouting it from the rooftops to

▼

take the power away. I grew up around blacks and have no fear of it. I grew up saying it as an expression." Brown's failure and Tarantino's lengthy absence from center stage muted the controversy. When he returned six years later with <u>Kill Bill</u>, the discussion was less about racism than about money. Rather than release the film in its entirety, Miramax, referred to in Hollywood as the house Tarantino had

▼

built, decided to split the film into two halves, released six months apart. The move seemed to be economically, rather than artistically, motivated but Tarantino, despite some early grumbling, didn't fight the decision. The first "volume" opened to mixed reviews in late 2003 but Tarantino's star, as bright as ever, propelled the film to a huge opening. The second volume added to his credibility, not

▶ just because it held the audience but won over a number of important critics, who had reserved judgment until they had seen both films. Not that their opinion mattered at all to Tarantino. In the spate of interviews he gave, he kept coming back to the fact that he was his own boss, and that he was making movies for himself. Oddly, for someone who has been so defined by his love of film,

▼

he did not seem all that concerned with his future projects or with his cinematic legacy. "If I were teaching a class...I could point out deficiencies I wouldn't allow in my own work, but I forgive it if I like it. A movie doesn't have to do everything. It just has to do a couple of things. If it does those things well and gives you a cool night, an emotion, that's good enough, man," he told Entertainment Weekly.

This low-key attitude continued with the almost startling admission that he didn't want to be an "old director". "A lot of the '70s movie brats have gotten old and it shows in their work and I don't want that. ...directors don't get better as they get older. I really do think directing is a young man's game – I don't want to be some old guy [in his 60s] pitching fucking scripts." But you know what, we don't buy it. As

▶ a line from Kill Bill, v. 2 goes, "What kills more old people? Retirement." As rich and smug as he may be, Tarantino was born to make movies and, our guess is, make movies he will. NF

335 BC	287 BC	830	1284	1455	1543	1564	1632	1683	1746	1755	1811	1818	1821	1837	1847	1853	1865	1868	1876	1877	1879	1886	1889	1890	1893	1898	1899	1903	1905	1906	1907	1914	1921	1926	1929	1932	1934	1937	1938	1939	1941	1942	1945	1946	1947	1948	1949	1950	1951	1952

Multiplayer Racing Games Virtual Racing starts a new arcade age of fast polygon multiplayer racing games. EVDZ

GEEK COMPUTER ICONS

Dorm Digirati
> see page 134

Myst Robyn and Rand Miller introduce groundbreaking graphics to the PC with the adventure game Myst, which sells more than 9 million copies. EVDZ

GEEK GADGET

Apple Newton John Sculley called it a personal digital assistant at the Consumer Electronics Show. But as a pda the Apple Newton was too expensive, too large and the handwriting recognition software too stubborn. The smaller, thinner and cheaper Palm Pilot introduced three years later did became a commercial success. EVDZ

Wired magazine's first issue goes to press and, as demand outstrips all expectations, gets reprinted multiple times, proving that the world of internet technology is less underground than it was perceived. NF

Cyberia Eva Pascoe founds the world's first internet café, Cyberia, a place where net-heads, geeks, designers, and coders meet and map out the future of the Net.

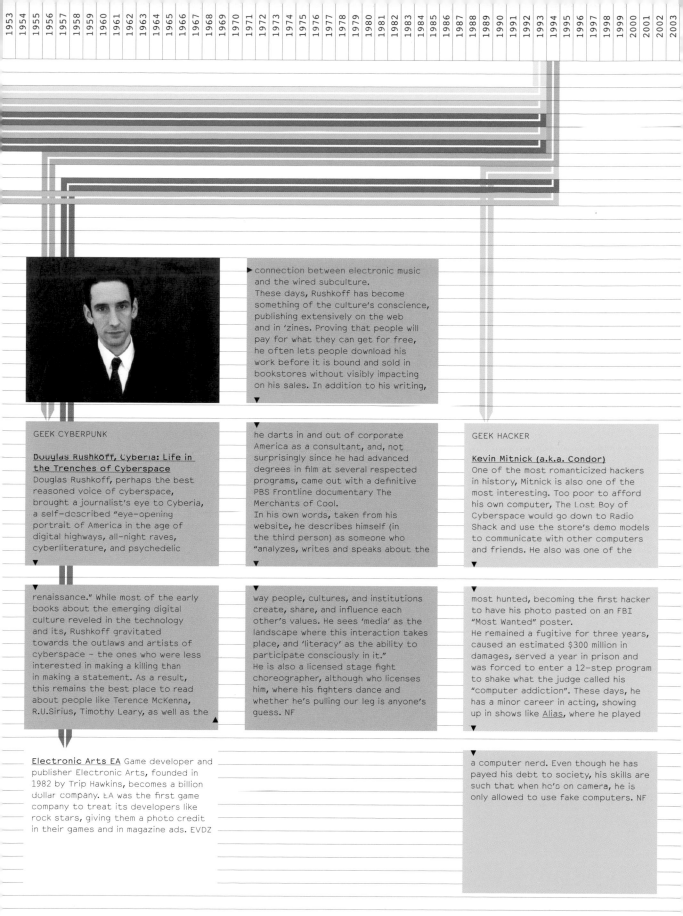

▶ connection between electronic music and the wired subculture.
These days, Rushkoff has become something of the culture's conscience, publishing extensively on the web and in 'zines. Proving that people will pay for what they can get for free, he often lets people download his work before it is bound and sold in bookstores without visibly impacting on his sales. In addition to his writing,

GEEK CYBERPUNK

Douglas Rushkoff, Cyberia: Life in the Trenches of Cyberspace

Douglas Rushkoff, perhaps the best reasoned voice of cyberspace, brought a journalist's eye to Cyberia, a self-described "eye-opening portrait of America in the age of digital highways, all-night raves, cyberliterature, and psychedelic

renaissance." While most of the early books about the emerging digital culture reveled in the technology and its, Rushkoff gravitated towards the outlaws and artists of cyberspace – the ones who were less interested in making a killing than in making a statement. As a result, this remains the best place to read about people like Terence McKenna, R.U.Sirius, Timothy Leary, as well as the

he darts in and out of corporate America as a consultant, and, not surprisingly since he had advanced degrees in film at several respected programs, came out with a definitive PBS Frontline documentary The Merchants of Cool.
In his own words, taken from his website, he describes himself (in the third person) as someone who "analyzes, writes and speaks about the

way people, cultures, and institutions create, share, and influence each other's values. He sees 'media' as the landscape where this interaction takes place, and 'literacy' as the ability to participate consciously in it."
He is also a licensed stage fight choreographer, although who licenses him, where his fighters dance and whether he's pulling our leg is anyone's guess. NF

Electronic Arts EA Game developer and publisher Electronic Arts, founded in 1982 by Trip Hawkins, becomes a billion dollar company. EA was the first game company to treat its developers like rock stars, giving them a photo credit in their games and in magazine ads. EVDZ

GEEK HACKER

Kevin Mitnick (a.k.a. Condor)

One of the most romanticized hackers in history, Mitnick is also one of the most interesting. Too poor to afford his own computer, The Lost Boy of Cyberspace would go down to Radio Shack and use the store's demo models to communicate with other computers and friends. He also was one of the

most hunted, becoming the first hacker to have his photo pasted on an FBI "Most Wanted" poster.
He remained a fugitive for three years, caused an estimated $300 million in damages, served a year in prison and was forced to enter a 12-step program to shake what the judge called his "computer addiction". These days, he has a minor career in acting, showing up in shows like Alias, where he played

a computer nerd. Even though he has payed his debt to society, his skills are such that when he's on camera, he is only allowed to use fake computers. NF

GEEK POP

John Digweed Unless you are part of the scene, one DJ is pretty much like any other. But if you care, DJs are as distinctive and heroic as any other musical or artistic genre. More than any other type of music, however, the electronic music community seems to thrive on small-pond wars, narrowly defined (and passionately

defended) sub-genres of sub-genres and a complete distrust of mainstream success. In trying to single out one DJ who cuts across genre to epitomize the idea of a contemporary DJ, you could do no better than John Digweed, the dance community's ambassador to the world.

Digweed was born in Hastings, England, the son of working class parents who owned a butcher shop. He spent his

childhood working there, and got his first exposure to mix tapes through an employee of the shop who was making them for the local club. An indifferent student who hated working in the butcher shop, he started moonlighting – over his parents' objections, who argued that a pub was no place for a young boy – in the local club while he was still 15. As it turned out, they had nothing to worry about. Digweed was

using the time to learn everything about clubs at the same time that he was coming in contact with enough alcoholics to convince him that was something he did not want to be. What he did want to be was a DJ. No one really thought it would come to much. When he confided in his guidance counselor at school, for instance, the counselor told the headmaster. The next day, at an assembly in front

of the entire class, the headmaster pointed Digweed out. "Take Mr. Digweed, for example. Mr. Digweed there thinks he's going to be a DJ," the headmaster announced, unable to keep the sarcasm out of his voice. "Well let me tell you; he's going to amount to nothing." (In 2002, accepting the coveted DJ of the Year award, he remembered to mention his headmaster. "He can go fuck himself," Digweed said,

enjoying the last laugh, 15 years later.) By that point, he was fully committed to music as a career. Juggling day jobs with late nights as a promoter and a DJ, he built his reputation, got his tapes to Geoff Oakes, who ran an important club called Renaissance, and one of the club's DJs, Sasha (who had been called the Son of God by a music magazine and was on his way to being the first of the DJ poster

boys). Recognizing Digweed's talent, they brought him in from the bush leagues. Although they made an Odd Couple, Sasha and Digweed pushed each other into rock star territory. Working together and individually, they stormed the clubs, continent by continent, until they had the largest electronic fan base in the world.

That, though, is only part of the story. Digweed, a butcher's kid with limited

education, not only became a citizen of the world, but a power broker with his hand in every aspect of the electronic music compendium, including club nights, a record label (Bedrock), a weekly radio show, soundtracks for films and television on top of thriving recording and DJ careers. He even acted in the movie Groove, getting the best reviews in the film essentially for playing himself. More to the point, he did it without

forgetting his love of gadgetry, his accessibility to the fans or his belief that even with the fortune and the fame, it's only worth it if its fun. And what's more fun than using a passion for music and a love of technology to escape a small town butcher shop and waltz into music history? NF

Marathon Bungie releases Marathon, the only noteworthy game for the Macintosh. EVDZ

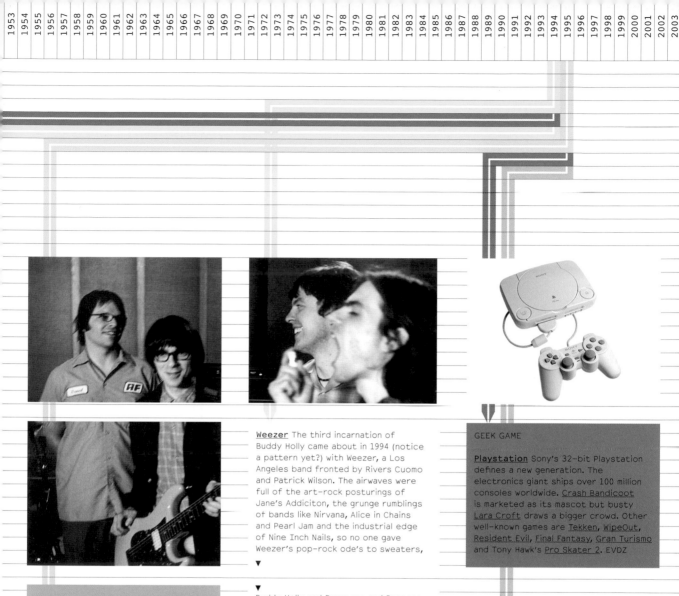

Weezer The third incarnation of Buddy Holly came about in 1994 (notice a pattern yet?) with Weezer, a Los Angeles band fronted by Rivers Cuomo and Patrick Wilson. The airwaves were full of the art-rock posturings of Jane's Addiciton, the grunge rumblings of bands like Nirvana, Alice in Chains and Pearl Jam and the industrial edge of Nine Inch Nails, so no one gave Weezer's pop-rock ode's to sweaters,

▼

Buddy Holly and Dungeons and Dragons much of a chance. But, as Rolling Stone said a decade later, in a rave review of the re-release of Weezer's classic album, Blue, Weezer became the great Geek rock band of all time – and did it without trying to be anyone other than who they were. As the review pointed out, Weezer's "broken-family soundtrack" captured white guys' self-consciousness and personal pain with

▼

so much power that their music would go on to inspire thousands of emo kids. The only hitch to all this is that these emo kids indeed love Weezer, they hate and won't claim the label "emo." So, since emo is just a three-letter word for geek, maybe we should just leave it at that. And wait for the next Holly incarnation which, if the 15-year resurrection holds true, should appear sometime very soon. NF

GEEK GAME

Playstation Sony's 32-bit Playstation defines a new generation. The electronics giant ships over 100 million consoles worldwide. Crash Bandicoot is marketed as its mascot but busty Lara Croft draws a bigger crowd. Other well-known games are Tekken, WipeOut, Resident Evil, Final Fantasy, Gran Turismo and Tony Hawk's Pro Skater 2. EVDZ

Windows '95 infiltrates just about every computer on the planet.

GEEK GADGET

Casio QV-11 Although Apple had released its QuickTake 100 a year earlier and Kodak its DC40 in March, it was the Casio QV-11 that opened the consumer market for digital cameras. It was small and featured a LCD-display on the back, enabling people to review their digital snapshots on the spot. EVDZ

GEEK INTERNET ICONS

<u>Dorm Digirati</u>
Tim Berners-Lee
Marc Andreesen
Jerry Yang & David Filo
Larry page & Sergey Brin
Linus Torvalds
Shawn Fanning

The modern personal computer may have been conceived at Xerox Palo Alto Research Center, a well-funded industrial lab filled with scientists, but Steve Wozniak and Steve Jobs opened up the market from a garage in Cupertino. The internet continued the spiral of downward mobility by being launched in the student dorm.
If you want to get technical, the internet was born on November 11,

1993 with the release of <u>Mosaic 1.0</u>. Sure, there were several other defining moments in the creation of the computer network. It started out in 1969 as ARPANET. This network switched to TCP/IP, the internet's core protocols on January 1, 1983. It was called NSFNet three years later when the National Science Foundation built its university backbone, sucking up Usenet and other networks while

they were at it. And it got a complete makeover when computer scientist <u>Tim Berners-Lee</u>, nowadays Sir Tim Berners-Lee, created the <u>World Wide Web</u>. His first website, info.cern.ch, went online on August 6, 1991. But those are really all just tech specs. It was the Mosaic web browser that brought the web, and with it the entire internet, to the masses because it let them access it from

their personal computers. And it wasn't some research ace at Microsoft, Apple, IBM, Intel, Sun, SGI or NEC that created it. No, it was 22-year-old <u>Marc Andreesen</u> – a student at the National Center for Supercomputing Applications of the University of Illinois – who programmed Mosaic. After graduation Andreesen capitalized on his momentum by creating Mosaic's successor, <u>Netscape Navigator</u>, and

becoming vice-president of the company that was built around it. Netscape's TPO in 1995 made him the hero of the internet bubble generation: a young geek who became a millionaire practically overnight.
He wouldn't be the only one. Just as the personal computer twenty years earlier offered young graduates like Wozniak and Jobs and college drop-outs like Bill Gates a chance for fame

and fortune, the internet was a diamond in the rough, a new game with only a few rules, a chance to invent something and an arena where you didn't have to start at the bottom and work your way up.
<u>Jerry Yang</u> and <u>David Filo</u>, for instance, were electrical engineering graduate students at Stanford University when they started filling their web directory called <u>Yahoo!</u>, indexing

the growing number of websites. "It started out as a way for us to keep track of things that we were interested in. A couple of friends started to use it. It was somewhat slow to catch on initially because we never really advertised it. It just grew by word of mouth and by people linking to it from their home pages," remembers Filo. Yahoo! incorporated in 1995. Its IPO followed a year later, making them multimillionaires too. Both Yang and Filo are still with Yahoo! as members of the management team. Two other Stanford students pulled a similar stunt. In 1996 Larry Page and Sergey Brin started a research project that led to the internet search engine Google in Page's dorm room. "When we set out in the kind of early Web days, we didn't decide to do online horoscopes or invitation services, but

version of the Unix operating system, at the University of Helsinki. He posted it online in 1991, free of charge and copyrights, and invited other programmers to e-mail him with their improvements.
They did. As a result, Torvalds has only written about two percent of today's Linux. And while he may not have become a millionaire, he has earned the respect of thousands of geeks around the

and everyone loved Shawn Fanning.
"I understood an idea like this could become popular, but at the same time I didn't think it was my implementation that would be so widely used," he said. And despite high-profile whining by stars like Metallica and Madonna, reports Fanning, "almost all of my interactions with artists were positive. Despite some questions about compensation, most artists

world. To him, that seems like an ample reward. "Making Linux freely available is the single best decision I've ever made," he says. "There are lots of good technical stuff I'm proud of too in the kernel, but they all pale by comparison." Although Torvalds' official title at Linux is project coordinator, he likes to think of himself as its Benevolent Dictator for Life. It's a title no one will begrudge him.

seem to understand that the future is a good thing." Perhaps but by mid-2001 a judge ordered Napster to shut its servers down to prevent further copyright violations.
Napster filed for bankruptcy in June 2002, only to re-appear as Napster 2.0 a year later, an online service selling music downloads legally. Fanning is no longer with the company but served as an advisor to 2.0 on the user

search, which is about information, which can make a real difference in people's lives," explains Brin.
By 1998, they had borrowed enough money from their family and their professors to found their own company. By the time this book is printed Google has had its highly anticipated IPO. This time around, the stakes were not just about incomprehensible personal wealth, but about social responsibility

For every one of these students, there are millions more who spend their dorm years happily downloading music and movies from the internet. And that is courtesy of college dropout Shawn Fanning, who created the MP3 filesharing program Napster.
There really was nothing like it when Fanning released it in the fall of 1999. It took the music business longer than the students to catch on. But

experience. He is living proof that no matter how big an industry has grown, one good idea can turn it upside down.
EVDZ

too. "Obviously everyone wants to be successful," says Brin, "but I want to be looked back on as being very innovative, very trusted and ethical and ultimately making a big difference in the world."
On the other side of the Atlantic, another student had already kickstarted the open source movement. At age 21 Linus Torvalds wrote the kernel of Linux, a free

once they understood that Napster was letting their prize demographic, the college market, download and swap music for free, the majors hit back, enlisting bands like Metallica and, determined to shut the service down, filing a massive class action suit against Napster.
The lawsuit had the opposite effect. Suddenly everyone knew about Napster; everyone loved free music;

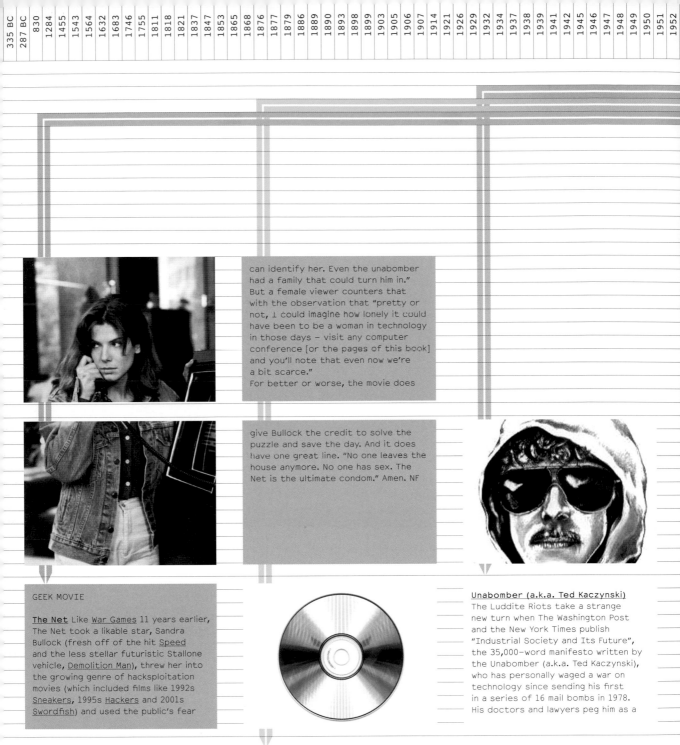

can identify her. Even the unabomber had a family that could turn him in." But a female viewer counters that with the observation that "pretty or not, I could imagine how lonely it could have been to be a woman in technology in those days – visit any computer conference [or the pages of this book] and you'll note that even now we're a bit scarce."

For better or worse, the movie does give Bullock the credit to solve the puzzle and save the day. And it does have one great line. "No one leaves the house anymore. No one has sex. The Net is the ultimate condom." Amen. NF

GEEK MOVIE

The Net Like War Games 11 years earlier, The Net took a likable star, Sandra Bullock (fresh off of the hit Speed and the less stellar futuristic Stallone vehicle, Demolition Man), threw her into the growing genre of hacksploitation movies (which included films like 1992s Sneakers, 1995s Hackers and 2001s Swordfish) and used the public's fear of technology as the backdrop to an otherwise by-the-book thriller. Most find the movie's premise and treatment of technological issues ludicrous. "This is the worst representation of a computer nerd ever," one male viewer, speaking for the majority, reports. "Even though she is supercute, we are supposed to believe that she has no friends, neighbors, family or co-workers who

Digital Versatile Disk (DVD) Sony and Toshiba finally agree on a single standard format for the Digital Versatile Disk (DVD) and it is launched later in the year. Geeks soon discover how to hack their DVD players to get around the regional codes that prevent DVDs from one country being played in another.

Unabomber (a.k.a. Ted Kaczynski)

The Luddite Riots take a strange new turn when The Washington Post and the New York Times publish "Industrial Society and Its Future", the 35,000-word manifesto written by the Unabomber (a.k.a. Ted Kaczynski), who has personally waged a war on technology since sending his first in a series of 16 mail bombs in 1978. His doctors and lawyers peg him as a paranoid schizophrenic, but many think Kaczynski, a Harvard grad with a MD from the University of Michigan who began a life of exile in the Montana mountains in 1971, is a modern poet.

Salon.com Real journalism validates the internet. David Talbot launches Salon.com, and before long the forward-thinking news and pop culture site becomes critically acclaimed by traditional media and fans alike for its competitive and innovative content. The site features columns by such prominent figures as Ariana Huffington and Camille Paglia, and plays host to The Well, the intellectual online community

founded in 1985. A long-time hold out against charging subscriptions, Salon.com succumbs to the pressure and begins charging users $30 for premium services in 2001.

GEEK HACKER

Vladimir Levin (a.k.a. unknown) One of the baddest of boys, this mathematical genius tore through St. Petersburg Tekhnologicesky University and reputedly conceived the first known international bank robbery over a computer network. Working out of London, he used a laptop to access Citibank's network. Using

codes and passwords he obtained from his foray, he transferred money from Citibank to accounts in five different countries. He hacked in 18 times and, in the end, whisked $3.7 million dollars into accounts he controlled. When Citibank discovered the funds were misappropriated, they contacted Interpol who arrested Levin at Heathrow Airport in 1995. He was unsuccessfully defended by a team of

lawyers, one of which he accused of being an FBI agent, and got a three year sentence and a $240,015 fine. NF

GEEK COMIC

Jimmy Corrigan, The Smartest Kid on Earth Nothing upped the graphic ante since Maus like Chris Ware's "festive and rompish simulacra" did. First released as a series of intricate, separately published chapters (in books that changed size and format every few issues) with elaborate fake ads and "interactive" puzzles that instructed

you to cut windows out of buildings with a scissor or perform origami rituals in search of the visual punch line), it was later anthologized into an award-winning hardback. From the first issue, it promised to be "the most trying and irritating production offered by the Acme Novelty Library so far". Guess what? They lied. It's the best. NF

335 BC	287 BC	830	1284	1455	1543	1564	1632	1683	1746	1755	1811	1818	1821	1837	1847	1853	1865	1868	1876	1877	1879	1886	1889	1890	1893	1898	1899	1903	1905	1906	1907	1914	1921	1926	1929	1932	1934	1937	1938	1939	1941	1942	1945	1946	1947	1948	1949	1950	1951	1952

▶ But, the book jacket also said – with an almost visible wink – that "The book you are holding is probably obsolete." If that was valid then, you can bet it's valid now. For while Negroponte was right far more than he was wrong, the changes he predicted in 1995 are almost old hat now.

In fact, the best reason to search the book out today is because of its book jacket, beautifully designed by Chip

GEEK CYBERPUNK

Nicholas Negroponte, Being Digital

Before he became a visionary of the Digital Nation, Nicholas Negroponte was an architect, so it makes a certain amount of sense that the New York Times described him as someone helping "to create the new cosmos towards which we are hurtling" at the same time that he writes about it.

Kidd with an intricate embossed plastic dust jacket (which he popularized with Donna Tartt's The Secret History in 1992). Since Negroponte is a famous design freak, it's ironic that the one thing you can still judge his book on is its cover. NF

The founder of MIT's Media Lab, for which he raised more than $50 million in 1980s money and which has been dedicated to the merger of newspapers, TV, entertainment and education since its inception in 1985, he wrote Being Digital, one of the first to go into detail about, in Negroponte's words, "what being digital will mean for our laws, education, politics, and amusements – in short, for the way we live."

Webby Awards Technology becomes congratulatory, Hollywood style, with the first annual Webby Awards. Modeled after the Oscars and Grammys, the contest honoring internet excellence is sponsored by the International Academy of Digital Arts & Sciences, with both outfits founded by Californian Tiffany Shlain. Only slightly less glamorous than the Oscars, if only for a noticeable absence of the other

GEEK HACKER

Johan Helsingius (a.k.a. Julf) Helsingius

was the world's most celebrated anonymous remailer until 1996, primarily because he posted the Church of Scientology's secrets on the web. In 1996, the Church sued him in a Finnish court, which ruled that Helsinguis had to include the real email address whenever posting new bulletins

kind of silicon, the Webbys become infamous for limiting its winners to five-word speeches.

and messages. To the dismay of tabloid journalists, he caved in before leaking anything about macho Scientologists John Travolta and Tom Cruise. NF

GEEK GAME

Quake Quake marks the breakthrough of online multiplayer gaming. There was such a buzz surrounding the game that the internet servers of id Software crashed due to the high traffic when the shareware version was uploaded. A lively subculture emerged in which players formed clans, spoke of frags and lag, made homebrew movies

RESFEST Digital Film Festival is a touring showcase dedicated to digital filmmaking, is launched. It is the first festival in the world to use the now-standard DLP digital projector. This year, the festival will travel to 14 cities internationally.

using the game as stage, and bought themselves 3D graphic cards for their computer. Nine Inch Nails, a.k.a. Trent Reznor, provides the music for id software's game, Quake. He's the first major artist to do so, and represents the new synergy between video games and the more established forms of popular entertainment.

GEEK MOVIE

Mars Attacks Tim Burton's comedy may not be his best film, but his campy throwback to 1950s Martian movies is a hilarious, cameo-filled adventure where Earthlings win – not because of our cunning, but because of our excruciatingly bad taste. **Mars Attacks** re-ignites the old Luddite adage: One bad country-western singer is worth

GEEK GADGET

Smart Phone Nokia's combination of digital voice and data services into the Communicator is actually the first so-called "smart phone." It made smart people drool. EVDZ

more than a warehouse of computers and hi-tech weaponry. NF

Y2K Hysteria Governments and businesses become aware that there is a potential bug in software programs that only use two digits to store the year, a common practice especially in earlier software. Such software will not be able to tell the difference between the years 1900 and 2000. Y2K hysteria around the Millennium Bug begins.

Porn Sites Traffic to porn sites, the killer app for E-commerce, peaks with 62 million Web pages devoted to sexual content. (Traffic has subsequently dropped by half.) People click out of CNN.com and instead turn to Playboy.com – to read the articles, of course.

Jennicam Jennifer Ringley sets up a series of video cameras in her home and transmits the images from her own Web site 24 hours a day. Jennicam becomes the first personal Web-cam site and attracts over 100 million visitors per week. Though this site does not feature sex, Web-cam sex sites soon appear as women in the sex industry take control using technology, and create their own online porn enterprises. This is not always a good thing.

condemns him to be a de-gen-erate in society. He works as a cleaner in Gattaca space center, while he wants to be an astronaut.

Nichols may not have had a lot of money to spend on special effects, but there's wit aplenty, especially in the inside jokes layered inside the movie: The name Gattaca by the way is entirely composed of the letters used to label the nucleotide base of DNA.

GEEK MOVIE

Gattaca They've got discrimination down to a science in Gattaca, Andrew Niccols' low-budget sci-fi thriller in which parents have their offspring genetically engineered to perfection. The main character Vincent though, played by Ethan Hawke, is a so-called invalid, a God's child who was conceived the old-fashioned natural way. This

The character Irene Cassini, played by Uma Thurman, is a reference to 17th century French-Italian astronomer Jean Dominique Cassini who discovered the gap in Saturn's rings. Saturn also happens to be the destination of the mission Vincent so desperately wants to join. The staircase Vincent uses is a replica of the DNA helix.

For all the intelligence and talent, not to mention the marquee value of Hawke

GEEK GAME

Super Mario 64 Mario 64 was the first great 3D video game. The game is set in kooky cartoon otherworld, stuffed full of bizarre puzzles and weird Japanese characters. Nintendo's superstar game designer Shigeru Miyamoto designed the game, and it is indeed a masterpiece – innovative, challenging, immersive and visually striking. It was also one of

and Thurman, at the time in the midst of a high-profile romance, lavished on the film, it still flopped at the box office. You can buy perfection, apparently, a lot easier than you can sell it. NF

the first games the feature precise "analog" control. The player is able to move Mario around the world with incredibly tight control.

It's easy to make him run, jump, he could rebound off of walls, creep slowly, do backflips... slide on his belly. The player is eventually forced to learn all the subtleties of Mario's moves, using them to beat the game in acrobatic fashion. MS

GEEK COMPUTER

Deep Blue The first defeat of a Chess Grand Master by a computer. After decades of the mental struggle between man and machine, IBM super-computer Deep Blue thrashes world chess champion Garry Kasparov. The tide is turning; technology is winning.

335 BC	287 BC	830	1284	1455	1543	1564	1632	1683	1746	1755	1811	1818	1821	1837	1847	1853	1865	1868	1876	1877	1879	1886	1889	1890	1893	1898	1899	1903	1905	1906	1907	1914	1921	1926	1929	1932	1934	1937	1938	1939	1941	1942	1945	1946	1947	1948	1949	1950	1951	1952

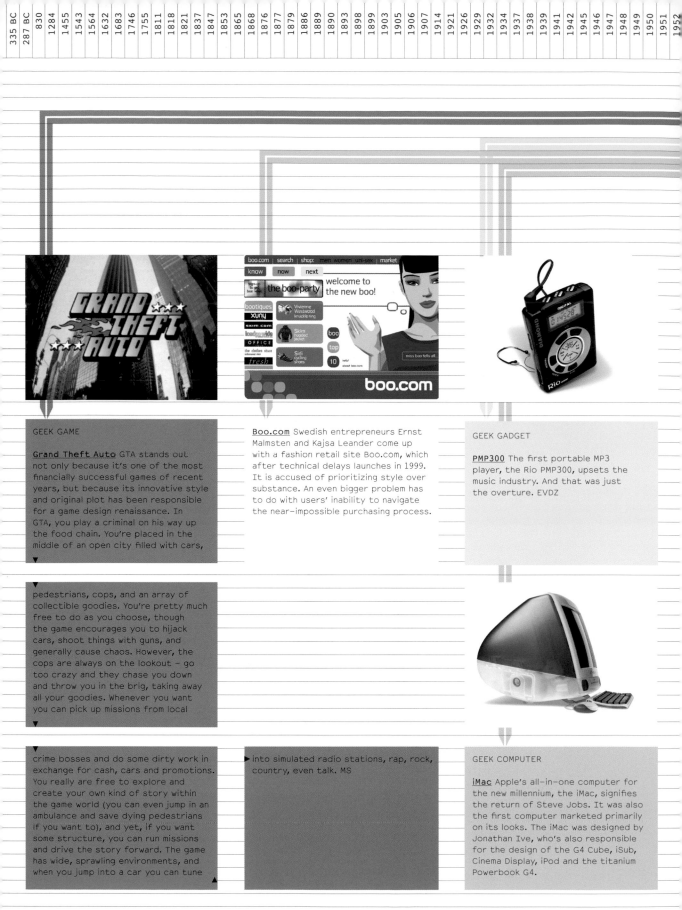

GEEK GAME

Grand Theft Auto GTA stands out not only because it's one of the most financially successful games of recent years, but because its innovative style and original plot has been responsible for a game design renaissance. In GTA, you play a criminal on his way up the food chain. You're placed in the middle of an open city filled with cars,

pedestrians, cops, and an array of collectible goodies. You're pretty much free to do as you choose, though the game encourages you to hijack cars, shoot things with guns, and generally cause chaos. However, the cops are always on the lookout – go too crazy and they chase you down and throw you in the brig, taking away all your goodies. Whenever you want you can pick up missions from local

crime bosses and do some dirty work in exchange for cash, cars and promotions. You really are free to explore and create your own kind of story within the game world (you can even jump in an ambulance and save dying pedestrians if you want to), and yet, if you want some structure, you can run missions and drive the story forward. The game has wide, sprawling environments, and when you jump into a car you can tune

into simulated radio stations, rap, rock, country, even talk. MS

Boo.com Swedish entrepreneurs Ernst Malmsten and Kajsa Leander come up with a fashion retail site Boo.com, which after technical delays launches in 1999. It is accused of prioritizing style over substance. An even bigger problem has to do with users' inability to navigate the near-impossible purchasing process.

GEEK GADGET

PMP300 The first portable MP3 player, the Rio PMP300, upsets the music industry. And that was just the overture. EVDZ

GEEK COMPUTER

iMac Apple's all-in-one computer for the new millennium, the iMac, signifies the return of Steve Jobs. It was also the first computer marketed primarily on its looks. The iMac was designed by Jonathan Ive, who's also responsible for the design of the G4 Cube, iSub, Cinema Display, iPod and the titanium Powerbook G4.

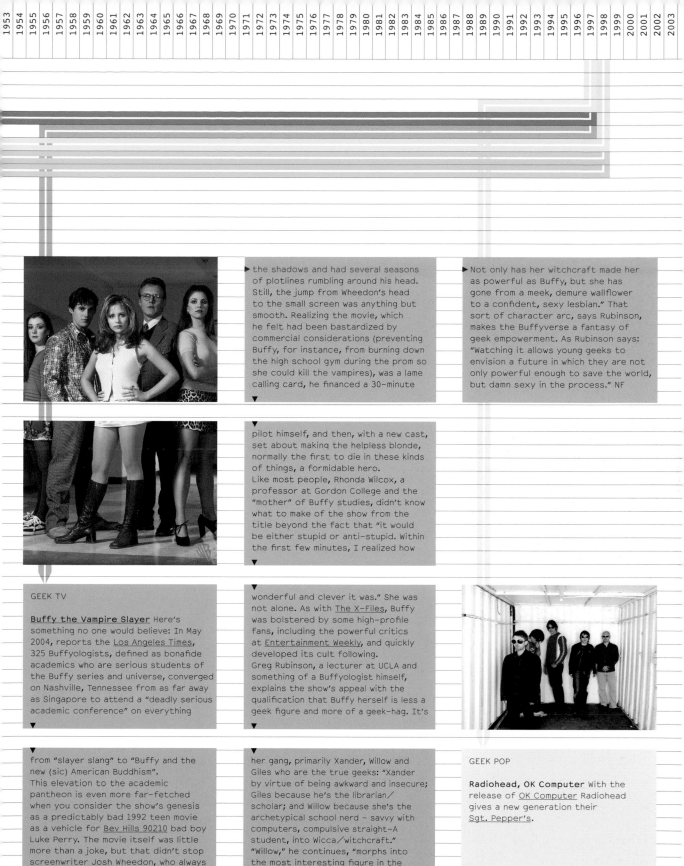

▶ the shadows and had several seasons of plotlines rumbling around his head. Still, the jump from Wheedon's head to the small screen was anything but smooth. Realizing the movie, which he felt had been bastardized by commercial considerations (preventing Buffy, for instance, from burning down the high school gym during the prom so she could kill the vampires), was a lame calling card, he financed a 30-minute ▼

▶ Not only has her witchcraft made her as powerful as Buffy, but she has gone from a meek, demure wallflower to a confident, sexy lesbian." That sort of character arc, says Rubinson, makes the Buffyverse a fantasy of geek empowerment. As Rubinson says: "Watching it allows young geeks to envision a future in which they are not only powerful enough to save the world, but damn sexy in the process." NF

▼ pilot himself, and then, with a new cast, set about making the helpless blonde, normally the first to die in these kinds of things, a formidable hero.
Like most people, Rhonda Wilcox, a professor at Gordon College and the "mother" of Buffy studies, didn't know what to make of the show from the title beyond the fact that "it would be either stupid or anti-stupid. Within the first few minutes, I realized how

GEEK TV

Buffy the Vampire Slayer Here's something no one would believe: In May 2004, reports the Los Angeles Times, 325 Buffyologists, defined as bonafide academics who are serious students of the Buffy series and universe, converged on Nashville, Tennessee from as far away as Singapore to attend a "deadly serious academic conference" on everything ▼

wonderful and clever it was." She was not alone. As with The X-Files, Buffy was bolstered by some high-profile fans, including the powerful critics at Entertainment Weekly, and quickly developed its cult following.
Greg Rubinson, a lecturer at UCLA and something of a Buffyologist himself, explains the show's appeal with the qualification that Buffy herself is less a geek figure and more of a geek-hag. It's

▼ from "slayer slang" to "Buffy and the new (sic) American Buddhism".
This elevation to the academic pantheon is even more far-fetched when you consider the show's genesis as a predictably bad 1992 teen movie as a vehicle for Bev Hills 90210 bad boy Luke Perry. The movie itself was little more than a joke, but that didn't stop screenwriter Josh Wheedon, who always knew there was a TV series lurking in ▲

her gang, primarily Xander, Willow and Giles who are the true geeks: "Xander by virtue of being awkward and insecure; Giles because he's the librarian/scholar; and Willow because she's the archetypical school nerd – savvy with computers, compulsive straight-A student, into Wicca/witchcraft."
"Willow," he continues, "morphs into the most interesting figure in the show over the course of the series. ▲

GEEK POP

Radiohead, OK Computer With the release of OK Computer Radiohead gives a new generation their Sgt. Pepper's.

335 BC	287 BC	830	1284	1455	1543	1564	1632	1683	1746	1755	1811	1818	1821	1837	1847	1853	1865	1868	1876	1877	1879	1886	1889	1890	1893	1898	1899	1903	1905	1906	1907	1914	1921	1926	1929	1932	1934	1937	1938	1939	1941	1942	1945	1946	1947	1948	1949	1950	1951	1952

GEEK GAME

Dance Dance Revolution by Konami becomes a craze in Japanese arcades. The dancing game is played with your feet. It is praised for helping obese players lose weight. EVDZ

GEEK GAME

Starcraft One of the most popular game genres on the PC is called "Real Time Strategy". These are basically war games – you harvest resources like gold, wood, crystals, and use what you find to build an army. You then use the army to crush your foes. These games require strategic thinking and good battle tactics. Oftentimes all
▼

GEEK MOVIE

Pi If geeks don't love science, technology, and computers, they surely love math. And if they're anything like Max Cohen, the biographical character in Darren Aronofsky's chilling brainteaser, they probably believe that mathematics is the universal language in these and all other facets of life. In Pi – a twisted mediation on
▼

players are given access to exactly the same soldiers and military nits – as in the perfectly-balanced game of chess, where both players start with the same chess pieces. The makers of Starcraft went a different route and created three different races for each player to choose from. Each race encourages a different tactic – some are more run-and-gun and some require the use of stealth and surprise. The
▼

the line between genius and insanity – Cohen slowly drives himself insane trying to prove that order exists in chaos – in this case, the New York Stock Exchange. NF

game spent years in fine-tweaking to ensure that no one race would have an advantage over another. Playing Starcraft with a group of friends on the internet is incredibly addicting. In Korea, the game created a "LAN Parlor" industry – rooms filled with computers hooked to the internet with the sole purpose of running Starcraft. Even Ben Affleck plays it. MS

Microsoft Anti-Trust Charges After nearly eight years of investigation, the US government, along with 20 states, indites Microsoft on anti-trust charges. A drama with proper high-court red tape, the trial seesaws in favor of each party until 2001, when Microsoft narrowly wins a ruling that would have split it into two companies. The monolith is, however, forced to let computer manufacturers choose their preferred system software without fear of Microsoft backlash, and to reveal portions of its software codes. Nine states out for blood object and seek further damages. Microsoft tries to persuade them and a host of other litigants by offering to pay for their court costs and pledging to donate a billion dollars worth of computers and software to low-income schools. No one is fooled, and Microsoft's offer is thrown out. The states eventually seek lesser charges, and Microsoft goes on to be sued by AOL Time Warner and Sun Microsystems.

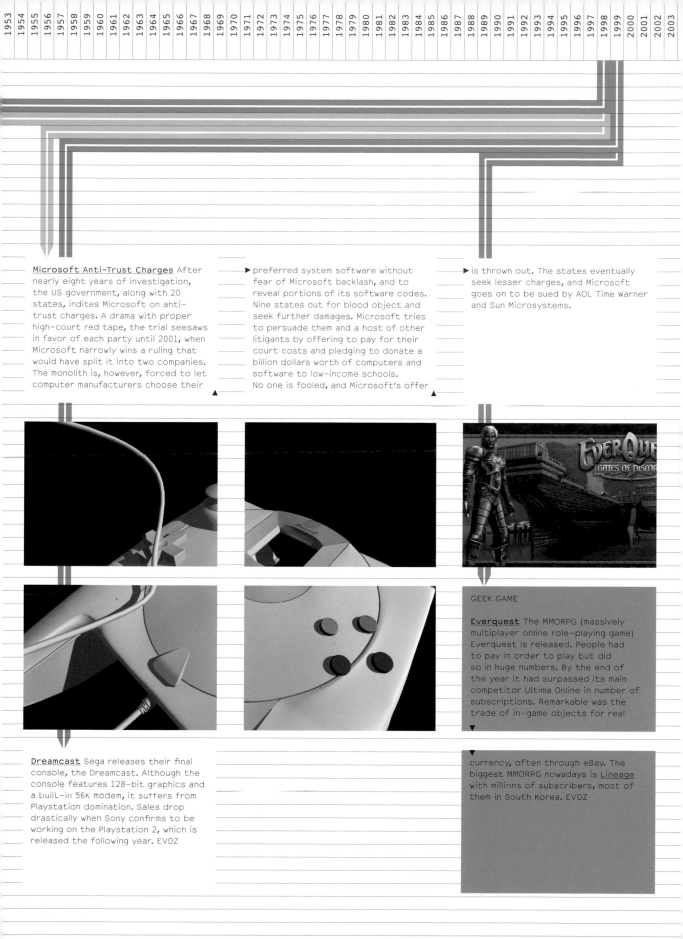

GEEK GAME

Everquest The MMORPG (massively multiplayer online role-playing game) Everquest is released. People had to pay in order to play but did so in huge numbers. By the end of the year it had surpassed its main competitor Ultima Online in number of subscriptions. Remarkable was the trade of in-game objects for real currency, often through eBay. The biggest MMORPG nowadays is Lineage with millions of subscribers, most of them in South Korea. EVDZ

Dreamcast Sega releases their final console, the Dreamcast. Although the console features 128-bit graphics and a built-in 56K modem, it suffers from Playstation domination. Sales drop drastically when Sony confirms to be working on the Playstation 2, which is released the following year. EVDZ

Strangely, no other network picked up the show either. And because the show's soundtrack was full of hits, the cost of licensing the music made the DVD prohibitively expensive to produce. So, for several years, fans swapped bootlegs and complained on the Web about the show's demise. Finally, a few fans started a petition demanding the DVD. The petition, which had thousands of names, gave series creator Paul Feig

GEEK CYBERPUNK

Neal Stephenson, Cryptonomicon
Neal Stephenson leaves no stone unturned. So on the back flap of the book's cover, there's a great shot of him as a boy, engrossed in a picture book; The First Book of Codes and Ciphers. Perhaps that, more than anything else, is why Cryptonomicon, his 900+ page opus, may end up being more

GEEK TV

Freaks and Geeks premiers on American television. A 1980s Michigan high school situation "dramedy" pares the burners (freaks) against the geeks and the rest of the school in the ultimate quest for acceptance.
Like Max Headroom, Freaks and Geeks was one of those out-of-nowhere series that created an instant

and executive producer Judd Apatow sufficient leverage to get a production company to spring for the song clearances and DVD release, including a limited edition yearbook. They even hired some of the petition organizers as research assistants who happily culled through all the old footage to come up with the DVD's bonus features. The release party – or, as they called it, the William McKinley High School

important than his other cyberpunk classic, Snow Crash (1992). Both have its fans, and Snow Crash is certainly the more streamlined and accessible of the two. But Cryptonomicon's got ambition, scope and power that hasn't been seen since Thomas Pynchon's Gravity's Rainbow.
The book interweaves two eras. The first follows two members of Detachment 2702, crypto analyst

community around it. And like Max Headroom, all the critical hosannas and fans' hand-wringing could not convince the network to give it more than one season.
A real loss to anyone who realized that shows such as Dawson's Creek or Felicity weren't terribly realistic. As one viewer posted, "The kids in Freaks and Geeks talk about sci-fi movies, get high, feel alienated by their parents,

Reunion – was held at Tower Records on Sunset Blvd. in Los Angeles. By the time the cast and crew show up in an old yellow school bus, the parking lot was packed with more than 500 people, some of whom had flown in from all over the country, happily signing yearbooks and reliving old high school memories. NF

Lawrence Waterhouse and his gung-ho, drug addled Marine pal, Bobby Shaftoe, in their crusade to crack the Axis military code in World War II. The second, which takes place in the late 1990s, chronicles programming geek Randy Waterhouse and the lovely Amy Shaftoe's adventures in an offshore data haven in Southeast Asia, trying to find hidden stashes of Nazi gold. Along the way there are

have confusing talks with the guidance counselor, etc. And these kids look like teens, with big glasses, young faces and zits."
That explains the visceral response, the critical acclaim and non-stop Web petitions pleading not to cancel the show. None of that phased NBC, of course, who casually cancelled the show after 18 episodes (not even bothering to air the last episode).

math problems, conspiracies galore and secret histories. Just like real life, as Stephenson would no doubt say. NF

out, the movie didn't age well, with an emerging consensus being that it was a triumph of style over substance. "If you like MTV, this is the best movie ever made," offered one message board post. "It scares me that people who saw this as a great movie may also vote," said another.

Even so, it had set a high visual standard, so the pent-up demand for the second and third sequels, which

GEEK MOVIE

The Matrix redefines cyberpunk and, in the only downside, assures Keanu Reeves of cinematic immortality. The DVD gives hundreds of thousands of people the excuse they need to buy DVD players. Although they grew up in Chicago under the shadow of Mies van der Rohe, the fraternal directors Wachowski are no fans of

were to be released within six months of each other, was palpable. In an instructive example of how "buzz" works today, the second movie, Reloaded, outgrossed the original by $400,000 in months. But, as with the Star Wars gang, the magic had migrated to New Zealand and to Hogwarth's, and no amount of spin could revive the franchise. So by the time Revolutions lurched into the theater, it was less a case of the

GEEK MOVIE

Office Space Despite Jennifer Aniston, Office Space did poorly at the box office. Instead it gained cult status on video. And rightfully so. The movie is a spot on comic jailbreak from the cubicles of modern office life at a Silicon Valley financial software company. The main characters plot a scheme ripping off their employer by rounding

"less is more". Instead, their tale of the "fight for the future" that pits men against machines is smorgasbord of breakthrough special effects, trendy production design, kung-fu choreography and half-baked metaphysics. The movie, which was budgeted at $63 million, became the watchword of cool. But, in an 11th-hour fumble, they threw it all away. It's not like they have anyone else

return of the king but of the emperor not wearing any clothes. NF

off payments to the next-lowest penny and deposit the proceeds in their checking account. Sounds familiar? "Yeah, they did it in Superman III. Also, a bunch of hackers tried it in the '70s. One got arrested." Director Mike Judge, of MTV's Beavis and Butt-head fame, successfully expanded his Milton cartoons that featured on Saturday Night Live into live action. The Milton character also plays a part in the

to blame, either. The film was dazzling eye candy but once everyone figured out the tricks, it went from cutting edge to parody and cliche by the time it picked up an Oscar for best visual effects. Even worse, as people got used to the look, they had no choice but pay more attention to the acting, script and plot. And while this cinematic Trojan Horse launched a million geek debates when it came

movie. The red Swingline stapler he is trying to protect so fanatically against supervisor Lumbergh became somewhat of a symbol of quiet rebellion among cubicle-bound employees. The red model didn't exist (it was painted red for visual purposes) but was in such demand after the movie's success on video that the company began selling a red stapler on its website. NF

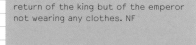

335 BC	287 BC	830	1284	1455	1543	1564	1632	1683	1746	1755	1811	1821	1827	1837	1847	1853	1865	1868	1876	1877	1879	1886	1889	1890	1893	1898	1899	1903	1905	1906	1907	1914	1921	1926	1929	1932	1934	1937	1938	1939	1941	1942	1945	1946	1947	1948	1949	1950	1951	1952

December 31, 1999: While the Millennium Bug self-destructs, the media anoints the geeks as "the new century's high priests". Like clergy of old, they forego Champagne toasts for around-the-clock shifts patrolling cyberspace for the potential bug. In the end, it's a total non-event.

GEEK GAME

Half Life Half Life took the first-person shooter formula, invented by id Software with Wolfenstein 3D and Doom, and perfected it by adding a great story. You play Gordon Freeman, a scientist working at "Black Mesa" a secret underground desert military base. The secret experiment you're working on malfunctions, sending the

▶ the end of the game, you feel like a real hero, single-handedly stopping an alien invasion and outsmarting your own government. If there's a video game equivalent to Citizen Kane, this is it. Oh, and lest we forget, the technology used to create Half-Life was released for free on the internet allowing hobbyists to tweak the code to their heart's content. The result? Counterstrike – a peacekeeper vs.

Napster goes live, pioneering person-to-person file sharing and creating one of the most frequently downloaded software applications in the history of the internet. Metallica wages war against 19-year-old, backwards-baseball-cap-wearing geek Shawn Fanning. In the end, Metallica et al may have won the battle, but we suspect Fanning may well win the war.

base into crazy sci-fi chaos. The game is full of inventive scenarios, the kind that require the player to adjust and react using wits and the tools at hand. The player must use a combination of shooting, jumping, crawling and puzzle solving to escape the base. The game's first-person perspective makes for an incredibly immersive experience – at all times the player experiences the world through Gordon's eyes. By

terrorist multiplayer shooting game that quickly became the most popular online multiplayer game in the world – with millions of fans. MS

GEEK ICON

Tony Hawk Back in the mid–80s, pro skaters hung out with misfits, outlaws and punks, made fun of athletes and turned their back on corporate changes. Then came the 1990s. Skate stars were geeks who invested their prize money in computer systems, built effective data bases, started their own companies, took meetings with companies like Disney, ESPN and Nike and, in the process, changed the sport. More than anyone else, Tony Hawk spearheaded the transformation. He grew up in San Diego and Orange County, in the heart of the action sports business. The most successful and probably the best pro ever, he became a role model to suburban boys all across the world. In time, these boys ended up running television networks such as MTV and ESPN, web sites, and video game companies. The first skater they turned to was Hawk. The first big move into the mainstream came in 1995, with ESPN's Extreme Games. To turn extreme sports like skateboarding into a major television event, competitions had to be invented, rivalries stoked (if not created) and sponsors wooed. Some veteran skaters wanted nothing to do with the program. Others, Hawk principal among them, couldn't do enough for The X Games.

"Because all our types of sports and music are viewed as the underdogs, there is a collective pride that we've come so far," Hawk told The Boston Globe in the summer of 2002. "It's almost like you are laughing at the fact that there is an endorsement that Schick Razors is sponsoring your tour, but at the same time you're happy they recognized you in that light."

"It's ok for me to be the one that everyone wants to epitomize the selling out of skateboarding." he continued. "I don't pay too much attention because I feel good about what I'm doing. I've always walked that line in getting sponsors that aren't in our industry. I just feel like getting those types of opportunities helps our skate companies grow."

The X Games did exactly that. By the time he nailed the 900, a trick that made national network news in the States, the only athlete who had higher name recognition than Hawk was Michael Jordan.

Activision, one of the video game giants, took Hawk to the next level. It wanted to develop a video game with a sports slant that would challenge Electronic Arts' John Madden's NFL. Hawk was the man to do it. "I'm 31," said Activision's Dave Stohl at the time. "Tony was the main guy when I was 13, and he's still the main guy now." A computer and video game freak, Hawk brought an authenticity to Tony Hawk's Pro Skater (now called THUG, for Tony Hawk's Underground). Since its inception, it has sold more than 12 million copies on every gaming platform, bringing in more than $625 million in its first three editions. Hawk himself has become the $10 million (a year) man. He's conquered TV, movies, books, magazines and video games. He owns and runs skate companies, clothing companies and production companies. The most decorated extreme athlete of our time, he proves that geeks now don't just get the girl. These days they also get the gold. NF

Melissa Virus New Jersey–based computer programmer David Smith creates and disseminates the Melissa Virus. Over 1,205,000 PCs and 53,000 servers are affected. Smith pleads guilty to the offense, and his case marks the first in which a hacker is convicted for computer-based crimes.

The Sims Outsells Myst and becomes the new number one PC game. The player can create and control the virtual everyday life of characters interacting with each other. Fifty percent of the buyers are women. EVDZ

GEEK CYBERPUNK

Jon Katz, Geeks: How Two Lost Boys Rode the internet Out of Idaho.
The story, which has a pretty even division between the characters' ups and downs, is okay. The real gem here is the opening chapter, which reads like The Geek Manifesto. Reading Katz's definition and description of geeks back in 2000 provided the inspiration

▼

for this book. In the early pages of Geeks, Katz forges a strong connection between the audio-visual guys (the true technologists) and the marginalized, "indie" artists and outsiders who are passionate about ideas as they are about living life according to their own rules. By the end of the introduction, you understand exactly how powerful geeks now are.
The book itself is a relatively quiet

▼

story, of two boys, neither very good nor very bad, from the Geek Club (an actual club) in a dead-end town in Idaho, and how their love of technology was their ticket to the big city. As they move to Chicago, however, Katz begins to mentor them, and then spends the last half of the book wondering if his efforts are unprofessional. It's an unnecessary, annoying tangent of hand wringing that,

▼

frankly, just gets in the way. Even so, Geeks is a humanistic demonstration of geek pride and culture. Like one of those made-for-television afternoon movies, it's sappy but if you're in the mood, sorta sweet too. NF

Al Gore Goes for Gold The American Vice-President who popularized the "information superhighway" during the 1996 Clinton campaign, goes for gold. (He uses the term to describe the era we live in, and makes the internet and technology a campaign issue.) He also runs a presidential campaign charitably described as robotic, but hires video wiz Spike Jonze to live with his family and make a video documentary making

▼

him "hip". Ironically, Gore does the unthinkable by managing to lose to George Bush Jr. in what is ascribed to computer error and fraud.

Internet Crash Boo.com closes, marking Europe's first major dot-com failure and the start of its internet crash. Its founders had burned through $120 million; say bye-bye to $12 Boo grapefruit cocktails, $50 entrees, private jets, and dreams of retiring at 27.

GEEK GADGET

Camera Phone Japanese J-Phone offers the first camera phone to its customers, the Sharp J-SH04. EVDZ

335 BC	287 BC	830	1284	1455	1543	1564	1632	1683	1746	1755	1811	1818	1821	1837	1847	1853	1865	1868	1876	1877	1879	1886	1889	1890	1893	1898	1899	1903	1905	1906	1907	1914	1921	1926	1929	1932	1934	1937	1938	1939	1941	1942	1945	1946	1947	1948	1949	1950	1951	1952

GEEK MOVIE

Donnie Darko On the surface Donnie Darko seems just another maladjusted suburban teenager movie. But this is no straightforward film. The very bright and troubled Donnie doesn't always take his medications and has an imaginary friend in a horrific bunny costume called Frank who is telling him the end of the world is near. The plot is quite confusing

▼

in a Twilight Zone and Stephen King way. So is adolescence but the central question from a sci-fi point of view is whether one can escape one's own time line, having been given a hint of its dramatic path. Will one's evasive actions avoid the outcome or subsequently lead you into its arms? After its release movie forums on the internet were buzzing with possible explanations. A key discovery for Donnie, played

▼

by Jake Gyllenhaal, is the book The Philosophy of Time Travel. It is for one a nice metaphor for the viewer's flashback to the late 80s thanks to the strong soundtrack. NF&EVDZ

GEEK GAME

Gran Turismo 3 GT is widely regarded as the most accurate videogame simulation of car racing. It's also jammed with hundreds of high-end cars, ie. total gearhead porn. The developers, Polyphony Digital, are famous for going millions over budget, fine-tuning every aspect of their games. For example, every wheel on

▼

every car is simulated individually, gripping the pavement accurately relative the amount of pressure on the tire and the amount of contact between the tire and the road. And of course the cars look identical to the real thing. To master this game can literally take years, but it's great fun for casual players too, if only because it feels so much like really driving an actual car. MS

GEEK GADGET

iPod
> see page 154

Web Site Fucking Machines takes Survival Research Labs and "Robot Wars" several steps further by bringing the robot into the bedroom and doing for sex toys what the lawnmower did for gardening.

GEEK GAME

America's Army For the first time in history a military organization, the US Army, releases a computer game to aid recruiting and public relations. America's Army is of course a multi-player first person shooter. Contrary to similar games like Return to Castle Wolfenstein or Call of Duty, one cannot play as the enemy. EVDZ

GEEK CYBERPUNK

John Cassidy, dot.com: The Greatest Story Ever Sold Of all the chronicles of the dot com boom and bust, few can match New Yorker/Economist financial writer, John Cassidy's. As he explains it, several things had to happen simultaneously. One was the rapid growth of the internet and the particularly rapid growth of electronic

▼

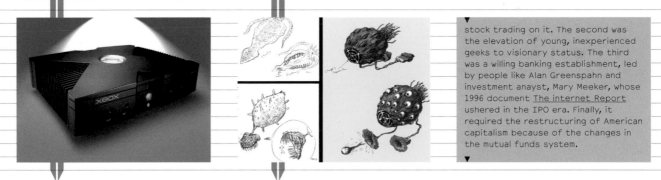

stock trading on it. The second was the elevation of young, inexperienced geeks to visionary status. The third was a willing banking establishment, led by people like Alan Greenspahn and investment anayst, Mary Meeker, whose 1996 document The internet Report ushered in the IPO era. Finally, it required the restructuring of American capitalism because of the changes in the mutual funds system.

▼

Xbox Microsoft joins the console contest and releases the Xbox. It's built around PC hardware and quickly becomes a favorite among computer hackers (turning it into a computer running Linux for example). At first the Xbox lagged behind Playstation 2 and the Gamecube but is steadily gaining ground. Its Xbox Live broadband-only service, has become the de facto standard for online gaming on consoles. EVDZ

Video Game Design The University of Southern California introduces a Master's in Fine Arts degree in video game design. With classes on video game theory and society being introduced in colleges across the world and pre-existing degrees in gaming in place at Georgia Tech and Carnegie Mellon universities, video games now infiltrate academia from coast to U.S. coast.

From that heady brew came the rags to riches to rags saga of players such as Bill Gates and Jeff Bezos and "synergistic" disasters like the AOL and Time Warner merger. Unlike many pop histories, Cassidy's sober, trust-inspiring reporting lends an appropriate gravity to the tale, so that the dot com bust becomes the ultimate train wreck, as impossible to look away from as it was to derail. NF

GEEK GADGET

<u>iPod</u>

▶ Somewhere around the mid–1990s, Jean Baptiste Mondino announced that he was no longer going to direct music videos. Music had changed, he said. The singer didn't matter anymore. Neither did the song or the album. Music was now fluid, ethereal and off the moment and he had better things to do with his time.
Time has proven him both right and wrong. Like Prince, Bowie, Cher, Simon and Garfunkel and God knows who else,

▼ Mondino came out of retirement and started doing music videos again. But his instincts were correct. Music was no longer as tangible. Where it used to lilve on vinyl or plastic, it now is on the hard drive or in your pocket. And, more and more frequently, it comes straight from the web, where it's just sitting, waiting to be downloaded.
Downloading has crippled the music business, with its bloated budgets and

▶ greedy bottom line, but it's been a boon to Apple. After companies like Rio promoted initial versions of MP3 players, the Mac design god, Jonathan Ive (he of iMac and iBook fame) and his staff shrunk the concept into one tiny object of tech lust, the iPod.
And they did it, as is their wont, by using design to create a status symbol. Say what you will about battery problems, arbitrary pricing and the

▼ behavioral consequences of a nation full of headphoned people bouncing to their own beats, ever since the fall of 2001, the iPod has been the essential gadget for people in the know. Throw in the fact that the iPod is really a portable hard drive, a DJ and a travel companion and it's virtually impossible to argue that the world is divided into two camps: those who have an iPod and those who want one. NF

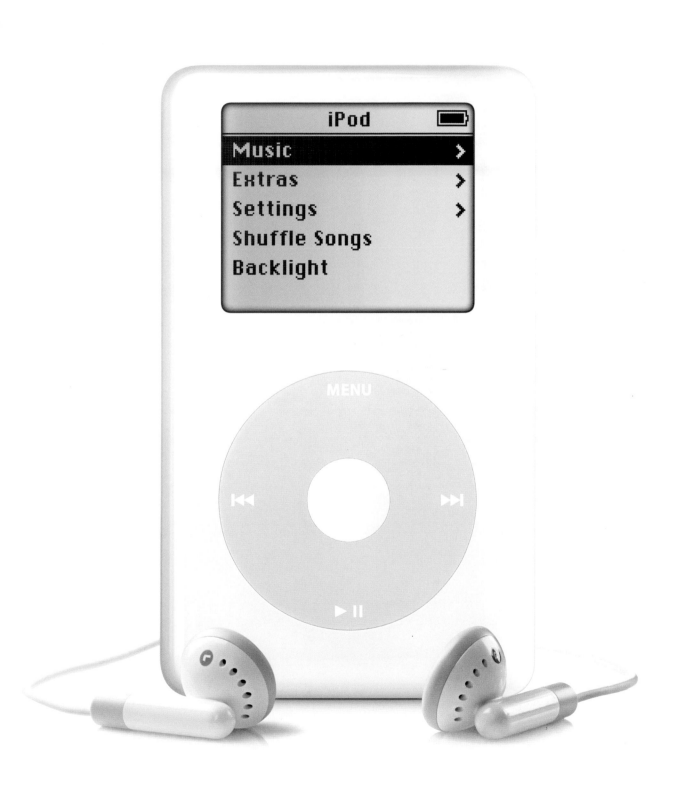

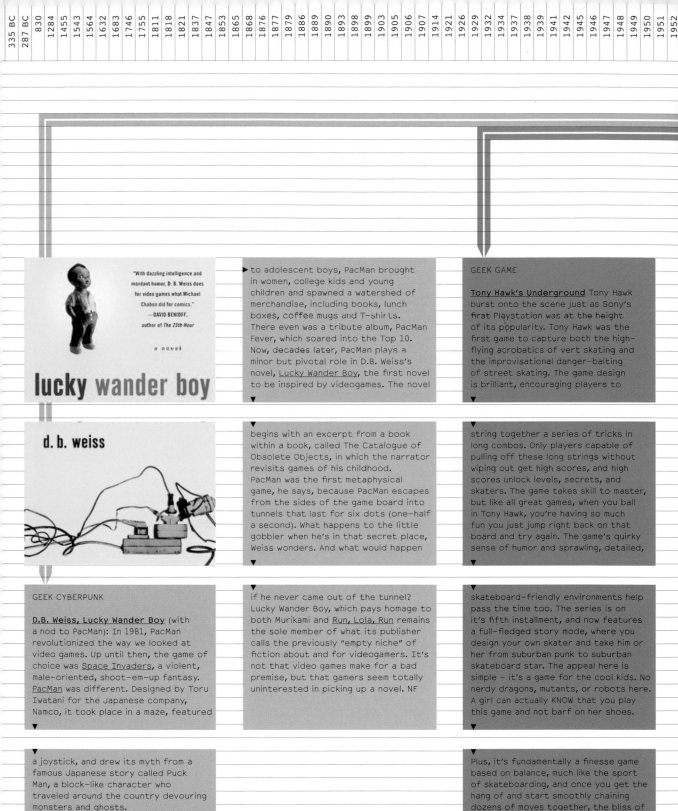

to adolescent boys, PacMan brought in women, college kids and young children and spawned a watershed of merchandise, including books, lunch boxes, coffee mugs and T-shirts. There even was a tribute album, PacMan Fever, which soared into the Top 10. Now, decades later, PacMan plays a minor but pivotal role in D.B. Weiss's novel, Lucky Wander Boy, the first novel to be inspired by videogames. The novel

begins with an excerpt from a book within a book, called The Catalogue of Obsolete Objects, in which the narrator revisits games of his childhood. PacMan was the first metaphysical game, he says, because PacMan escapes from the sides of the game board into tunnels that last for six dots (one-half a second). What happens to the little gobbler when he's in that secret place, Weiss wonders. And what would happen

if he never came out of the tunnel? Lucky Wander Boy, which pays homage to both Murikami and Run, Lola, Run remains the sole member of what its publisher calls the previously "empty niche" of fiction about and for videogamers. It's not that video games make for a bad premise, but that gamers seem totally uninterested in picking up a novel. NF

GEEK CYBERPUNK

D.B. Weiss, Lucky Wander Boy (with a nod to PacMan): In 1981, PacMan revolutionized the way we looked at video games. Up until then, the game of choice was Space Invaders, a violent, male-oriented, shoot-em-up fantasy. PacMan was different. Designed by Toru Iwatani for the Japanese company, Namco, it took place in a maze, featured

a joystick, and drew its myth from a famous Japanese story called Puck Man, a block-like character who traveled around the country devouring monsters and ghosts.
The Japanese team, for obvious reasons, made Puck a Pac, and proceeded to mint money. Within the first 12 months, over 100,000 arcade games were sold in the States alone. Unlike other games, which appealed primarily

GEEK GAME

Tony Hawk's Underground Tony Hawk burst onto the scene just as Sony's first Playstation was at the height of its popularity. Tony Hawk was the first game to capture both the high-flying acrobatics of vert skating and the improvisational danger-baiting of street skating. The game design is brilliant, encouraging players to

string together a series of tricks in long combos. Only players capable of pulling off these long strings without wiping out get high scores, and high scores unlock levels, secrets, and skaters. The game takes skill to master, but like all great games, when you bail in Tony Hawk, you're having so much fun you just jump right back on that board and try again. The game's quirky sense of humor and sprawling, detailed,

skateboard-friendly environments help pass the time too. The series is on it's fifth installment, and now features a full-fledged story mode, where you design your own skater and take him or her from suburban punk to suburban skateboard star. The appeal here is simple – it's a game for the cool kids. No nerdy dragons, mutants, or robots here. A girl can actually KNOW that you play this game and not barf on her shoes.

Plus, it's fundamentally a finesse game based on balance, much like the sport of skateboarding, and once you get the hang of and start smoothly chaining dozens of moves together, the bliss of intense gaming sets in. Certainly not for everybody, but a kick nonetheless. MS

GEEK GADGET

Trilobite Robot Vacuum Cleaner We made it. The future is finally here. Swedish Electrolux launches its Trilobite robot vacuum cleaner. Just sit back and put up your feet. EVDZ

Nokia N-Gage Nokia tries to combine a cell phone and a Game Boy into a killer combo. The result, called N-Gage, is rather disappointing. Especially the design is poor. To insert a game one has to remove the back cover and access the battery compartment. Making a call is also quite hilarious. The speaker is in the side edge of the hybrid device. Hence the nickname "taco phone". EVDZ

ACKNOWLEDGMENTS I am not a geek, so there are many people who helped bring this book about. Initially it was to be the cover story of a short-lived magazine about electronic music I edited called, <u>Revolution</u>. It was the brainchild of Jonathan Simpson-Bint and Matt Firme, then president and editorial director respectively of Imagine Publications, who brought me into the dot-com era pushing and screaming.

Right along with them were my senior editor, Chelsea Kalberloh, who was working on the story when the magazine went under, and to Matt Sammons, a video game designer and true friend who took me under his geek wings and provided a foundation from which I could appreciate the subculture. Next came Femke Wolting of Submarine, who got the concept immediately and secured a grant that funded a PDF file magazine for which Chelsea, English geek extraordinaire Rob Davis and I wrote the bulk of the timeline, and to graphic design studio Coup, the art directors who we pursued, knowing that this project had their name on it.

The grant money long gone, this soon became a labor of love, which soon attracted a lifesaver called Femke Dekker, whose intelligence and shared appreciation of KXLU radio, made the completion of the book possible and, later, the invaluable input from Dutch editor Erwin van der Zande.

Reflecting the realities of publishing today, this team worked under now normal constraints: a skeletal staff; extremely limited financial resources; compressed deadlines and tight page limits. As a result, we've undoubtedly made some mistakes. We've included people or events that you may question and, almost certainly, left some deserving things and people out. And we're operating from a perspective that favors what we know best, which is the States and Western Europe.

Having said that, we've given it our all. So thanks to all, including the hometown crew of Jodi MacArthur, Seth Mannheimer, Jeff Krintzman and Lori Armstrong, to Matt Sammons and Mindi Levine, to Sasha Coe and John Digweed for their continued support, friendship, to Steve Reiss for networking skills beyond belief, and inspiration, and, especially, to Chelsea, the Femkes, Rob, Peter, Erica and Bruno, who were so smart, dedicated and fun to work with. Also a word of thanks to our publishers for believing in us, and a special thanks to Rietje van Vreden for her valuable support. Now it's your turn. Let us know who or what you think we missed. It's not like we thought this was going to be the last word on geek chic. Actually, we hope it's just the beginning.

Neil Feineman
1/2/2005

Glasses Courtesy of Mansell Collection (Photo Willibrord Church, The Netherlands); Nikolaus Copernicus www.frombork.art.pl, Nicholaus Copernicus Museum Frombork, Poland; Coffee Koffie In Nederland by P. Reinders, Th. Wijsenbeek, Walburg Pers (1994); Benjamin Franklin Autobiography of Benjamin Franklin. J. Bigelow, Franklin Center, Franklin Library (1984); Geek The Dictionary Men: Their Lives and Times. R.W. Holder, Bath University Press Library, University of Bath (2004); Luddite Riot The Leader of The Luddites. Mess, Walker and Knight, Sweetings Alley (1812); Galileo Galilei Galileo, Colin A. Roman, G.P Putnam's Sons New York (1974); Mary Shelley Wollstonecraft www.adelaide.edu.au; Difference Engine aima.cs.berkeley.edu" Artificial Intelligence: A Modern Approach, S. Russel and P. Norvig. Prentice Hall (2002) Picture by Charles Babbage; Telegraph Portrait Gallery of Eminent Men and Women in Europe and America. Evert A Duyckinick. Johnson Wilson & Company, (1873); Alexander Graham Bell www.si.edu, Smithsonian Archives, USA (neg. no. 9823-C); Coca-Cola www.cocacola.nl, Coca Cola Enterprises, The Netherlands; Nikola Tesla www.berkeley.edu, Berkeley University of California, USA; Thomas Alva Edison Thomas Edison and Electricity, Steve Parker, Belitha Press Ltd. (1992) picture Mansell Collection; Aspirin www.bayer.nl, Bayer AG, The Netherlands; MSG www.jpo.go.jp" www.jpo.go.jp, photo by: Ajinomoto Co., Inc.; Albert Einstein Einstein's Legacy; The Unity of Space and Time, W.H. Freeman and Company (1985); RUR www.stetson.edu, Stetson university of Florida, USA; Metropolis Courtesy of Friedrich-Wilhelm-Murnau-Stiftung, ditributed by Transit Film GmbH; Universal Turing Machine www.nsa.gov/museum, National Cryptologic Museum, USA; Alan Mathison Turing www.berkeley.edu, Berkeley University of California, USA; Batman www.dccomics.com, DC Comics Inc.; Enigma www.nsa.gov/museum, National Cryptologic Museum, USA; Wonder Woman www.dccomics" www.dccomics.com, DC Comics Inc.; Mountain Dew www.mountaindew.com, PepsiCo Inc.; LSD (dr.Albert Hofmann) www.drugsyndicate.com; Dan Dare Pilot of the Future, Frank Hampson, Arthur C. Clarke, Hawk Books.; If I ran the Zoo (Dr. Seuss) If I Ran the Zoo, Dr Seuss, Random House Books for Young Readers www.usps.com, Commemoratove stamp, United States Postal Service; Isaac Asimov Isaac Asimov's Robot Visions, Isaac Asimov, Roc Reissue edition (1996) Illustration out of the book by Ralph McQuarrie; Peanuts www.snoopy.com, United Feature Syndicate Inc.; Jimmy Saville www.bbc.co.uk/totp2, British Broadcasting Corporation, UK; The Day the Earth Stood Still www.moviebunker.com; Lincoln Futura www.lincoln.com, Ford Motor Company; Gog www.jeffbots.com; Juan Garcia Esquivel perso.wanadoo.fr, photographer unknown; Sputnik web.ccr.jussieu.fr, Centre De Calcul Recherche et Reseau Jussieu, photo by: Gerard Auvray; Hush Puppies Hush puppies advertisement taken from Playboy; Ambassador Atom www.astro-boy.net; Buddy Holly 1984, NCB, All rights reserved, made in Denmark; The Original Twilight Zone www.rodserling.com, Rod Serling Memorial Foundation, USA; The Original College Bowl www.cinema.ucla.edu, LA Film and Television Archives, USA; Fantastic Four www.marvelcomics.com, Marvel Enterprises International Ltd.; The Incredible Hulk www.marvelcomics.com, Marvel Enterprises International Ltd.; The Jetsons www.goldenlands.com, Golden Lands CollecLables Studios; The Amazing Spider-Man www.mlcomics.com, ML Comics; James Bond (Dr.No) www.mgm.com, Metro Goldwyn Mayer Studios Inc.; Birkies www.birkenstock.com, Birkenstock Orthopädie GmbH, Germany; Moog www.moogmusic.com; Kiss Me Quick www.fantafilm.it, Fanta Film Festival, Italy; Lost In Space www.lostinspacetv.com, New Line Productions Inc.; Volvo 1400/140 www.volvo200.org, photo by: Jan Wilsgaard; David Bowie www.davidbowie.com, David Bowie; Mr. Rodgers Neighbourhood www.rodserling.com, Rod Serling Memorial Foundation, USA; A Space Odyssey Photo by: DEFD/TCS; Technics sp10 www.panasonic-europe.com/technics, Matsushita Electric Europe; Floppy Disk Courtesy of Mansell Collection; AMC Gremlin AMC Pacer advertisement taken from Playboy; Kraftwerk Album Cover Computerwelt, Kling Klang product 1981, EMI Electrola GmbH; Brian Eno www.brianeno.com, Opal Ltd; Computer Space www.computerhistory.org, Nutting Associates Inc. (Computer Space promotional photo c. 1971); Sinclair Executive www.vintagecalculators.com, Nigel Tout; Westworld www.stuntman.co.nz; Soylent Green www.mgm.com, Metro Goldwyn Mayer Studios Inc.; Rubiks Cube ce.et.tudelft.nl, Technische Universiteit Delft,The Netherlands; Michael Jackson www.bbc.co.uk/totp2, British Broadcasting Corporation, UK; MITS Altair 800 www.computermuseum.20m.com, Popular Electronics, front-page January 1975; AMC Brigade AMC Pacer advertisement taken from Playboy; Synthesizer www.synthmuseum.com, Synthmuseum Watertown, USA; David Byrne www.feelee.ru; Microsoft www.computerhistory.org, Ed Thelen; Apple I www.apple.com, Courtesy of Apple Computer, Inc.; Bill Gates Photo by: Doug Wilson, Corbis/TCS; Steve Jobs & Steve Wozniak Courtesy of Apple Computers Inc.; Demon Seed www.hyperleap.nl; Joystick www.thosewerethedays.de; Apple II Apple II Owners Manual '82-'83, courtesy of R. Jansen, the Netherlands; Close Encounters of The Third Kind www.columbiatristarfilms.com, Columbia TriStar Motion Picture Group; Heavy Metal www.imagenetion.com, Image NetIon; Star Wars Star Wars Movieposter, Twentieth Century Fox; Atari VCS www.pixeleye.net, Pixeleye; Elvis Costello www.feelee.ru; Space Invaders www.arcadeclassics.co.uk, Arcade Classics Inc.; Sinclair Zx90 www.uknet.net/gallery, UK Network Services; Andy Kaufman's Funhouse www.lubetv.org, Lube TV; Depeche Mode www.depechemode.com, Venusnote Ltd; John Draper aka Captain Crunch www.wideweb.com; Ms. Pac-Man batman.homelinux.com; IBM Personal Computer www.ibm.com, IBM Corporation; The Beastie Boys Album Cover Licensed To Ill, 1986, Def Jam Records; Osborne I www.ornitron.com; Commodore c64 www.uknet.net/gallery, UK Network Services; Morrissey www.bbc.co.uk/totp2, British Broadcasting Corporation, England; Bladerunner Copyright Warner Bros. Studios, courtesy of Stichting Skrien, the Netherlands; Tron Courtesy of © Disney.; Sixteen Candles Courtesy of © 1984 Universal City Studios, Inc.; Zelig www.bu.edu, Boston University, USA; CD www.feelee.ru, photo by D. Deji; Wargames www.mgm.com, Metro Goldwyn Mayer Studios Inc. & Ua Studios; Revenge of The Nerds www.imdb.com Internet Movie Database; Transformers www.vegalleries.com, Marvel/Sunbow Studios; Max Headroom www.techtv.com, G4 Tech TV, photographer unknown; Challenge of the Gobots www.hasbro.com, Hasbro; Apple www.apple.com, Courtesy of Apple Computer, Inc.; The Terminator www.mgm.com, Metro Goldwyn Mayer Studios Inc. & Ua Studios; William Gibson's Neuromancer Photo by Chris Saunders; Richard Stallman www.gnu.com, Free Software Foundation; Electric Car www.sinclair-research.co.uk; Commodore Amiga www.the.feds.are.lookingat.us; Alexei Pajitnov www.math.sciences.univ-nantes.fr, Université de Nantes, France; Nintendo Famicom www.nintendo.com, Nintendo of America Inc. & Famicom; Short Circuit www.delos.fantascienza.com; Batman the Dark Knight www.dccomics.com, DC Comics Inc.; Pixar www.pixar.com, Pixar Animation Studios; Ferris Bueller's Day Off www.dvdtown.com, DVD Town; PC Convertible www.ibm.com, IBM Corporation; A Legend of Zelda: A Link From the Past www.zeldalegends.net, Nintendo of America Inc.; Redbull www.redbull.com, Red Bull GmbH, Germany; Akira www.bandaivisual.co.jp, Tokyo Movie Shinsha, Japan; Robert Morris mit.edu, MIT Lab for Computer Science, USA; Family Matters www.kellie.de; Gameboy www.nintendo.com, Nintendo of America Inc. ; SimCity www.ea.com, Electronic Arts Inc.; Tetsuo I www.vialeweb.com; The Simpsons www.thesimpsons.com, Fox Broadcasting Company; John Perry Barlow www.eff.org, Electronic Frontier Foundation; Eric Steven Raymond; tuxedo.org; Linus Torvalds www.linux.org, Linux Online Corp.; The World Wide Web www.gabaynet.com, J.Jonathan Gabay; Douglas Coupland: Generation X Generation X: Tales for an Accelerated Culture, D. Coupland, St. Martin's Griffin; 1st ed edition (1991); Spike Jonze www.spike-jonze.tk, photographer unknown; Mosaic archive.ncsa.uiuc.edu, NCSA, USA; MiniDisc www.malechite.com; Aphex Twin www.shift.jp.org, Shift, Japan. photographer unknown; Moby Photo by: Danny Clinch, courtesy of Mute Records Limited, UK; Janeane Garofalo www.threerivertechreview.com; William Gibson / Bruce Sterling: the Difference Engine Difference Engine, W. Gibson and B. Sterling, Spectra; Reissue edition (1992); Street Fighter II www.capcom.com, Capcom USA Inc.; Neal Stephenson: Snow Crash SnowCrash, N.Stephenson, Spectra; Reprint edition (2000); The X-Files www.foxhome.com, Twentieth Century Fox Home Entertainment LCC.; Richie Hawtin www.vh1.com, photo by: Nicola Kuperus; Quentin Tarantino www.efriends.pnet.pl,

Baseline's Encyclopedia of Film; Myst www.ubi.com, Ubisoft Entertainment, USA; Apple Newton www.apple.com, Courtesy of Apple Computer, Inc.; Wired www.wired.com, The Condé Nast Publications Inc.; Cyberia www.cyberiacafe.net, Cyberia Internet Cafe; Douglas Rushkoff: Cyberia www.rushkoff.com; John Digweed www.johndigweed.com; Weezer www.du.edu, University of Denver, USA; Casio QV-11 www.casio.com Casio Computer Co. Ltd.; Playstation www.us.playstation.com, Sony Computer Entertainment America Inc.; Dorm Digirati Photo by Marleen van de Kerkhof; Digital Versatile Disk www.sony.com, Sony Corporation of America; Unabomber www.iath.virginia.edu, University of Virginia, USA; Jimmy Corrigan: the Smartest Kid On Earth Jimmy Corrigan: The Smartest Kid on Earth, Chris Ware, Pantheon (2000) ; Nicholas Negroponte: Being Digital mit.edu, MIT Lab for Computer Science, USA; John Helsingius (aka Julf) www.julf. com, Johan Helsingius; Quake www.idsoftware.com, ID Software Inc.; Resfest Digital Film Festival www.resfest.com, photo by: N. Akiws; Mars Attacks www.kino.com, photo by: L. Erw; Smart Phone www.nokia.com, Nokia Group, Finland; Jennicam www.peepingmoe.com, Jennifer Ringley; Super Mario 64 www.consolenetwork.it, no.wikipedia.org/w/index.php?title=Super_Famicom&action=edit" \o "Super Famicom" Super Famicom & Super Nintendo Entertainment System; Gattaca www.colombia.com, Columbia/Tristar Studios; Deep Blue www.ibm.com, IBM Corporation; Grand Theft Auto www.chez.com, Take Two Interactive Software Inc.; Boo.com www.boo.com/boo, Fashion Mall Inc.; PMP300 www.diamondmm.com, Diamond Multimedia; iMac www.apple.com, Courtesy of Apple Computer, Inc.; Buffy the vampire slayer www. fox.com, Fox Broadcasting Company; Radiohead: OK Computer www.sanborns.com, Sanborns; Dance Dance Revolution www.jeffmcbride. net, McBride/Bowers family; Starcraft www.fictionalworlds.com, copyright © 2001–2004 Bill Tellefsen; Dreamcast www.sega.com, Sega Europe Ltd.; Everquest www.sony.com, Sony Corporation of America; Freaks and Geeks www.emissions.ca Emissions, Canada; The Matrix www2.warnerbros.com, Warner Bros. Studios; Office Space © 1999, Twentieth Century Fox – All rights reserved; Napster www.napster. com, Napster LLC.; Half Life www.half-life.com, 2004 Valve Corporation; Tony Hawk Thrasher Magazine, 10th anniversary issue, (1991) High Speed Productions Inc, USA; The Sims outsells Myst www.ea.com, Electronic Arts Inc.; Camera phone www.sharp.nl, Sharp Corporation, Japan & N. Ajade; Gran Turismo 3 www.us.playstation.com, Sony Computer Entertainment America Inc.; America's Army www. americasarmy.com, U.S. Army, USA; X-Box www.microsoft.com, Microsoft Corporation; iPod www.apple.com, Courtesy of Apple Computer, Inc.; D.B. Weiss: Lucky Wander Boy Lucky Wander Boy, DB Weiss, Plume Books, USA (2003); Trilobite Robot Vacuum Cleaner www. electrolux.com, Electrolux Group; Nokia N-Gage www.nokia.com, Nokia Group, Finland